Costa Blanca
Mountain Walks

volume 1: west

ABOUT THE AUTHOR

After wartime service in the navy, Bob Stansfield had a career in the police force, becoming superintendent, then lecturing in law in East Anglia. Bob is a lifelong mountain lover, and has walked, climbed and skied in most of the high places of Britain and in many parts of the Alps. He was a part-time instructor with Outward Bound and a voluntary warden in the Lake District, and also founded the first police climbing club.

Bob and his wife, Kathy, retired to the Costa Blanca in 1986. There they helped to found the Costa Blanca Mountain Walkers, a group which went on to thoroughly explore the walking possibilities of the region. Bob has written walking articles in local newspapers and published a series of walking guides locally. A selection was published by Cicerone in 1995 as *Mountain Walks on the Costa Blanca*. In this new edition, in two volumes, Bob has updated and expanded the scope of the first edition to give unrivalled comprehensive coverage of the area.

ADVICE TO READERS

Readers are advised that whilst every effort is taken by the author to ensure the accuracy of this guidebook, changes can occur which may affect the contents. A book of this nature with detailed descriptions and detailed maps is more prone to change than a more general guide. New fences appear, waymarking alters, there may be new buildings or eradication of old buildings. It is advisable to check locally on transport, accommodation, shops etc., but even rights of way can be altered, and paths can be eradicated by fire, landslip, forest clearances or changes of ownership. The publisher would welcome notes of any such changes. The website www.geocities.com/bobstansfield includes a full and current programme of walks and updates.

Costa Blanca Mountain Walks

volume 1: west

Bob Stansfield

2 POLICE SQUARE, MILNTHORPE, CUMBRIA, LA7 7PY
www.cicerone.co.uk

ISBN 1 85284 330 6 2nd edition
(ISBN 1 85284 165 6 1st edition)
First published 1995
Second edition 2001
Reprinted 2004

A catalogue card for this book is available from the British Library.

Acknowledgements

Like the first edition, these walks represent a selection of the results of exploratory work done by the leaders of the Costa Blanca Mountain Walkers, and I am again glad to acknowledge their help and generosity in allowing me to chronicle their discoveries. Whilst I have received unstinted help and encouragement from a legion of fellow walkers, especially in bringing my walks up to date, some need a special mention here.

I wish to record my gratitude to the following: Kees Andriessen, Bill Assheton, Derrik Ayrton, Clive Axford, Chris Batnick, Malcolm Blakeney, Jack and Anita Bremner, Gladys Brettal, Jenny Carter, Vicky Carter, Brian and Aileen Evans, Peter Fallows, Maurice and Eunice Gibbs, George and Betty Goddard, Kaithe Greene, Roy and Sharon Hancliff, John Hemmons, Jim Johnston, Roger Massingham, Alan Myerscough, Peter Reason, Jean Ryan, Maurice Scholer, Vincent and Elena Schultz, and Eric Taylor.

Finally I am pleased to be able to record my gratitude to those readers who took the trouble to let me have suggestions for improving the book, and I have thanked them individually.

My dear wife Kathy, my most constant mountain companion for more years than we both care to remember, can no longer walk, but I am grateful for her unstinted collaboration in the preparation of this edition.

I take the greatest of pleasure in dedicating my work to her with love and gratitude.

Bob Stansfield
CALPE 2001

CONTENTS

SIERRA AITANA/CAMPANA/PONOCH

THE AITANA WAY

VAL DE ARC

BENIDORM AREA – SIERRA HELADA/SIERRAS DE CORTINA

SIERRA SERRELLA/AIXORTA

VAL DE ALGAR

VAL DE GALLINERA

GALLINERA WAY

NORTH-WEST SIERRAS

WESTERN SIERRAS

COSTA BLANCA MOUNTAIN WAY

APPENDIXES

Bernia-Pinos Valley Walk with ridge
photo by Bob Stansfield

Foreword to 1st edition

When I commenced my exploration of these mountains of Las Marinas, I started a new mountain log-book which I called 'The Fragrant Fells'. I hope that readers will agree that the title of this book is both literal and apt. Wherever you walk in these beautiful mountains of the Levant, you will brush aside, or crush beneath your boots, a great variety of fragrant herbs, the like of which you would normally be buying in small packets at Sainsburys or Tesco's. How often has a soft warm breeze wafted a new, tantalising scent across my track, the source of which I have often had difficulty in tracing.

These are truly the mountains of my old age. In my more youthful years, only the Alps seemed to matter, except, of course, for my beloved Lake District and other British hills. Spain never called, mainly because it didn't seem to have any Alpine tradition or famous mountain guides to inspire the young climber with their memoirs, nor was there anyone like Gaston Rébuffat to fire the imagination with magnificent photographs.

When, in later years, I did eventually discover the mountains of Las Marinas, it was love at first sight and they have filled my declining years with a joy which equals, if not surpasses, the fading memories of those heady days on the Aonach Eagach, the Black Cuillin, Striding Edge, Crib Coch, Dow Crag and the Milestone Buttress, and even our modest Alpine tours.

If I can inspire and help others to share and appreciate these wonderful and neglected mountains of Las Marinas, I shall be more than content. To all who use this guide, I wish many happy mountain days, which I hope they will treasure always, as I do.

Bob Stansfield
Calpe, January 1995

Foreword to 2nd edition

There have been many changes since the first edition was published: mountain walking has become a major attraction, and accommodation, waymarkings and facilities for camping have improved.

This edition not only provides an update but also adds further day walks and two extended walks in the area. The biggest problem has been achieving a balanced selection, and sadly some favourite walks have had to be left out. Those keen to find their own walks need have no fear: there is an almost unlimited scope for further exploration by future generations of walkers.

Bob Stansfield
Calpe, August 2001

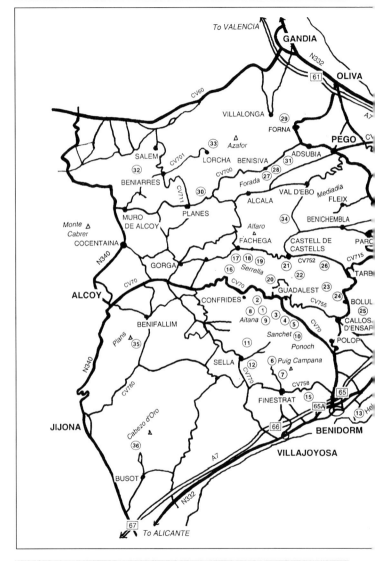

STARTING POINTS FOR THE WALKS

Numbers in circles show
approximate starting points of the walks

Numbers in boxes show
autoroute junctions

0   15 km

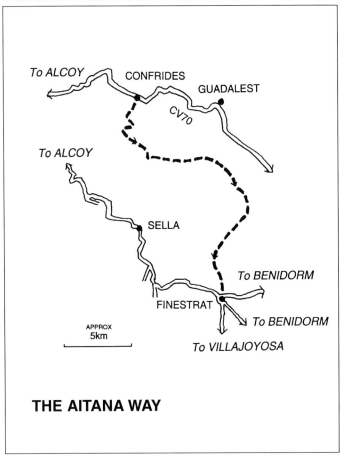

THE AITANA WAY

See page 71

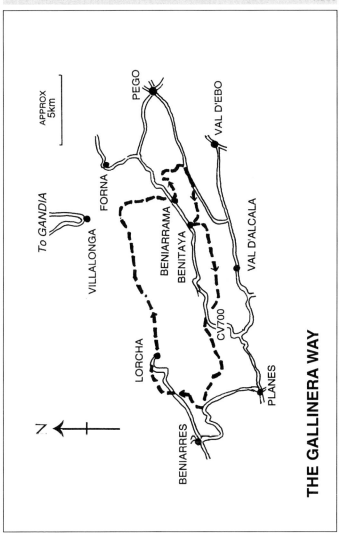

THE GALLINERA WAY

See page 173

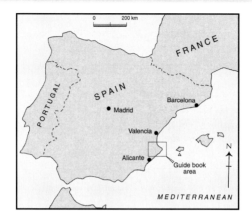

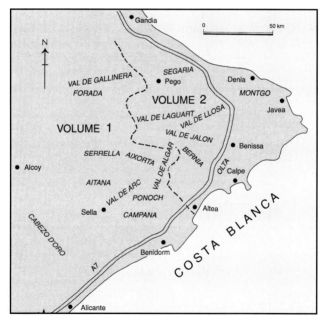

INTRODUCTION

The rugged mountains of the Costa Blanca offer wonderful walking in a landscape of pinnacled ridges, enormous crags, and shady pines. Orange and almond groves enhance the valleys, whilst attractive mountain villages provide hospitality, offering a taste of the real Spain, far removed in character from the developed coastal strip.

Mountain Walks on the Costa Blanca volumes 1 and 2 are simple, easily understood guidebooks, written to enable both visiting and resident mountain walkers to share the delights of ascending and traversing this most satisfying and picturesque mountain area of the Costa Blanca. The two volumes divide the region roughly into west and east. Volume 1 covers the area north and west of Benidorm, while volume 2 covers the area to the north of Calpe.

The guide is not offered in any way as a manual for mountain walking. Readers are assumed to have acquired these skills elsewhere. Some modest strolls are included, which are suitable for walkers of any age or ability, and the guide also offers advice on the differences between walking in these mountains and those of Britain.

Costa Blanca

The region known as the Levant, bordering the Mediterranean, includes the Costa Blanca, which runs from Denia in the north to Torrevieja in the south. The walks in this book fall within Alicante, part of the Costa Blanca and one of the three provinces of Valencia, an ancient kingdom with its own language, customs and flag. Spanish kings, and more recently a dictator, have tried hard to prohibit such manifestations of local pride, and until the recent restoration of the monarchy and the move towards democracy, the language, local costumes and fiestas were prohibited by law. Now there is a spirited revival, Valencia is a region with autonomy and its own government, and the flag proudly flies alongside the national one. Don't be at all surprised to hear country folk speaking Valenciano or a mixture of both languages, and nearly all notices, including road signs, are in Valenciano.

Spain, like France, has now named all its coasts in the interest, no doubt, of tourism. Luckily, the development of tourism has largely been confined to the coastal strip, where vines and oranges have given way to villas, apartments and the major resort of Benidorm. Inland, however, the countryside remains (with one or two exceptions) unspoiled, with the country people still making a living from agriculture. It is not many years ago that Benidorm was a poor fishing village, and women walked barefoot to Callosa de Ensarria to sell fish in the more prosperous inland town.

With the exception of Switzerland, Spain is the most mountainous country in Europe, and the Costa Blanca is no exception, with the mountains coming right down to the sea. By far the greatest concentration of mountain scenery is to be found in the north of the Costa, in the district known as Las Marinas, and these are the mountains traversed by the Costa Blanca Mountain Way (see 'The Costa Blanca Mountain Way' section).

The Costa has excellent communications, and on the coast accommodation is lavish. Inland, over the past years hotels and accommodation have improved greatly and there are now good hotels in most of the valleys.

The climate is typically Mediterranean, the rain falling mainly in spring and autumn in heavy downpours. This gives the region over 300 glorious mountain days, although not everyone will want to be on the hills in the middle of a hot August day, when even at 1000m it can be 98°F (37°C).

The Area Covered by the Guide

This comprises mainly two *comarcas* (local authorities) of the province of Alicante, La Marina Baja and La Marina Alta (lower and higher). The area is easily identifiable on maps as the large promontory between Valencia and Alicante.

The ridges and valleys of the mountains radiate roughly from the city of Alcoy, 50km from the coast, like the fingers of a hand. The most northerly valley is that of the Rio Serpis, and is actually in the *comarca* of Safor. Next comes the beautiful Val de Gallinera, famous for castles and cherries. Further south, is the remote Val d'Ebo and the Val d'Alcala, accessible only by negotiating the acute hair-pin bends on the most difficult, but most picturesque, road in the area. Then there is the Val Laguart, a lovely unspoiled valley, with a road which leads right to its head and continues across the Caballo Verde ridge at Col de Garga. The road continues, again with many a hair-pin, down into the next valley, that of the Rio Jalon, probably one of the most attractive valleys for tourists due to the picturesque situation, ringed by high mountains, with the broad lower valley ablaze with the blossom of thousands of almond trees in the spring (February). It is the only mountain valley which has been granted appellation status for the wines it produces. Further south, another tortuous mountain road negotiates the side of the Pinos Valley to reach the high plateau of the Bernia. The next valley, that of the Rios Guadalest and Algar, is without doubt the most popular with tourists, and the road has been improved to accommodate the many coaches which bring them daily from Benidorm. Despite this the valley remains unspoiled. Set amongst the highest peaks of the region, with the added attraction of the only large stretch of open water, the Embalse de Guadalest, justifies its reputation as the most beautiful of valleys. The final valley is that of the Rio Sella, which leads inland from Villajoyosa to cross the Aitana Ridge at Paso de Tudons.

The Mountains

It is a mistake to classify a mountain solely by its height – its form is much more important. The mountains of the area are modest in height – 1000m (3300ft) on average. Some, however, reach 1558m (5000ft). But they all have the true characteristics of a mountain – rocky summits, sheer crags, deep gullies and ravines, exciting ridges and pinnacles, and, above all, magnificent views. In addition they have the distinct advantage of accessibility with good approaches by road to the high plateaux or passes, and can all be climbed comfortably in a day, many in a few hours. No need here for cable-cars, mountain huts or a long walk in before you can even set foot on the mountain.

Geology

'The Alpine structures of Southern Spain, south of the MESETA, are divided into three units of BETICS (sensu stricto), SUB-BETICS and PRE-BETICS' (C.B. Mosley, *Field Guide to the Costa Blanca*). For those like me, ignorant of the finer points of geology, this means limestone with some nostalgic intrusions of gabbro. The limestone, a sedimentary rock, is easily eroded by the chemical action of the rain, and rivers soon disappear underground, forming a network of shafts and caverns beloved of the potholer. There are many areas of limestone pavement, with their fissures (grykes), which make for difficult walking. Much of the rock is friable, and on some of the ridges 'jug handles' are liable to come away in your hand. Despite this, there are a lot of difficult climbs put up on great walls of solid rock, particularly on Puig Campaña, Peñon d'Ifach, Toix and Altea Hills, the Sella area and Monte Ponoch.

Travel To and Around Costa Blanca

By Air

There is an international airport at Valencia, which is sometimes used by those visiting the north of the Costa Blanca, but by far the most popular is the airport at Alicante, El Altet, which is much used by package tour operators. There are taxis (rather expensive) and a bus service to Alicante Bus Station from the airport. All tour operators provide coach transport from the airport, and hire cars are available here, but it is better to hire your car in advance.

By Road

The main trunk road, CN332, runs down the coast, giving access to all the resorts. Only Benidorm, however, is so far by-passed, so at peak times there can be delays in passing through the towns.

The A7 *autopista* (motorway) is superb except for the fact that you have to pay rather dearly for this service. As a result of this toll charge you will find it uncrowded, even in the height of summer.

Minor roads may be narrow by British standards, but have an excellent surface. *Caminos rural*, even narrower, will take you high into the mountains, and usually have a good surface. Forestry roads give access, even to the summit of some mountains, but are only really suitable for four-wheel drive vehicles due to the variable surface, steep gradients and the tendency to disappear after a storm.

Roads often have kilometre marker stones (indicating, for example, Km.31). These are used in the guide as useful reference points.

Bus Services

The service from Alicante city is extensive, and operated by Alcoyana.

Ubesa (Union Benissa) operate a service from Alicante to Valencia, with links to other towns along the route. Benidorm has a municipal service, including a service in the tourist season to Algar and Guadalest. Other resorts along the coast have a limited service solely to satisfy local needs.

The bus service to mountain villages is either non-existent or extremely poor, and this means of transport is virtually useless for those who wish to engage in mountain walking.

Information from Central Bus Station, Plaza de Seneca, Alicante (Tel: 522 0700).

Trains

Alicante has main-line connections with the rest of Spain and Europe. The main line runs inland to Valencia via Alcoy.

El Trenet, a narrow-gauge, single-track railway owned by the provincial government of Alicante runs daily services from Alicante to Denia. This line is extremely picturesque, especially between Benidorm and Benissa, where the track runs close to the Corniche. This is not a speedy service, as the train stops at every station, and some trains do not run from Altea to Denia, turning back at Altea del Olla.

With the exception possibly of Calpe, and the halt of Ferrandet, the line is of little use to mountain walkers. From Calpe station there is a bus service to the base of the Penon d'Ifach, and from Ferrandet you can step out onto the Olta route. The railway company has commissioned a local mountaineer to survey a number of walks from stations along the route.

For train information contact:

> R.E.N.F.E. (Main Line),
> Avenida de Salamanca,
> Alicante

> F.G.V. (Coastal),
> Ferrocarriles de la Generalitat,
> Avenida de Villajoyosa, 2
> Alicante.

Taxis

Taxis are identifiable by the green light fitted to their roof. Costa Blanca taxis are far more expensive than those in Madrid and Barcelona. They are certainly not an option for the walker wanting a day out in the mountains.

Car Hire

This is by far the best option for the visiting mountain walker. The smaller cars are very reasonable to hire, sturdy and reliable. They can be booked in Britain as part of a package, available at the airport or at your hotel. For pre-booking in England a recommended firm, which has proved reliable and gives good value for money, is Premier Car Hire (Tel: 01279 641040). A current British (EEC) driving licence is generally acceptable. There are even small four-wheel drive vehicles available for hire, but be sure to book in advance for this type of vehicle.

Accommodation

There is plenty of accommodation of every description to be found on the Costa Blanca. Hotels, hostels and apartments abound. There are also *casas de huespedes* (boarding houses), *pensiones* (guest houses), *fondas* (inns) and *casas de labranzas* (farm houses) to be had, and the Provincial Tourist Board (Patronata Provincial de Turismo), at Esplanada de Espana, 2 Alicante, will supply a list of accommodation. Hospitality can be found, however rudimentary, even in the remote villages.

Package Holidays

These are very good value, especially if you take a 'special offer', which allows the tour operator to choose your hotel and resort within the Costa Blanca.

Hotels

Benidorm has more hotel beds than any other resort in Europe, so it is more than likely to be offered by your travel agent. There are also good hotels at all other resorts, and an excellent *parador* (state-run luxury hotel) in Javea. There are motels alongside the CN332 at Gata le Gorgos, Oliva, Vergel and Calpe.

Apartments

There are hundreds of these at the main resorts, and are extremely popular with the Spaniards as well as other nationalities. Apartments usually have minimal cooking facilities. Shopping in the popular resorts is easy and food is reasonably priced. Unlike France, shops do not open very early; they close for an early afternoon siesta, and stay open in the early evening. The largest supermarkets open longer, some even on Sunday. Self-catering is not a problem, due to the relatively cheap menus available in bars and restaurants.

Villas

Most letting agents can supply a list of villas for rent, to suit individual needs, and most include the use of a private swimming pool. These are very good value, especially for a large party.

Youth Hostels

Youth Hostel Aubergue La Marina is situated next to La Comita Campsite: take the first turning right leaving Moraira towards Calpe. The director is Amparo Franqueza, and the hostel offers accommodation for 130 in 2-, 4- and 6-bedded rooms. Usual activities including mountaineering (opened September 1994).

Camping

Many mountain villages have now established campsites. Notable campsites ideal for walkers are at Calpe (Camping Municipal, high on the flank of Olta), Camping Val Laguar at Campell, Finestrat, and at Alcala de la Jovada. The Provincial Tourist Board produces a list of the commercial coastal sites – but these are expensive and far from ideal for walkers. General information is available from:

> Agrupacion Nacional de Camping de Espana
> Duque de Medinaceli 2
> Madrid

> Oficina de Turismo Tourist – Info
> Explanada de España 2
> 03002 Alicante (Tel: 521 22 85 & 520 00 00)

> Oficinas Municipales de Informacion Turistica
> Avda. Europa
> 03500 Benidorm (Tel: 586 00 95)

> Oficinas Municipales de Informacion Turistica
> Avda Ejércitos Españoies 66
> 03710 Calpe.

In England a list of camp sites and information is available from

> Spanish National Tourist Office
> 57–58 St James's Court
> London SW1 (Tel: 0171 499 0901).

There is no need for a Camping Carnet in Spain. Camping libre, or camping off-site, is popular with the Spaniards. The advice of the tourist board is to ask the Ayuntamiento (Town Hall) in the villages for permission and advice. Camping Libre may be restricted in certain areas which are vulnerable to forest fires.

Accommodation Inland

There are two mountain huts that provide accommodation.

- Refugio La Figuera on the Col de Molinos, Km.18, on the CV721, Pego to Val de Ebo Road. Enquiries Town Hall (Ajuntamiento), Pego.

- Casa Refugio Font de L Arc, Camino de Val, Sella 03579, Tel 96 587 2102 or 96 594 1019. 4km from Sella at the end of the surfaced section of the road leading to Paso de los Contadores and Benimantell. Sleeping accommodation and rock climbing guides. For directions see Route No. 12.

Where to Stay

This is very much an individual choice depending on the area in which you intend to walk, but Calpe is considered to be the central point on the coast. From Calpe, in 15min, you can be across the Pass of the Windmills, ready to start your exploration of the beautiful Jalon Valley. In 30min, you can enter the Val Laguart, which will take you high into the mountains, or explore the Pinos Valley, which will take you to the high plateau of the Sierre Bernia, or go south to the thriving inland town of Callosa d'Ensarria, through extensive groves of citrus fruits. From Callosa d'Ensarria, you have to decide whether to visit the Algar Valley with its attractive waterfalls, or to head into the Guadalest Valley, without doubt the most beautiful and picturesque valley of them all.

In 45min, you can be in the interesting town of Pego, ready to explore the unspoiled valley of the Gallinera, with its four castles, six typical Spanish villages, all with Moorish names and, at the head of the valley, lies the beautiful Barranca Encantada (Enchanted Valley). Just a kilometre before you reach Pego, you might be tempted to turn off with the signs for Val d'Ebo, and climb, for 9km on the steepest, most dramatic, but definitely the most scenic road on the Costa (count the alpine bends, if you can drag your eyes away from the views).

Going south, in one hour you can be in Finestrat, a beautiful village, built on top of high cliffs, with casas colgadas (hanging houses) on the south side, pretty Hermita, set in beautiful gardens, on the highest point. From here, you get fantastic views of Alicante's second-highest mountain. Puig Campaña. In a further 15min, you can be in the mountain village of Sella.

This itinerary may be of some use in deciding where to stay on the Costa Blanca, but wherever you stay on the coast, you will have easy access to the mountains. All the times refer to leisurely driving on provincial roads. For those in a hurry, and with unlimited funds, the A7 *autopista* will reduce the times given considerably.

Communications

Telephones

Telephone kiosks are not always reliable. Although they look modern and efficient, they can gobble up your small change and still not connect you. Often you will find that the machine will not operate because the cash container is full. A much more sensible idea is to use the facilities of a Locutorio, a manned kiosk, where the operator will connect your call for you. They are more expensive but efficient. Most bars have pay phones which always seem to work, but the problem is the noise of the TV. Using the phone in your hotel bedroom may be efficient, but the charge can be excessive.

Fax

There are facilities in most hotels, and public facilities (commercial) at all the resorts.

NOTES FOR WALKERS

Rights of Way

The Spanish law of trespass would seem to be basically the reverse of the English common law, where there is no general right of access to land, even common land, without statutory or common law rights. I am advised that in Spain you may wander at will, providing that you obey a few sensible rules. You should not commit damage, hunt, light fires, and so on, and you should not enter private land by climbing walls or fences. Where land is plainly private or the owner has given notice of privacy, you should respect his wishes. Many unsurfaced roads can be chained with a notice 'Camino Privado' or 'Camino Particular', but these notices are to restrict access by motor vehicles and do not normally affect walkers. In addition the Spanish civil codes give many absolute rights of access which can only be removed by statute. These include all riverbanks, lakes and the coast, access to the top of mountains and to historical sites, castles, *ermitas* (sanctuaries), and springs and wells.

Waymarkings

Some walks are well cairned; others may have no waymarkings. Where there could be confusion on a route, I have always preferred to build a cairn; only where it cannot be avoided do I desecrate the countryside with a paint marker. But do not confuse these markers with the boundary marks made by surveyors, which generally include a number preceded by a dot in a circle. When I first explored these mountains, I discovered lots of small metal crosses, and was much impressed by the religious devotion of the local people. I now know that they originally marked private hunting areas, and the notices on them had been blasted off by poachers.

Weekends, Fiestas and Hunting

At weekends and fiestas you can expect the countryside, with its narrow roads, to be crowded, especially the picnic spots. Another hazard, which needs to be taken seriously, are the hunters. Spain's hunting seasons vary according to the prey, but generally extend from

October to January. Game (rabbits, hares, pheasants, partridge, thrushes, etc.) can only be slaughtered on Sundays and fiestas. Wild boar are no luckier, they may be done to death on Thursdays and fiestas. This means that the frustrated hunters bang away at everything that moves on the few days when they can use their hunting licences, and a prudent mountaineer leaves them to it, unless he wishes to have his head mounted on a hunter's wall as a trophy!

Route-finding

In the mountains, due to the *garigue* (spiky vegetation), you cannot enjoy true cross-country walking as you can in Britain and the Alps. Here, I am afraid, there is no such thing as walking from peak to peak on a carpet of heather. Pursuing a direct route can be time-consuming, wearisome, painful and sometimes dangerous. The relief felt on reaching a rough but reasonable path is a joy to be savoured after this type of experience.

All the screes I have found so far will not 'run', and progress down them is painful, slow and dreary, with the possible exception of the north scree on Puig Campaña (see Route 7).

Mule tracks between villages seem to follow the easiest line, along a valley bottom or over a col, and there are still tracks to most of the castles and *fuentes*. If you are forced to climb terraces, try to look for the access provided for the mule at the end of a section. It may take a little more time, but it is easier. Trails made by hunters are well waymarked by empty cartridge cases and empty tins of seafood (I wonder if fishermen eat tinned rabbit?).

Country Code

- Respect all property – if you shelter in an abandoned *finca* (farmhouse), do no damage and leave no litter.

- Prevent fires – do not leave glass around, and make sure cigarettes are extinguished.

- Leave no litter in the countryside – take it home with you.

- Do not pick growing fruit – remember it is the farmer's livelihood.

- Do not uproot or pick wild flowers – take seeds only.

Forest Fires

Every summer, many hectares of forest are destroyed by forest fires, as it only takes a spark to ignite the tinder-dry scrub. There is no doubt that some fires are caused deliberately, either by arsonists or by the owners in order to gain permission to develop the land. Most, however, are due to carelessness, either by the farmers themselves, a cigarette end thrown from a vehicle, or by the townspeople having a traditional Sunday paella in the country. Campers, probably the most careful people, can suffer when the local government imposes a ban on camping during high fire-risk periods.

La Conselleria de Medio Ambiente (Council for the Environment) has laid down new procedures for dealing with forest fires. Especially when the dreaded Poniente wind blows like a gale from the west, the Met Office will update the following gradings for seven areas within Valencia every 48 hours:

- **prealerta** – all services on stand-by
- **alarma** – mobilisation of all forces at disposal of the *conselleria*, the civil governor and the forestry brigades
- **alarma extrema** – notification of all police, fire, Guardia Civil and mayors of all towns and villages in the area.

During alarms traffic will be checked, and restricted in the mountain areas affected. Walking and camping may be banned or restricted by police and Guardia.

Water

In the Costa Blanca, all public water supplies are fairly reliable and drinkable, but it is advisable to check locally. In the mountains there is normally no surface water, and the streams, running underground, are not subject to pollution. There is hardly any use of chemical fertilisers. Wherever there is an old *finca*, there will be a well, but unless there is evidence of recent use it is advisable to treat it with caution. If in doubt, use sterilising tablets as a safeguard.

Clothing and Equipment

It is assumed that readers are experienced in mountain walking, hence this section can be kept short. Although very heavy clothing is not needed, do make sure that especially in winter you have reserves of warm clothing, including a windproof anorak and trousers. Shorts cannot be recommended in the mountains as they do not protect you from the spiky vegetation, nor do they conserve core heat in an emergency. If walking in summer, always have a long-sleeved shirt and a hat, and carry barrier cream to protect you from the sun. You also need lots of water and some salt tablets. Any comfortable ankle boot with a good cleated sole will suffice.

Emergencies and Medical Care

It is advisable that at least one member of the party has basic first aid training, and that each member has a small simple first aid kit for their own use.

There is no volunteer mountain rescue organisation in Valencia; each incident is dealt with on an *ad hoc* basis by the Guardia Civil (Tel: 522 11 00), who will organise the rescue in conjunction with the Cruz Roja (Red Cross), which is organised on a local basis and is manned by young conscientious objectors as an alternative to doing military service. There is no official ambulance service either, and private ambulances are expensive. In addition, the Guardia Civil or the Cruz Roja will probably make a charge for their services, especially if a helicopter has to be brought in. It is, therefore, essential that adequate medical insurance cover is taken out.

Most large towns now have Insalud (National Health) Medical Centres, which are staffed 24 hours a day. At Denia and Villajoyosa there are excellent hospitals with full facilities. Denia hospital is on the southern edge of the town (under Montgo mountain), and the one at Villajoyosa is on the northern outskirts on the CN332. Both are well signposted.

Membership of the Federacion Espanola De Deportes De Montana y Escalada, Calle Alberto Aguilers, 3 – 4 o, izda, 2815, Madrid confers the usual services of mountain organisations, including full medical, recovery and the like in case of a mountain accident or illness.

Farmacias (Chemists)

Spanish pharmacists are most reliable. Many Spaniards seek their advice, and in the villages they often carry out first aid treatment. Remember, however, that in the villages their opening hours are restricted, and even in the towns they close for the siesta.

At night, on Fiestas and Sundays, there is always a Farmacia Guardia open, but you may have to go to the nearest large town. Information may be obtained from the local police or posted on the pharmacy shops.

Maps

The official Mapas Militar are at 1:50,000, the nearest thing to the UK Ordnance Survey maps. The detail and printing, however, are far from OS standard, and buying a new edition does not guarantee an updated map. I find that it pays to keep old maps. They are often more reliable, as the editor of the series is capricious, to say the least, in removing information from new editions. It also takes a very long time before new roads are shown on the maps, and the vast network of forestry and rural roads remains unmarked. There are also the 1:25,000 Ministry of Public Works (M.O.P.U.) maps, produced by the Institutio Georgrafico Nacional, who produce the Mapas Militar. These maps are still based on the old 1:50,000 grid system, with four sheets to the area covered. The printing is better and new roads are shown (still not the rural and forestry), but on some sheets important detail is missing which appeared on old smaller-scale maps. The contours and the spot heights on some sheets of Mapas Militar are questionable.

Maps Required For Las Marinas

1:50,000 Mapas Militar

Jativa	29-31	(795)
Alcoy	29-32	(821)
Benisa	30-32	(822)
Villajoyosa	29-33	(847)
Altea	30-33	(848)

1:25,000 M.O.P.U.

796	I Gandia	III Oliva IV Denia
795	Jativa	Sheets I – IV (Xativa, Real de Gandea & Albaida, Villalonga)
822	Benisa	Sheets I, II & III (Orba, Benisa & Tarbena)
823	Javea	Sheets 1 & 3 (Javea & Benitachell)
847	Villajoyosa	Sheets II & IV (Relliu & Villajoyosa)
821	Alcoy	Sheets I – IV (Muro, Alcoy, Planes, Alcoy and Castell de Castells)
848	Altea	Sheets 1, 2 & 3 (Altea, Calpe & Benidorm)

Road Maps

These are quite good, but are at times misleading to say the least. They have the annoying habit of not showing road numbers for provincial and minor roads, which walkers use a lot. And there are glaring mistakes on some, such as showing a dam which failed 20 years ago and the wetlands below Pego as a vast lake. Some roads which were completed years ago and now have an official number are shown as mule tracks.

Michelin	1:400,000	Central/Eastern Spain 445
Firestone	1:200,000	Costa Blanca T28
M.O.P.U.	1:200,000	Province of Alicante (based on Mapas Militar)

Map Suppliers

Many newsagents and bookshops now display a sign showing that they supply Mapas Militar, but don't get excited – their stock-keeping is atrocious. I list suppliers who are (more or less) reliable.

Altea	Newsagent near Supermarket Pepe Clara, Calle Ingen Munoz, in centre of town
Alicante	Librea International, Altmir 6, near Town Hall
Benidorm	Librier Atlas, Calle Valencia
Calpe	Papeleria Vasquez, Av. Gabriel Miro and other branches
Jalon	The Sweetie Shop, on main road just before you reach the river (English)
Valencia	Papeleria Regolf, Mar2, side street near Cathedral and Zaragoza Gardens
In England	Stanfords 27A Floral Street London WC2E 9LP
	The Map Shop 15 High Street Upton-upon-Severn Worcs WR8 OHJ

Both stock the military maps plus smaller scale tourist maps of the area.

Place Names

In this text I have endeavoured to keep to Castilian Spanish when recording place and feature names. There is, however, a spirited revival of the use of Valenciano (similar to Catalan), the old language of the province. The older Mapas Militar always use Castilian, but all the new editions of Mapas Militar, and the new 1:25,000 edition, use Valenciano exclusively for place names and mountain features. This could cause some confusion to those familiar with the Castilian names. Appendix 3 contains a glossary of Valenciano terms for most mountain features.

When to Walk?

The Weather

Residents on the Costa do not, generally, walk in the mountains when it is raining, nor do they do so until the tracks have dried out. This may have British walkers rolling on the floor, but there are 300 plus dry days in this idyllic climate, and to cancel a walk now and again because of the weather is no great loss.

The climate on the mountains closest to the sea is much the same as on the coast, with two exceptions. The coast, under the maritime influence of the Mediterranean, does not suffer from frost at all, whereas inland, and over 300m, you will get regular frosts in winter, and even some snow higher up on Aitana and Serrella. The dry conditions on the coast are not reflected in the mountains, which get a slightly higher rainfall and much mist in winter, when the coast is clear.

But the region's 16in of annual rain has to fall some time, and generally the spring and autumn months can include short periods of wet, unsettled weather. The end of the year, Christmas, then New Year are normally settled and sunny, but generally the unsettled periods are short and clear up quickly. Probably the only safe prediction as to the weather is that from mid-June to mid-September you will be extremely unlucky if you get a wet day, as drought is the general rule throughout this period. Some time during September/October, the Gota Fria arrives. This consists of tempests and torrential rain which occur when the cold moist air stream from the north meets the overheated Mediterranean at the end of the summer. There is very heavy rain for many continuous days, resulting in landslides, floods and general devastation, much to the 'surprise' of the local authorities – it has only been happening since the Carthaginians were here! The only conditions really to be avoided are torrential rain during the Gota Fria. For the rest of the year, as long as you avoid unsettled conditions and are well equipped, walks can be attempted in comfort.

All village bars have TV and a copy of the local paper, *Informacion*, on whose penultimate page is a detailed weather forecast for the day. Be prepared for snow on the ridge tops of Serrella and Aitana.

The Costa does not have the same variation in daylight hours as Britain. At the summer solstice (June 22nd), there are sixteen hours of daylight, and at the winter solstice (Dec 22nd) ten hours. There is a slightly shorter twilight period than in Britain. The months from May to July give the greatest flexibility in planning your walks in daylight; a winter walk needs very careful planning.

Temperature

Winter temperatures are not to be compared with those encountered when hill-walking in Britain, but on the highest mountains windproof clothing is required, as on exposed ridges the wind can bite deeply. The generally sunny conditions give moderate temperatures during the day even in winter, but when the sun goes in the drop in temperature, added to the wind-chill factor, can be dramatic.

From mid-June to early September, the sun is very high in the sky, and temperatures often rise to over 90°F (over 35°C), with no appreciable drop due to altitude. Precautions against sunstroke, sunburn, heat exhaustion and cramps (this last is due to lack of salts) should be taken seriously.

Temperature Chart (°C)

	max	min	average
Jan	16	7	12
Feb	17	6	10
March	20	8	14
April	22	10	15
May	26	13	18
June	29	15	23
July	32	19	26
Aug	32	20	28
Sept	30	18	22
Oct	25	15	18
Nov	21	10	14
Dec	17	7	11

Dogs

Dogs merit this special note because of the many problems encountered in Spain. Dog owners must hold a current inoculation certificate against rabies, and a colour coded tag must be worn by the dog. Generally, for dogs over 30kg in weight, the dog needs to wear a muzzle in public places. During the hunting season, only licensed hunting dogs (usually very friendly) can roam at will; others need to be on a lead in the mountains (they might otherwise be shot in mistake for a fat fox). Letting a dog roam is not a good idea because of other hazards. The undergrowth hides fissures, pot-holes and abandoned wells, which could prove fatal if a dog falls down them. During the spring, hunters put down poisoned bait to try to get rid of foxes, wild cats, etc., and so protect the game. The law requires that the poison be put out only at dusk, and removed at dawn, but like many Spanish laws it is hardly ever able to be enforced.

There are natural hazards, too, for an inquisitive hound. Both viper and scorpion wounds can cause the death of a dog unless promptly treated by a vet, and the processional caterpillar can also poison a dog. If eaten or taken in the mouth, the swelling can cause asphyxiation. Finally, there is the sand fly, which comes out at night, and whose bite can carry **Leishmaniosis**, a very dangerous disease. So, if camping, take a pup tent as well! Ticks are a special problem in this area because the winters are not cold enough to control them. If they bite humans there is the possible risk of catching Lymes Disease, which will require prompt medical treatment.

Flora

The botanist calls the region's dry, rocky terrain *maquis* or *garigue*, and the plants which prosper through the long hot summer are tough and spiky. Cross-country walking is, therefore, quite painful, and can be dangerous as the undergrowth can hide fissures.

The vast variety of wild flowers, however, add to the enjoyment of walking, and tends to make botanists of us all. Of course, only those species tolerant of lime flourish, but throughout the year there is always some joy to be discovered by the wayside or clothing the slopes of the mountains. The most impressive display is in the early spring, when the valleys are filled with almond and orange blossom. The slopes become clothed in the pink and white of the Mediterranean heath mixed with the yellow of anthyllis, and later, the broom and gorse. Giant asphodels and fennels, and verbascums, add to the display. Many cultivated species such as phlomis (yellow and purple), antirrhinum and gladioli grow wild here, and underfoot are grape hyacinth, miniature iris, crocus and an orange tulip (*Tulipa Australis*), and blue flax makes the slopes of Montgo look like a garden. Flora unique to this area include the rusty foxglove (*Digitalis obscura*) and, usually on some of the scree, the tiny rush-leaved daffodil (*Narcissus requienii*). In the woods the orchids flourish: venus, bee, spider and purple pyramid. On the tops the unusual hedgehog broom (*Erinacea anthyllis*) is to be admired. Even in July, the beautiful pink centaury (*Centaurium erythraea*) still blooms along with the red valerian (*Centranthus ruber*), and on the shady side of a crag or a bridge blue throatwort (*Trachelium caeruleum*) flourishes. Rock roses, cistus and potentilla still bloom on the high ground.

Summer heat and lack of water reduces the display, but those plants that have adapted to these conditions continue to bloom. Be prepared to walk on a carpet of herbs, lavender, sages, thyme, rue, curry plant and cotton lavender, which succeed in the high places. In autumn, once the Gota Fria is over, there is another surge of bloom, but not as dramatic as in the spring, and shade and moisture-loving plants take advantage of the autumn season to bloom – pennywort, hart's-tongue fern and violets, for example, which cannot tolerate the rest of the year's harsh conditions. Wild roses and blackthorn bloom again on the high slopes.

Wildlife

The wild flowers are a joy, but the wildlife of this area is a disappointment, due to over-hunting. Spaniards are inveterate hunters, but do not restrict themselves to game. Any wild bird (except the hoopoe, whose killing is said to bring bad luck) is a prime target, and it is said that in certain areas even large dragon-flies are not safe! Birds are still indiscriminately shot for food and netted, using water as a bait or by employing a bird-lime made of boiled wine. The more colourful specimens are trapped, using a captive bird as a lure, then sold in small cages as song birds to end their days on a town balcony.

The ornithologist needs luck and patience, but there are eagles to be seen, most harriers, many warblers and, on the crags, choughs, but quite naturally they avoid man like the plague. The most colourful birds, hoopoe, roller and bee-eater, are not mountain birds, but may be seen in the valleys. Such pheasant and partridge which have escaped the gun may also be seen. There is, however, compensation for the keen twitcher in the wetlands of La Albufera and the Marjal Mayor near the coast.

Wild boar, foxes, lynx (a protected species), hares and rabbits still roam the high places, but are rarely seen. Lizards and snakes are common in summer, and the dear little geckos come out at night to hunt mosquitoes, moths and so on. Toads (*Bufo bufo sapo comun*) the size of your hand frequent the damp places of the *Fuentes* and wash-houses.

Flocks of sheep and goats are to be seen grazing under the watchful eye of the pastor (shepherd), with his motley collection of dogs, and in some valleys, where there is reliable water (like the Val de Infierno), bulls are grazed, always, thankfully, supervised by a herdsman.

The ancient, abandoned *salinas* (salt pans) under Penon d'Ifach at Calpe are to be designated a Natural Park. The *salinas* attract a great variety of waders and water birds including the greater flamingo, which now winters here in flocks exceeding 100 birds.

Beware!

The only poisonous snakes found in Spain are the vipers, and of the three species only one, Vipera La Tast (*Vibora hocicuda*), is found in this region. It is very easy to recognise, with a triangular head, yellow-coloured, with a wavy line down the spine and dots on each flank. It can grow to 73cm, but more normally measures 60cm. It avoids man, but it may be found basking on a rock. The bite of a viper needs urgent medical attention, as does a scorpion sting. You are unlikely to meet a viper on your walks, but the following advice is useful.

- Remember that snakes are very active in warm weather especially the middle of the day.
- Be careful where you sit down. Do not move rocks (scorpions like the shade too) and remember that snakes live in walls.
- Wear breeches, gaiters or just tuck your pants into your socks. You cannot blame a snake for mistaking your trouser leg for a suitable bolt hole.
- Treat all snake bites as poisonous and get medical aid as soon as possible. Even non-poisonous snake bites could cause problems.

Bees are best avoided. You will find that the farmers move their small, wooden hives about the mountains to take advantage of the nectar which is available all the year round. The best advice is, of course, to leave the bees well alone to continue making their delicious honey, keep moving and carry some hydrocortisone.

The processional caterpillar (*Thaumet opea pitycampa*) is a menace in pine forests. This creature spins its nest in the pine trees, which defoliates the tree, and can kill small saplings. In the spring they form a chain to find a hole in the ground in which to pupate. Processions 2m long are not unusual. Every part of this creature is poisonous, especially the hairs which disintegrate to form a noxious powder, which causes severe skin rashes. Having unintentionally slept with two of these creatures, I cannot advocate too strongly that you shake out clothing and bedding. The most effective antidote for the rash is vinegar, although olive oil and lemon juice are also recommended. Hydrocortisone will not necessarily work.

OTHER INFORMATION

Food and Drink

These days there is not a lot of difference in shopping in Spain, compared to the UK, as even the smaller shops have adopted self-service, and those who are self-catering need only make a shopping list of the Spanish names and be able to convert the euros to their sterling equivalent.

Bread: the standard white *barra* is regulated as to size and price by government decree. It is absolutely scrumptious when fresh, but within a short time becomes a lethal weapon. There is a vast variety of other bread, all of which are more expensive.

Fish: The Costa Blanca is awash with every conceivable variety of fish, from squid to lobsters, to sea bream, swordfish, fresh tuna and salmon. The Spaniards are addicted to the salted and dried cod, always traditionally brought to this region from Galicia in the north.

Meat: There are a lot of amateur butchers, so watch out for bone splinters. Mutton is extremely difficult to locate, and the lamb is slaughtered far too early, with the result that you do not get fine lamb chops or fillets. Pork, on the other hand, in any form, is absolutely delicious, as is the veal.

Cheese: Foreign cheeses are now imported in great variety. Spanish cheeses from the north, especially La Mancha (Manchego), a mixture of goat and sheep cheese, are first class.

Fruit and vegetables: There is a bewildering variety available in the markets and shops, all of excellent quality, and the season extends well beyond that in Britain (e.g. strawberries from February to July). Oranges are available all the year round, and ridiculously cheap. There are many exotic varieties readily available: melons, artichokes, asparagus, avocados, kiwi fruit, figs, dates and lots of almonds.

Wine

In this bounteous land it is a tradition to make your own wine, and most farmers do so, but mostly only for their own use. Whilst the main wine-growing areas are to the south, near Alicante, which has its own *denominacion*, the Costa Blanca area still grows a lot of vines, and there are bodegas (wineries) at Gata le Gorgos, Teulada, Benissa, Denia, Javea and Jalon, the only mountain valley to produce wine commercially.

The land, climate and quality of the vines has meant that from early times this land has been a prolific producer of extremely drinkable wine, which has kept a great many people happy, despite lack of pedigree. If in doubt, drink red.

There is now the Cosejo Regulador de la Denominacion de Origen which grants *appelacion* status each year to those wines which reach a certain standard, and there are many excellent wines, of diverse variety, granted this status.

Sherry, Montilla (poor man's sherry) and Cava (not a champagne but most people are fooled), and the local Moscatel, a lovely sweet desert wine, are surely well known outside Spain already.

The 'Appelacion' is produced by the Bodega de la Pobre Virgin at Jalon (capacity 1,700,000 litres), where you can join the coachloads of tourists in tasting the wine (*degustacion*) and purchase some, from the vat, or in the bottle. For the expert, the whites are from Moscatel grapes and the reds and rosados from Gironet. Teulada holds a wine festival in October when you can join in the fun and sample the new vintage.

Most restaurants will supply a very drinkable wine with the menu. Valencian, Alicante, Jumilla and the wines of Murcia are the most popular. More select wines are available on the wine list. In the mountains you often receive a generous jug of home brew, but seldom a good white, due to the fact that there is little call for anything but red by the locals. If Tio Paco's brew proves a little daunting, mix a spritzer by adding a little soda water or lemonade.

Restaurants

As might be expected, the restaurants in the towns and on the coast are more sophisticated and expensive, but even here there are good inexpensive small restaurants. In addition, there are the ubiquitous oriental restaurants which are always excellent value. There is even a McDonalds in Benidorm and Denia, and take-aways are now quite common (por llevar).

One of the good things that Franco decreed was that all restaurants should provide a simple menu consisting of starter, main course, sweet, and bread and wine for a fixed price. This law has now lapsed, but a great many restaurants still offer a good meal at an attractive price. The Jalon Valley has over thirty excellent restaurants which cater for every taste and pocket. However, at weekends and fiestas you will be lucky to get a table unless you book well in advance. When the almond blossom is in bloom, the Jalon restaurants are full every day.

In the mountains, you must generally accept more spartan fare, provided mainly to the taste of the locals, not the tourists. Nevertheless, it is possible to dine cheaply and well in the most unlikely localities. In the mountain bars and restaurants, you can nearly always get salad and pork chops with wine and bread, accompanied by the ever-present *patatas fritas* (chips). *The Marling Menu Master*, published by William and Clare Marling has proved invaluable.

Tipping

Spaniards seldom tip anyone. Foreigners, it seems, are expected to do so according to most guidebooks. Only give a very modest one after a good meal with good, attentive service.

Village Bars

Most villages have at least one bar, and it serves as a social centre. Opening hours vary with the demands of customers. There is usually a corner reserved for the pensioners of the village, where they can talk and play cards and dominos. The bar will always have some food available, although it may only be an omelette or tapas (snacks), and there are TV, local papers and a telephone. Once open, the bar remains so until the last customer leaves at night. Dogs are generally not allowed in the bars.

One cannot really complain about the inflated prices for refreshment on the coast. Even in some Spanish bars just inland from the coast, there is a sliding scale of charges for drinks, despite the law that charges must be prominently displayed. The lowest price is for family, friends, and favoured customers, the middle price is for normal customers, and those foreigners who are regulars, the highest price is for foreigners, tourists, and anyone the patron takes a dislike to! Normally, country and mountain village bars will give you a friendly welcome, even though they may be curious about you, and like to know what you are doing in their village.

Costa Crime – A Warning

The crime rate on the Costa is no worse than in other European holiday resorts, but many holidays are marred or even ruined by ingenious, determined, charming thieves and fraudsters.

Be most vigilant when in crowded places, markets, airports, fiestas and even supermarkets of anyone who approaches you, however charming and genuine they may appear. Ploys such as offering you a carnation, begging, telling you that you have a stain on your jacket, that you have dropped some money or have a puncture are common. By all means watch the Trileros, who perform a three-card trick with a potato and a pea. It is quite an act, but never join in, and watch out for the pick-pockets who also join in the fun. On some motorways gangs stop tourists pretending that there is a fault in their vehicle, then rob them. At beauty spots thieves watch where you put your valuables as you leave your car on the car park, then break into it. Even in your villa, do not leave valuables on show. Anything that you can do to make life more difficult for the criminals will result in them looking for an easier victim. Happily the mountains are, at the moment, free from problems.

WALKING ROUTES

Gradings

Gradings, despite all efforts to be objective, are never entirely successful, and eventually each individual grades a walk subjectively. These grades always err on the side of caution. I hope that those younger and fitter walkers will not be too disappointed by finishing some of the walks a little earlier than the time given. There will be more time to spend in the local bar.

Timing

These allow for occasional short stops but not for longer breaks. Remember that the weather and temperature can considerably extend the time given if you are to enjoy the walk.

Route Grades

Scramble (Sc)   Rock work below the rock climbing grades

Strenuous (S)   Steep, rough, and require the ability to get your knee under your chin

Moderate (M)   Good general standard of walking, with reasonable gradients

Easy (E)   Exactly what it says, but remember that it is still a mountain walk

Stroll (St)   A gentle amble of 2–3 hours in majestic scenery, with a handy restaurant at the end.

If two grades are used, the first grade takes priority over the second (ie. moderate/strenuous means a moderate walk with some strenuous sections).

Maps

The maps listed in the route information at the start of each walk are 1:50,000 Mapas Militar.

List of Walks

	Grade	Km	Walking time (hrs/mins)	Ascent (m)	Alt. (m)	Start
SIERRA AITANA/ CAMPANA/PONOCH						
1 Aitana Summit	M	12	4	500	1558	Fuente Partagas
2 Confrides Castle	M	7	2.30	300	1100	Loma del Castellet
3 Peña Mulero	St	14	3.30	590	1300	Font Moli
4 Peña Roc	S/M	8	4	460	1129	CV70
5 Sanchet	S	16	7	925	1175	CV70
6 Ponoch circuit	M	14	5.30	720	1181	above Finestrat
7 Puig Campaña	S/Sc	14	6	1060	1410	Font Moli, Finestrat
THE AITANA WAY						
8 Day 1 Confrides to the Aitana Summit	M	10	3.40	592	1558	Confrides
9 Day 2 Summit to Paso del Contadores	M	25.5	10.30	400	1558	Font Moli, Benimantell
10 Day 3 Paso del Contadores to Finestrat	M/S	25.5	6	400	1050	Rest. Vipas, Benimantell
VAL DE ARC						
11 Peña Devino and Alto de la Peña Sella	M	13.5	5.30	360	1160	Val Tagarina
12 Sella to Benimantell	M	16	7	500	1000	Sella
BENIDORM AREA – SIERRA HELADA/SIERRAS DE CORTINA						
13 Traverse of Sierra Helada from Benidorm	S	10	4	1000	438	Benidorm
14 Sierra Helada from Albir	M	7	3	438	438	Albir
15 Sierras de Cortina	E	7	2.30	170	520	Finestrat road
SIERRA SERRELLA/AIXORTA						
16 Serrella Summits and Pla de la Casa	S	13	7.45	600	1379	Puerto Confrides
17 Agulles de la Serrella	Sc	7.5	6	759	1359	Cuatretondeta
18 Pla de la Casa from Fachega	S	12	5.45	614	1384	Fachega
19 Malla de Llop from Famorca	S	12	5	669	1361	Famorca
20 Serrella Castle from Berniarda	E	9	3.30	650	1050	Berniarda

	Grade	Km	Walking time (hrs/mins)	Ascent (m)	Alt. (m)	Start
21 Serrella Castle from Castell de Castells	M	11.5	4	400	1050	Castell de Castells
22 Sierra Aixorta Circuit	M	15	5	418	1218	Pla De Alt
23 Morro Blau from Pla De Alt	S	12	6	750	1126	Callosa d'Ensaria
VAL DE ALGAR						
24 Bolulla Castle	E	9	4	480	739	Bollulla
25 Algar Valley Walk	M	11.5	4	150	320	Algar Falls
26 El Somo Circuit	M	18	5	600	875	Val de Alt
VAL DE GALLINERA						
27 Forada Ridge	M	17.5	6.15	600	912	Benisiva
28 Almisira via Alto de Chap	Sc	14	5	457	757	Benirrama
29 Forna to Villalonga and Rio Serpis	M	10	5	200	350	Forna
30 Val de Encantada and Ermita del Santo Crista	M	11.5	4.30	210	604	Planes
31 Gallerina Way						
Day 1 Beniarrama to Benisiva	M	17	5.30	300	757	Beniarrama
Day 2 The Forada Ridge	M	17.5	6.15	500	912	Benisiva
Day 3 Benisili to Lorcha	M	20	6	250	660	Benisili
Day 4 Lorcha to Benirrama	M/S	18	8.30	600	1015	Lorcha
NORTH-WEST SIERRAS						
32 Benicadell	S	10	6.45	684	1104	Gayanes
33 Lorcha to Villalonga and Rio Serpis Valley	M	20	7.30	225	–	Lorcha
34 Punta de Alfaro and Barranco de Malifi	M	13	5.30	500	876	Cova Alta
35 Sierra de la Plans	M	6.5	3.30	431	1331	Benifallim
WESTERN SIERRAS						
36 Cabeza d'Oro	M	10.5	5	866	1207	Busot

COSTA BLANCA MOUNTAIN WAY
37 Stages 1 to 6 (see p215)

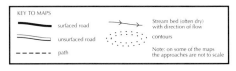

KEY TO MAPS

— surfaced road

— unsurfaced road

- - - path

→ Stream bed (often dry) with direction of flow

⋯ contours

Note: on some of the maps the approaches are not to scale

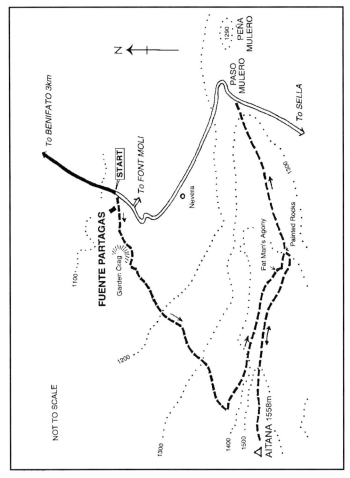

N ←

To BENIFATO 3km

START

To FONT MOLI

PASO MULERO

PEÑA MULERO

1290

To SELLA

Nevera

1300

FUENTE PARTAGAS

Garden Crag

Fat Man's Agony

Painted Rocks

1100

1200

1300

1400

1500

AITANA 1558m

NOT TO SCALE

Sierra Aitana/Campaña/Ponoch

1: AITANA SUMMIT

Grade:	**moderate**
Distance:	**12km**
Time:	**4hrs**
Ascent:	**500m**
Maps:	**Alcoy 821 (29–32), Villajoyosa 847 (29–33)**

The highest of Alicante province's mountains is no Matterhorn, not even a Puig Campaña, but a broad ridge of high ground stretching east to west from Polop to Puerto de Tudons on the Sella to Alcoy road. This mountain is easily identified by the white radar domes on the western summit.

The summit itself is occupied by the military, who also have the easiest ascent, by a road leading off east from the Puerto. Sadly, this road is out of bounds. Our route will approach from the north, by way of the Simas de Partagas – a set of giant fissures which form a line of impressive cliffs above the Guadalest Valley. Whilst this is a moderate walk, most of it is rough walking with few good paths, and the crossing of the Partagas is a rock scramble.

Making a Start to the Fuente de Partagas

Leave the CV70 beyond Guadalest near Km.31, and turn left with a sign to Benifato (watch out for this, there is little warning), and go towards the village. Just as the houses start, turn right (south) along a narrow surfaced road next to a house named Casa la Foya. This is an access road which winds upwards for 3km until it becomes unsurfaced at a low building – the *Fuente* Partagas. Here you will find picnic tables, and the Partagas stream running down the road. The road continues to climb left, and goes south-east to the Paso Mulero and Sella – this will be your return route.

Towards the Partagas Rocks

Behind the *Fuente* can be seen the solid wall of double cliffs which are the Partagas, and it is necessary to first outflank them by turning them on their western end. To do this, strike up west-south-west, keeping a prominent crag (Garden Crag) on your right, towards a small col, then seek out an indistinct path which zig-zags upwards in the same direction, following it until the masts on the summit of Aitana are visible. Look back now, and you will see that the impressive Garden Crag is, in fact, cultivated nearly up to its summit, and you have glorious views of the coast, Penon d'Ifach, the Bernia and Mala del Llop, with Confrides Castle just below the ridge.   20mins

Carry on heading for the summit masts for a while, passing a *deposito* (water storage tank) and a spring, until you reach a large flat area which gives onto a broad shelf running almost parallel with the main ridge. You can now see all the summit installations.   *1hr 10mins*

To Fat Man's Agony

Change direction now to south-east to follow below the Partagas cliffs away from the summit. You have now outflanked the lower cliffs, and now have to cross another band to join the main ridge of Aitana itself. The track moves slowly upwards towards another small col, but soon has to cross some scree, and you can now actually touch the crags. Ahead is a jumble of rocks filling a gully. A prominent yew tree will be seen high up, and a gap in the rocks to the left of it. This is Fat Man's Agony, and your route. Behind you, high up on the ridge, is a small rock window. Scramble up the rocks, pass the tree and go through the gap, and you have crossed one of the Simas de Partagas. Turn left as you leave the gap, and traverse until you meet a path near some painted rocks – souvenirs of past speleological explorations. Look back into the fissures, they are very impressive.   *1hr 30min*

At these painted rocks, turn right (due west) and climb along the edge of the fissures to reach the broad summit of Aitana, the highest point (not quite 1558m but near enough) accessible to the public in the whole province.   *2hrs*

Wonderful Views

From the summit can be seen the second and third highest peaks in the province, Puig Campaña (1410m) looking south-east, and Mont

Cabrer (1389m) to the north-west. Further access to the west is prohibited, so views in the direction of Alcoy are limited. In all other directions, however, the vistas seem endless. It is not often that you can pick out the square tower of Cocentaina Castle (north-north-west). Confrides, Serrella and Guadalest Castles are also visible to the north-east.

An ice-pit, or *nevera*, was a necessity in ancient times for keeping food fresh. It was always dug on the northern slope of a hill in order to be shaded from the sun and to be near the snow-line. The best example to be seen, still with part of the roof intact, is on Mont Cabrer near Concentaina. Below you on the northern flanks, see how many of these circular pits you can spot. You will visit one on your descent.

Enjoy your time on the roof of Alicante and if, by any chance, you wear a hearing-aid, do switch it off if the radar is operating – the bleeps will drive you mad!

Descents

If you have become 'hooked' on 'Fat Man's Agony', then by all means reverse the ascent route. A recommended alternative is to follow the ridge down and over Peña Alta to Paso Mulero, and the road back to the *fuente*. It is a very scenic route, noted for some prickly vegetation and few paths until the road is reached.

To Paso Mulero

Go south-east first down the ridge to avoid the fissures until you reach the painted rocks. Now the route will be generally east, following the edge of the cliffs wherever possible to avoid the vegetation. Look back to enjoy magnificent views of the dramatic land-slips which have occurred on Aitana, probably caused by the great earthquake in the 17th century. The route is rather undulating between small summits, one of which is Peña Alta, until the road to Sella can be seen below.
2hrs 30mins

Keep going ahead until a reasonable path appears, which leads you down to the pass, and turn left along the good forestry road, which will lead you back to your transport at *Fuente* Partagas.   *3hrs 30mins*

Visit to Nevera

It is easy going now, the good road leading west towards the *fuente*. After about 10min, start to search the left-hand side of the road for the remains of a *nevera* – about 100m from the road – and try to visit it. There was once, of course, a stone and wood roof, but the pit and its access doors can still be seen.

Rejoin the road, and head back to the *Fuente* Partagas and the hospitality of the Venta de Benifato on the main road.   *4hrs*

2: CONFRIDES CASTLE

Grade:	moderate
Distance:	4km; from Benifato 7km
Time:	2hrs–2hrs 30mins
Ascent:	300m; from Benifato 440m
Map:	Alcoy 821 (29–32)

Confrides Castle attracts other names. Benifato claims it, and somehow it has gained the name El Castellet. It is apparently the only castle on Aitana, and stands on an isolated turret of rock at the end of a northern spur of the mountain, with a commanding view of the whole of the Guadalest Valley. Within sight are two other castles, its sister on the other side of the valley, Serrella, and in the centre of the middle valley Guadalest Castle itself. We will approach the castle from Benifato (southeast).

A pleasant walk on good tracks, but care is required for the final ascent to the castle over rocky ground. Purists may leave their transport at Benifato, and walk a pleasant 3km on the metalled road through almond, cherry and pear orchards. Others may wish to take their transport higher up the road.

Making a Start

Leave the CY70 beyond Km.31, and turn left, signed Benifato. The sign comes on you rather suddenly around a bend in the road, and is easily

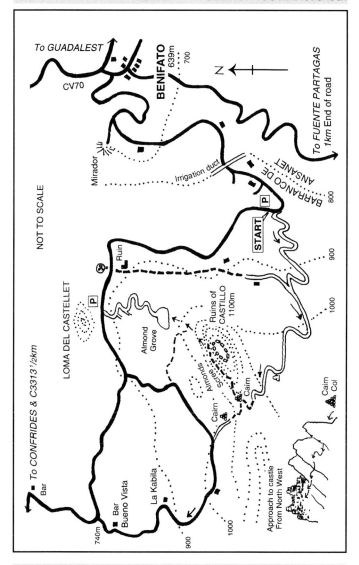

NOT TO SCALE

To GUADALEST

CV70

BENIFATO 639m

700

N ←

To FUENTE PARTAGAS
1km End of road

Mirador

Irrigation duct

BARRANCO DE ANSANET

800

START

P

900

Ruin

1000

LOMA DEL CASTELLET

P

Almond Grove

Ruins of CASTILLO 1100m

Almonds Scree

Cairn

Cairn

To CONFRIDES & C3313 1/2km

Bar

Bar Bueno Vista

La Kabila

740m

900

1000

Cairn Col

Approach to castle From North West

missed. Almost immediately, a very tight turn is needed to join an unclassified road on the right, leading over Loma de Castellet to Confrides. There are helpful waymarkings at all junctions to prevent you wandering off onto side roads. Ignore a forestry road leading off to the right, and after 3km a side road on the left (red markers) is the start of your walk. A few cars can be accommodated on the roadside, but a larger party should park 2km further on at the summit of the road, and walk down the road to the starting point. *(allow 20mins)*.

The red waymarks on the wall will help you throughout this route, although your first objective, the col between Aitana and the castle, is clearly visible most of the time. The unsurfaced road twists and turns to gain height, and at first heads towards Aitana. Pass a sign *'Finca de Castillo'* on the right, and now you have clear views of the summit of Aitana, with its white globular radar domes. *15mins*

You now have a good view of a great gully cut into the flank of Aitana (Barranco de Alfafani). Ignore a side track going left, then pass a boulder on the left-hand side with lots of paint on it, and then two metal gateposts on the right. At this point, say goodbye to Aitana, as you pass through a few mature pines and the track steepens for the final pull up to the col, now clearly visible. Reach the col with its prominent cairn. *35mins*

The Col

You now have a view to the north-west and the upper Guadalest Valley. The best route to the castle is on the western side of the crags and needs care, although there are a number of good paths. First, however, keep to the eastern side of the first rock pinnacle, before zig-zagging upwards, heading for the 'Front Doorway'. Towards the top, beware of side paths leading to impressive view-points, and watch out for a shaft which leads to an underground cave system. In winter, walkers can warm themselves in the 'warm' air from the caves. Go through the gateway and into the castle ruins. *1hr 10mins*

The Castle

The ruins are impressive – there is a good part of a tower, pieces of a castellated wall, and a cistern with stone pipes remaining. The views, as might be expected, are also sensational, with the whole of the valley laid out before you, and offer a good opportunity to test your map-reading skills by identifying all the villages and summits in the area.

Descent

In addition to reversing the approach route, there are other routes on the western side which can be used.

Before leaving the castle it is a good idea to check your chosen descent route, especially the one to Lomo del Castellet. The key to the descent is a small circular grove of almonds north-east of the castle, from which a surfaced road leads to Lomo del Castellet.

A. Descent to Lomo Del Castellet

Leave the summit and retrace the route to the col. Just before reaching the cairn, turn sharp right to find a good track leading across the screes directly under the castle crags (north-east). The track ends in a broader track leading from a single terrace of almond trees which is the route to Confrides. From here to the small almond grove, cross over the Confrides track, until you see a marker, then follow a good surfaced road and turn right to reach Loma del Castellet. This route now has red waymarkings. Refreshments and meals are available at Venta de Benifato on the main road below the village. *45mins*

B. Descent to Confrides

Follow the normal route and then turn left and follow the surfaced road down to Confrides, passing through a farm La Kabila and by the restaurant Buena Vista to reach the main road just outside the village. *35mins*

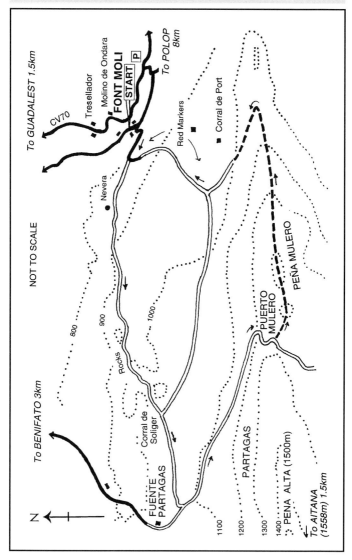

3: PEÑA MULERO

Grade:	**moderate/strenuous**
Distance:	**14km**
Time:	**3hrs 30mins**
Ascent:	**590m**
Map:	**Villajoyosa 847 (29–33)**

Aitana (1558m) is the highest mountain in Alicante province, difficult to identify except by the distinctive white Radar domes installed by the Americans on the summit. The East Ridge stretches down towards the sea and the mountain Peña Mulero. From halfway along the ridge, Peña Mulero is equally difficult to identify at close quarters, but from across the valley its summit crags can be seen above the village of Benimantell. There are lots of good roads but the summit traverse is rough walking.

Getting There

Font Moli is a charming hamlet on a back road which runs from Km.8 on the CV70, from Polop, on the outskirts of Guadalest, and joins the Confrides road, in the village of Benimantell. There are signs on both roads to El Tresellador Restaurant to help you. Amongst the small collection of houses is the old water mill and an attractive picnic site at the *fuente*.

To the Nevera

Either climb the steep path to the left of the *fuente* or walk round by the broad road, heading north-west, to seek out another unsurfaced which leaves the main road (our return route) and heads almost west along terraces between almond groves, with a view of Confrides Castle and Aitana ahead of you. As the road twists and turns, note a well preserved *nevera* (ice pit), on the right-hand side of the road, used many years ago to make ice from snow. This one has lost its roof. Above, ahead of you are some attractive rocks and pinnacles, and the road climbs through them to reach the ruins of an old *finca*.   *30mins*

Towards Fuente Partagas

Behind the *finca* ruins there is a good broad track which heads in a south-westerly direction towards a small col, from which there are good views of the summit of Aitana, with its array of aerials and the huge white radar domes. Below the summit note the impressive crags and fissures of the Simas de Partagas. Pass a small cultivated depression and a small shelter, and there is another ruined *finca* on the skyline as a track joins from the left and ends your western tack. Above can be seen the rough road which climbs to the Puerto de Mulero, and continues down into the Val de Tagarina and to Sella. In another fifteen minutes the road from Partagas joins from the right, and you can now look down on the *fuente* with its old *finca*, used to provide accommodation for walking groups and for fiestas. The village of Benifato is down below you in the valley.   *1hr*

To the Puerta de Mulero

From the col head upwards, east, without any path, but with some red markers to help, until you reach the broad crest of the ridge, with its cairn.   *2hrs*

There are now excellent all-round views especially to the east, towards the coast, with Peña d'Ifach, Moraira Castle, Villajoyosa and Benidorm with the Isle of Tabarca.

Continue along the ridge, as near to the edge of the impressive cliffs as safety allows, on intermittent paths still going east. Pass a small depression, access to a pit hole, with ancient ropes still in place, until the path start to descend to a small col, where you can see that the ridge bends to the south towards Peña Roc. Here find a small rock gateway with a red square marker (hunting rights), and the way off the ridge.   *2hrs 30mins*

Descent to Font Moli

First descend north-east on a rocky path through almond groves to a good broad track, with marker posts also with red square markers. The track from Corral de Solinger and Partagas joins from the left, and the route now heads north-east to rejoin the ascent route with good views of the Guadalest Valley below. The Tresellador, 0.5km along the road north-west to Benimantell, will provide excellent traditional fare and is the nearest restaurant, but in the valley there is an extensive choice.   *3hrs 30mins*

4: PEÑA ROC

Grade:	**strenuous/moderate**
Distance:	**8km**
Time:	**4hrs**
Ascent:	**460m**
Maps:	**Altea 848 (30–33), Villajoyosa 847 (29–33)**

This is a rocky peak which guards the western portal of Paso de Contadores, which in itself is the effective end of the long Aitana Ridge as far as walkers are concerned. Progress further east, towards Ponoch, is strictly the province of the rock climber. The pass is easily identifiable from the Polop to Benimantell road by the pointed crag which forms the eastern portal opposite to Peña Roc.

The first hour of this traverse is on a good forestry road, which crosses the pass and descends via the Barranco del Arc to Sella. It is, in itself, a good pre-prandial stroll for those who only came to dine at one of the three excellent restaurants near the start of the walk. The next section includes two or three strenuous rock climbing pitches and a steep loose gully, and can only be recommended to those who can cope with and enjoy these conditions. Walkers can still reach the summit of Peña Roc by reversing the descent route, which is, however, still rather strenuous.

Getting There

Take the CV70 road from Polop to Benimantell, and near Km.6.8 find three restaurants, the Ponsoda, Vipas and Rincon de Juan, where walkers can leave their cars and make arrangements for refreshments at the end of the walk.

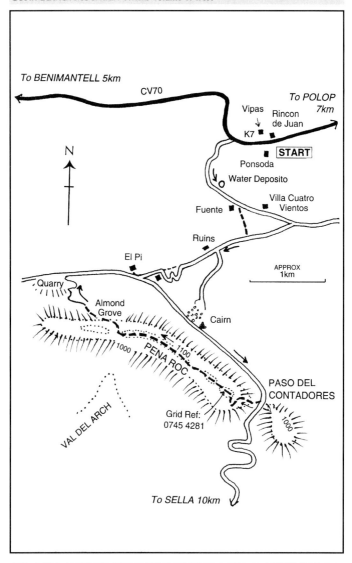

To the Paso de Contadores

A few metres to the west of the restaurants, near Km.7 and a small villa, an unsurfaced road goes off south-east (left) climbing gently past a green water deposit on the left to reach *Fuente* Almaquer, with its troughs and cisterns. *15mins*

From the *Fuente*, a rough track goes directly up to join the road at a higher level for those who are obsessed with cutting corners or in a hurry. Otherwise, continue along the road, passing a house, Quatro Vents, and at a junction change direction to the right, heading north-west until you reach an old *finca*. Near this *finca*, a grass road on the left provides a short cut, but necessitates a scramble through boulders at the end. Continue along the road in a north-westerly direction until, at a cairn at a junction, the road to the pass is joined by turning left.

Continue in a south-easterly direction, parallel with and under the impressive crags of Peña Roc, and pass through the portals of the Paso del Contadores. *1hr 15mins*

From the pass, there are extensive views north, down into the Guadalest Valley, whilst to the south, walkers can admire the deep valley of the Barranco del Arc.

The Ascent of Peña Roc

Face west and note a reddish buttress with an eroded pinnacle on its right. The route is first a scramble up the broken ground towards the pinnacle, then traverse left to reach the base of the buttress. Don't forget to look down through the crags towards Montgo. Now follow the buttress wall for a few metres, descending a little, to find a narrow cleft, which provides a short moderate-grade climbing pitch, giving access to the gully itself. The ascent is very steep and loose, and contains two or three nice little rocky problems. I have seen similar gullies graded as rock climbs in England, and it needs great care. With a large party the ascent will, of course, take much longer, and the danger of being struck by dislodged rocks is obviously greater. Once at the throat of the gully, it is easier to go left, and then scramble up to the summit rocks. *2hrs 10mins*

The Summit

The rocky crest of the mountain has magnificent views in all directions. To the south, Puig Campaña dominates the scene, then, just a little

Peña Roc photo by Maurice Gibbs

west, the beautiful curved arête of El Realet. South-west, look directly down the broad valley of Barranco del Arc to Sella, with the Murcian mountains in the far distance. To the west of the valley can be seen Peña Devino, and to the north the Guadalest Valley, then Montgo to the east.

Traverse of the Ridge and Descent

Now follow the arête westwards, taking care to keep only as close to the northern edge, with its sheer drops, as your experience and weather conditions permit. There is no path. As the ridge broadens, a track appears; follow this until a col is reached. Once the track starts to climb towards Peña Mulero, escape from the ridge on the northern side to seek out a rough path. So far, no markers on this route.   *2hrs 40mins*

The indistinct path traverses downwards, crossing scree and heading west towards a large quarry, which can be seen below. Reach an almond grove, from which a good track leads west towards the quarry.   *3hrs*

From the quarry, the road continues in a north-easterly direction, and when you come to a small *casita* (El Pi), turn off left to join the ascent route again. Descend via the *Fuente* back to the main road and refreshments at hand.   *4hrs*

5: SANCHET

Grade:	**very strenuous**
Distance:	**16km**
Time:	**7hrs**
Ascent:	**925m**
Maps:	**Altea 848 (30–33), Villajoyosa 847 (29–33)**

To the west of the beautifully situated town of Polop de la Marina, rightly famous for its sweet and bountiful water supply, the skyline is dominated by the great bulk of the mountain Ponoch (the Sleeping Lion). A much more elegantly shaped mountain, Sanchet, is often ignored. To me, the contrast of Ponoch's great buttress with the shapely pinnacles of Sanchet is a joy to behold, especially from the terrace of one of my favourite bars, El Tosal in Chirles.

This walk is not to be taken lightly. Whilst it is true that the walk in and the walk out are extremely pleasant, with exceptional views, the ascent and traverse of Sanchet's ridge need stamina and mountaineering skills in keeping with the route, which has now been waymarked in some parts. The reward, however, is a view of almost every Sierra in the Marina Alta, and even beyond, with enough jagged ridges to satisfy most mountaineers.

Getting There

Polop lies on the road from Benidorm to Parcent, and from Polop follow the CV70 road, which runs north-west to Benimantell. There are bars in Polop and Chirles on the way to the start, which is at Km.2.

To the Casa De Dios

The route is a circular one from Casa de Dios, and there is a choice of two starts. The route from Km.2 is shorter by 1.5km, but involves 100m

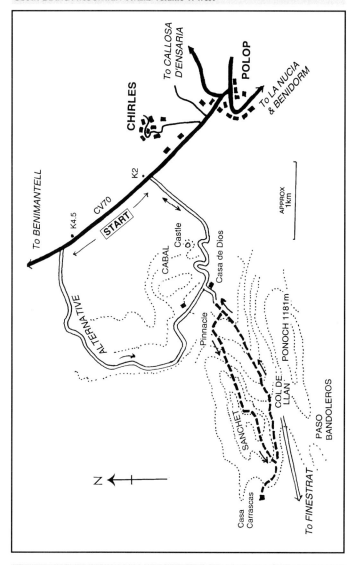

or so of extra ascent. The route from Km.4.5 is longer, but starts higher up the mountain and is less strenuous. Both routes take about 1 hour.

Park your transport near Km.2, or, if you have the nerve and wish to shorten the route, you can take a car to Casa del Dios, but the road is rough and unreliable. Start by walking south-west, passing between tall bamboo screens which help to protect delicacies such as nisperos, kiwi fruit and avocados, until you pass between two reservoirs which supply water for the fruit. To the right are the crags of Cabal, with a small castle on a spur of rock. After passing through a small rock gateway, you can see ahead a small *finca* with an outside kitchen (it must be hell out there when the Gota Fria strikes!). On the skyline is Collada de Llan. This is your return route at the end of the walk. To the right of the Collada can be seen a shapely pinnacle, which is the next objective. The road now zig-zags upwards, until in 20 minutes it reaches a substantial house, Casa de Dios. The walk so far makes a pleasant stroll, with extensive views for those who do not wish to go higher, and the little castle can be ascended in a few minutes.   *1hr*

For the alternative route, find a reasonable parking place on the south side of the AP1704, and about Km.4.5 follow a broad unsurfaced road close to a sharp bend, which leads towards the mountain. The road contours gently, generally south-east, until you arrive at Casa de Dios. This road is passable by 4x4 vehicles, or those with a total disregard for the welfare of their car.   *1hr*

Casa de Dios to the Pinnacle

From the Casa de Dios, follow the road (sometimes chained) which goes (south-west) towards the Collada, but after about 20 minutes, as the road ends, note a cairn and yellow arrow pointing towards some crags. Break off right, and head for the base of some shattered strata along a narrow footpath for about 10 metres, then move right (east) making for a rocky gully, which must have once contained waterfalls. The massive rock pinnacle is above you to your left, and ahead you can see some shattered upright stratas of rock. Once these have been reached, you will find a broken 10 metre wall, which needs care to surmount. Above the wall, walk for a few metres to find a more modest wall, which leads to the final easy scramble to an upper terrace and easier ground. At this point, head for some pine trees, and then go diagonally right to the base of some cliffs, which make up one of Sanchet's arêtes (the mountain is made up of two parallel arêtes). Once at the base of the cliffs, you will find a modest path, which climbs through *bancales* (terraces) to a col, from which you can visit the top of the pinnacle in about 5 minutes. The pinnacle is joined to the mountain by a narrow arête. *2hrs 50mins*

Pinnacle to the Summit

From the col near the pinnacle, aim upwards and right towards the skyline until the way ahead can be identified. To the west is the trough between the two ridges of Sanchet, and it is necessary to descend for a short while until, by climbing decayed *bancales*, the final col is gained. If you can spare the time, go to the edge of the northern arête for dramatic views of the Val del Arch before starting the ascent of the ridge to the summit.

Move up some loose scree, keeping as best you can on firm rock along a rake, until you are able to gain a rocky arête, which is in a corner where another arête joins the ridge. Once you have made the rock moves on to the arête, you become aware of the 300 metre sheer drop on the other side, so test all holds carefully. Now cross, with care, some moderate rock to gain the summit cairn, with probably the best all-round views in the Marina Alta. To the south-east Ponoch dominates the view, with the Paso del Bandeleros between it and its neighbouring peak. Puig Campaña looks every bit the second highest mountain in the province, and Benidorm and Alicante appear to the south and south-west. *3hrs 30mins*

The Ridge

From the summit follow easier but still very tough ground, keeping south-west just below the rocky crest of the ridge for easier progress, until in about an hour the descent reaches a mule-track, which contours round the western end of the mountain. This track comes up from Casa Carrascas, the extensive *finca* seen below. *4hrs 45mins*

Turn left (east) along this track, which is quite well-worn and does have some yellow and white markings. You will find this track a pleasant contrast to the last few hours' scrambling, and eventually, below, can be seen a broad road coming up from Finestrat to the Collada de Llan, whilst ahead the summit of Ponoch can be seen. At the end of this section, you reach the broad flat slabs of the Collada. *5hrs*

Collada de Llan to Casa de Dios

From the Collada there is a good track down the valley, in a north-easterly direction, passing the cave on the right-hand side, which will lead in about an hour straight back to Casa de Dios. Some waymarkings have now been provided on this part of the route, which keeps to the left-hand side of the valley. During the descent, you can still enjoy excellent views, and pass once more beneath the pinnacle of Sanchet, which was the first objective.   *5hrs 50mins*

Most people descend from Casa de Dios in about half the time shown, spurred on, no doubt, by the hospitality which awaits them at Chirles and Polop.   *7hrs*

6: PONOCH CIRCUIT

Grade:	moderate
Distance:	5hrs 30mins
Time:	14km
Ascent:	720m
Maps:	Altea 848 (30–33), Villajoyosa 847 (29–33)

Ponoch (1181m) is a massive bulk of a mountain, a neighbour of Puig Campaña (1410m) and of Aitana (1558m), the second and the highest mountains respectively in the province of Alicante. It is also a close neighbour of the elegant Sanchet (1175m). Ponoch sprawls to the south-east of the town of Polop, and the resemblance to a sleeping lion can best be seen from the next town of La Nucia, when the oblique winter sun makes the massive lower eastern crags look like the animal's mane, and a subsidiary spur takes on the appearance of the animal's haunches. This route tackles the mountain from the south-west, just above Finestrat, and provides a long and satisfying day amongst majestic crags, with the province's highest peaks as constant companions.

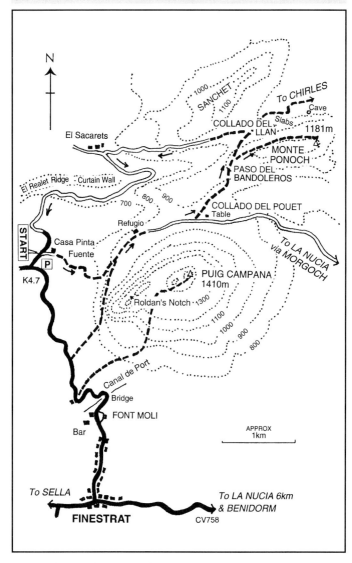

Getting There

The picturesque mountain village of Finestrat, with its *Casas Colgadas* (hanging houses), which rival those of Cuenca, is our starting point. Make for the popular *Fuente* Molino (Font Moli), 1km to the north, on a good surfaced road. Pass over a bridge, Canal de Port, on a surfaced road for 4.7km, passing the starting points for the ascent of Puig Campaña and to Collado del Pouet (direct) on the right, admiring as you go the steep crags of the south face, so favoured by rock climbers. Park eventually at a road junction with a signpost for PRV13 to Ponoch.

To Collado Del Pouet

Take the broad surfaced road (with waymarkings) right, to the north-east (the main route goes on to Sella), and after 5 minutes turn off right onto another track, almost east, to pass Casa Pinta. Pass close to the house and its water troughs, and follow red markers through trees upwards on a rough track heading for Puig Campaña, and eventually join a good path marked in red and white, which will join the path up to the refugio and Collado del Pouet. This track now runs north to reach Refugio Vera Catadral, a fine name for a tin hut with tin beds, used by rock climbers. Beyond the refugio, the track broadens (it leads down to La Nucia via Margoch), and reaches Collado del Pouet, with a large flat boulder to rest on.

In spring, this area is ablaze with the blue Hedgehog Broom (*Erinacea anthiyllis*), not a plant to tamper with due to its fierce spikes.

To Paso Del Bandoleros

Above, on the left of the track, note a red crag with a cave which will be passed on the climb up to a small col on the ridge of Ponoch, the summit of which is visible to the north-east. The path is indistinct at times, but heads for the cave; then scramble through some small pinnacles to reach the west ridge of Ponoch.   *2hrs*

There are now extensive views to the north, mainly Aitana, Sanchet, Cabal with Chirles Castle, and in the distance the village itself. Below is Collado de Llan, a broad plateau with many outcrops of flat rock, where the route up from the north-east joins us.

*Approaching Paso del Bandoleros
from Collado del Pouet*

To the Summit

To the east the ridge leads up to the summit, but there is no regular path due to the scree, and some might find it a bit energetic. Rock climbers and scramblers will keep to the rocky arête, only leaving it at a deep gully under the summit. Others should keep to the left-hand side of the ridge, until the deep gully on the south side marks the start of a short scramble to the summit, with its cairn. *3hrs*

The grassy summit of the mountain is a delight, with views to the north of Penon d'Ifach, Bernia and Montgo on the coast. To the south even the castle of Santa Barbara, on its rock, in the centre of Alicante can be seen. There are views along the ridge, east towards Sella and Cabeza d'Oro, with El Realet, an impressive arête which will be passed on the return route, in the foreground.

The grassy summit drops invitingly down to the eastern buttress, overlooking Polop, known as the 'Lion's Head'. However, this diversion would involve an extra 2km of walking and, worse, a drop of 300 metres, which would have to be climbed again.

Peña Roc to Aitana (Walks 1, 3, 4)

Benimantell, Aitana and Confrides Castle (Walks 1, 2)

Sanchet from Paso del Bandeleros (Walks 5, 6, 10)

Descent – Via El Sacarets and El Realet

Retrace your steps towards the col, leaving the ridge when you can see a good path heading for the slabs of rock, and the good path over the col. Turn left, west, along a good track, which after passing a spring becomes a road and descends to a substantial farmhouse, El Sacarets. Here the road changes direction, south-east to negotiate a broad valley, then settles back to south-west heading for a gap in the arête of El Realet, called locally the 'Shark's Teeth'. Pass between the crags, and the good road now leads back to Casa Pinta and your transport.

5hrs 30mins

Finestrat is well equipped to offer hospitality, after which you may wish to climb up to the *ermita*, on top of a rock, for some more wonderful views.

7: PUIG CAMPANA

Grade:	strenuous/scramble
Distance:	6hrs
Time:	14km
Ascent:	1060m
Maps:	Villajoyosa 847 (29–33)

Puig Campaña (those in the know pronounce it 'Putch'), at 1410m, is the second highest mountain in Alicante. Second it may be in height, but no other mountain, including its big brother Aitana, can hold a candle to it for sheer beauty and fine mountain form. The south-western buttress and ridge is most distinguished, and includes the famous 'Roldan Notch', a fault which has left a square hole in the ridge. From Alicante to Campello and Villajoyosa the buttress presents a fine sight. From Benidorm it provides a dramatic backdrop to the popular resort, but it is from Finestrat, the mountains' 'Zermatt', that the most intimate views can be enjoyed. The south-western ridge is much relished by rock climbers, and there are a number of routes, most of them quite hard. Each year there is a climbing fiesta hosted by local clubs and the town council. Each year, too, hundreds of walkers reach the summit by means of the 'tourist

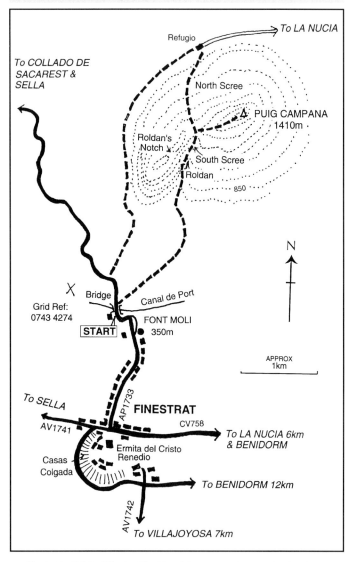

route' up the Great Gully. Many are not mountaineers but adventurers who just had to climb the Puig. A few years ago, when a German mountaineer donated a handsome log book for use on the summit, it was full before the year was out.

This route follows the tourist route to the summit and then offers an alternative circuit for the dedicated and experienced mountaineer and 1000ft scree run down the north face of the mountain. The Great Gully, in which you will spend a great deal of this walk, is definitely not a walker's paradise, but the views from the summit ridge are worth the effort involved.

Getting There

Finestrat, 12km from Benidorm on the CV758, is the most 'Alpine' of Costa villages, built on a cliff with its *casas colgadas* (hanging houses), and with most intimate views of The Puig and the route up the Great Gully. The top of the cliff is crowned with an ancient *ermita* and a formal garden, the centrepiece of which boasts 'Finestrat, centre of the universe'. The village is well worth exploring and has lots of restaurants and bars. To the north of the village is another attraction, the Font Moli, with its gushing jets of pure mountain water. Drive past the *fuente* and continue upwards on a narrow road toward the Puig, and once over a small bridge park your transport and look for a waymarked track (red and white) which heads north towards the base of the Great Gully.

Towards Great Gully

This very well-worn and clearly marked track heads just east of north towards the boulder-strewn area at the base of the Great Gully, and there is little need for any directions. On arriving at the base of the gully just start climbing.   *45mins*

The Great Gully

Settle down now for a long, hard slog up to the main col. Steady walkers might allow at least two hours for this section. There is no route to follow, but by using mountain skills and keeping to the right of the stones where you can discover little zigzags, you can find the least uncomfortable way. The gully bed is a mixture of large boulders, mixed scree and some vegetation, all of which is unstable. A ski pole is useful.

Do be careful if you are a large party to stagger your routes so as to prevent a dislodged boulder causing injury to those following below. You will dislodge more than a few, and remember to shout 'below' to those on the receiving end.

On the way up spare a glance to the right, where a large pinnacle is supposed to represent Roldan the Giant who lived on this mountain. There are a number of delightful folk stories about him and the notch on the south-west ridge. Roldan's daughter was abducted, and the giant flew into such a rage that he kicked the ridge and sent a huge part of it into the sea. This is now Benidorm island. Hard-headed and unromantic geologists disprove this, as Benidorm Island is not the same rock as the Puig. Another tale is that his wife was destined to die at sunset and the giant cut the notch to give her a few more minutes in the setting sun.   *2hrs 24mins*

To the Summit

Now reap the reward for your privations in the gully and tread a lovely marked track along the ridge east to the main summit, with its cross and letter box. As might be expected the views are magnificent: only to the north is there some restriction due to Aitana, and you cannot view the third highest peak Monte Cabrer near Alcoy. But the rest of the panorama is enough to make your stay on the summit most memorable. There are particularly good views of Cabezo d'Oro, near Busot, and Sierra de Aguilar y de la Grana at Rellieu.   *3hrs*

Descents

For most folk descent is again by Great Gully, which is more hazardous and uncomfortable than the ascent. You will not cut down the time on the descent.

Descent by the North Scree

This is a very sporting alternative. From the main col face north and find a well-defined track leading down the face; after a few minutes it turns into the only decent scree run on the Costa. When the scree runs out traverse left for a short distance to find another piste equally delightful until you are forced to breast the gorse and heather down to a good wide track which has come from the Collado del Pouet and La Nucia. If you are really lucky you should arrive at the metal refugio (climbing hut) used by local rock climbers as a base for the northern climbs. *1hr*

Turn left, generally south-west on a good, marked track which circuits the South-Western Buttress and leads you back to the surfaced road, about a kilometre from the start. *2hrs*

On the path up Puig Campaña

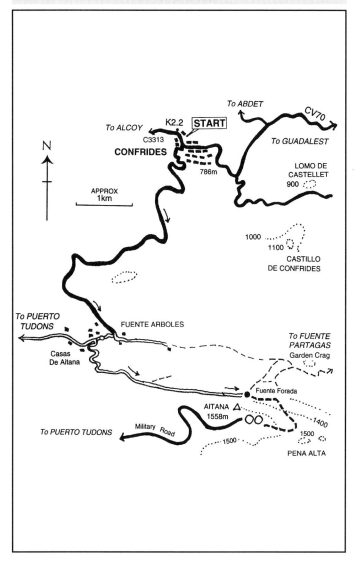

The Aitana Way:
from the highest summit towards the sea

This three-day walk (see map p.12) follows the East Ridge of the highest mountain in the province of Alicante from the summit to Finestrat, as near to the sea as the mountains reach. The main route covers about 42.5km, with about 2000m of ascent. For those who choose to climb to the summits of Sanchet and Ponoch, this will involve nearer 48km of walking, with 2500m of ascent. If you insist on climbing Puig Campaña (not described, but reverse Route 7), the province's second highest peak, then the grand total will be in the region of 50km, with 3560m of climbing.

8: DAY 1 – CONFRIDES
TO THE AITANA SUMMIT

Grade:	moderate
Distance:	**10km**
Time:	**3hrs 40mins**
Ascent:	**592m**
Maps:	Alcoy 821 (29–32),Villajoyosa 847 (29–33)

Aitana, at 1558m, is without doubt the highest piece of ground in the province of Alicante, but it is equally, without doubt, at first sight a most unpromising peak for the mountaineer, especially when seen from Guadalest Valley or Sella. If it were not for the great spheres of the radar installations on the summit, it would be difficult to identify. On closer inspection, however, the northern face of the ridge is made up of a continuous band of steep crags and there is much evidence of earth movement, slips and even earthquakes, where whole sections of the mountain have contorted and left deep cracks which are the delight of cavers.

The Way follows the whole ridge, even after it changes direction, south, at Peña Roc, and will take you from the summit to Finestrat (about 40km) and even over Puig Campaña, if you still have the strength, as a last tour de force.

First, of course, you must gain the summit of Aitana, and there are a number of routes from which you can choose.

- Military Road from Puerto Tudons on the Sella to Alcoy road (A170). This would be perfect: a good surfaced road, starting high at 1000m, leading across the southern flank directly to the summit. There is one important difficulty, the road is a restricted military area. I have known those who have gambled on the armed guards being asleep, and made it by this route, but don't forget that there are still terrorist groups active in Spain, and it is not worth the risk of spoiling the walk by having one of your party shot!

- From Puerto Tudons via *Fuente* Arboles. This route takes about one hours' walking to get to the *Fuente*. If you are in a hurry, you can normally drive cars to the *Fuente*.

- From *Fuente* Partagas, 3km above Benifato, where a marked track climbs towards the cliffs and joins the other routes near Fat Man's Agony. The route which I have chosen to describe, and which is so far unpublished, is the route to the summit from Confrides via *Fuente* Arboles.

Getting There

Confrides, at 786m the highest village in the Guadalest Valley, lies on the CV70, about 9km beyond Guadalest. There are a number of bars and some good restaurants, and very good accommodation is available at the Hostal Pirineo, on the main road.

To Fuente Arboles

Leave the *hostal*, cross the road, and go up the main street of the village, Calle St Antonio, passing a *fuente* on the left, and take the first narrow street on the right, which goes up between houses to gain a surfaced road. In five minutes, fork right onto a concrete road, with a wire mesh fence on your right and pass the gate of a house, El Pouet San Ignacio. Ahead you can see Confrides Castle on a jagged spur of Aitana, and over to the left the route over the Serrella Pass can be seen passing under Serrella Castle, overlooking Guadalest. Bear right at a junction and ignore a track to the right, settling down to some well spaced zig-zags, as the path starts to gain height, on a western track. Behind you, the end of the Bernia Ridge has the look of the Matterhorn from this angle.   *25mins*

Now the antennae on the summit of Aitana are in view ahead. Below, to the right, will appear the motor road climbing up towards Puerta Confrides and Alcoy. Serrella's two summits also appear with the peak of Pla de la Casa behind them. The road now contours round a barranca, passes a small casita, and now Monte Cabrer, near Alcoy, appears on the skyline. Down below is an old ruined *finca* with an *era* (threshing floor). As you breast a rise, there are more little casitas as you near the hamlet of Casas de Aitana. Still moving east, you see the western buttress of Aitana and swing east, parallel to the ridge. All of the summit of Aitana is now visible, and across the level cultivated area, with its casitas, can be seen another track, climbing under the summit towards Fuente Forata. Now the road levels, and below on the right can be seen the *Fuente* and the *casitas*, many being restored as weekend homes, known as Casas de Aitana.   *1hr 30mins*

To Fuente Forada

Leave the *Fuente* and take the forestry road which climbs up, south towards Aitana, and zig-zags steeply, ignoring as you go two tracks which lead downhill to the left. Note the large split boulder on the right of the road and the missing section below, on the left. On this section you will pass four *neveras* (ice pits) so keep a look out for them. The road finally makes one or two last zig-zags to gain height and arrives directly beneath the masts on the summit.

You may be tempted to go up directly to the summit, but I cannot offer any advice as to a viable route, or what the effect of your head appearing at the perimeter fence would be on the military guards!
2hrs 30mins

Look over your shoulder and to the north-west to see Benicadell, whilst ahead is the Bernia Ridge, Montgo, Col de Rates, Segaria and even Isadoro, on the coast at Benitachell.

In ten further minutes you are directly under the radar domes, as the track drops a little to reach a level *era* with the third *nevera* and the *fuente*, with its trough, whilst behind you is the *Forat*, a hole in the rock high above your head, from which the spring gets its name.   *2hrs 40mins*

To Fat Man's Agony

Go up right of the *nevera* and there is now no regular path over broken ground and scree, as you head for a cleft crag on your left, heading north, with the fourth *nevera* below.   *2hrs 50mins*

The track leads slowly upwards towards another small col, but soon crosses more scree until you can touch the base of the crags. Ahead is a jumble of rocks filling a gully, with a prominent yew tree growing at the top, and over to the left there is a gap in the rocks which is Fat Man's Agony, our route through the Partagas. You can still see behind you the small *forat* passed earlier on. Scramble up the rocks and pass below the tree and through a gap in the rocks, which is Fat Man's Agony, and you have passed through one of the Simas de Partagas.

Turn left as you leave the gap and traverse above the fissures until you meet a path near some painted rock, souvenirs of past speleological explorations. Look back, down into the deep fissures; they are very impressive, caused by earth movements or quakes. At the painted rocks, join a path which climbs west, along the edge of the fissures to reach the broad summit of Aitana, 1558m. You are now as high as you can get in the province of Alicante.   *3hrs 40mins*

Wonderful Views

From the summit can be seen the second and third highest peaks in the province: Puig Campaña (1410m) to the south-east and Monte Cabrer (1389m) to the north-west.

Further access to the west is restricted by the military, so views towards Alcoy are limited, but in other directions, as might be expected, the vistas are endless. Enjoy your time on the 'Roof of the Province', but if you wear a hearing aid, switch it off when the radar is switched on, otherwise the bleeps will drive you mad!

9: DAY 2 – SUMMIT TO PASO DEL CONTADORES

Grade:	moderate
Distance:	25.5km
Time:	10hrs 30mins
Ascent:	400m
Maps:	Villajoyosa 847 (29–33), Altea 848 (30–33)

This is the start of the Aitana Way proper – the traverse of the ridge east towards the sea, and the best part of the walk. You have already walked 11km in 3 hours 40 minutes, and there is now at least another 7 hours' walking ahead, making the whole section 25.5km and a total of 10.5 hours of actual walking. You should, of course, allow a generous margin for rests and also ensure that you have transport waiting at the end of the day.

Descent from the Summit to 'Painted Rocks'

Reverse the ascent route down to the col at the Simas de Partagas, the fissures where past cavers have left painted mementoes on the rocks.

4hrs

To Puerta Mulero Via Peña Alta

This traverse along the northern edge of the escarpment, east, towards the sea, provides exceptional views along the ridge towards Peña Roc at the end of the section. There are good views too of Puig Campaña and Ponoch in the distance. Eventually the coastal mountains Sierra Helada (Benidorm) and Peñon d'Ifach with Sierra Toix (near Calpe) will come into view. Below, on the north side are excellent views of the Guadalest Valley, whilst behind, to the west, are dramatic views of the great cracks and landslips which form the Simas de Partagas. To the south are the barrancas which lead down to Sella.

There is seldom a reliable path since the pastors ceased to graze their sheep and goats here and headed for the coast and their fortunes.

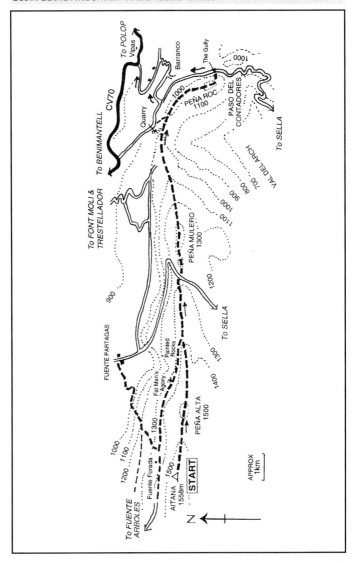

There are five buttresses to traverse before you gain the Puerta, and the best advice is to keep as near to the edge of the escarpment as your experience, the weather and prudence dictate, as here, at least, there will be a minimum of vegetation. Soon you will get views to the south of a forestry road coming up to the pass from Sella, but the pass itself remains hidden until the last moment.   *5hrs 15mins*

To Peña Mulero and Peña Roc

There is no path to help the ascent of the eastern side of the pass, but there may be some red markers. Just head upwards through the rocks and scrub, and in a short while you will reach a broadish ridge with a number of cairns, one of which has got to be Peña Mulero's summit.

Continue along the ridge, east, until you get a good view of your next objective, the crags of Peña Roc. It is now clear that, just before the Peña, the ridge curves to the south.   *5hrs 40mins*

Now follow the ridge in an easterly direction until you find a hollow with a pot hole. This is a good place to shelter if the weather is bad; old rotting ropes seem to suggest that this is an entrance to a cave system.

Carry on, losing height now to a col where there are red markers on a rock gateway on the north side. This is a way off the ridge which in a short time leads to a good track to Font Moli.   *6hrs 40mins*

Carry on now, keeping where possible close to the escarpment on the south side. At times there is a faint path as you drop down to another col before the crags of Peña Roc. In the col you will find another way off the ridge on the northern side which will take you to a quarry, then to join our descent route to the valley.   *6hrs 40mins*

Both hands and feet are now needed as you take to the rocks to follow the arête to the summit of Peña Roc and in half an hour reach its spectacular summit. The views down into the Barranco del Arch, leading down to Sella, with the Murcian mountains in the far distance, are particularly good.

To the west is Peña Divino and Aitana and to the east Montgo.
                   8hrs 10mins

Descent to Paso del Contadores

Unless you are prepared to retreat to the last col again, there is no real option but to commit yourself to descending Nasty Gully, which is on the east side of the pinnacle, overlooking the pass.

This is the penance we all have to pay for the glorious hours spent on the ridge, and it will normally only last about an hour. The gully starts quite broad but loose, and then narrows, and one or two small boulder problems are encountered. Eventually you enter a narrow groove, Asshetons Delight, which in turn releases you from the gully onto the scree beneath some red-coloured crags. Move over to the north (left) and there is a reasonable path down to the forestry road seen below.

Paso del Contadores (the Pass of the Counters) is quite a common name for a narrow pass where a shepherd could check his flock. I was very fortunate to meet an old shepherd from Confrides who, as a boy, would take his father's flock over the pass to Villajoyosa to graze by the riverside during the summer months. There were no telephones, but he says that his father always knew when to be at the pass to check the flock as it returned to winter pasture.   *9hrs 10mins*

The ridge on the east side of the pass is strictly for experienced rock hoppers, and walkers must take a lower route and descend by way of the forestry road to the valley. At first the road runs under the northern crags of the Peña. It then turns to the north (where the route from the quarry joins it) and then to south-west for a while until it reaches a junction and turns left for the valley. Just before this junction look for a marker which indicates the start of the third and last section of The Way. Pass a villa, Quatro Vientos, the *Fuente* Almanaguar on the left-hand side, with its troughs and *deposito*, and finally reach the motor road near Km.7 CV70, where there are three excellent restaurants in which to end a glorious mountain day.   *10hrs 30mins*

10: DAY 3 – PASO DEL CONTADORES TO FINESTRAT

Grade:	moderate/strenuous
Distance:	25.5km
Time:	6hrs
Ascent:	400m
Maps:	Villajoyosa 847 (29–33), Altea 848 (30–33)

This final section of The Way does not include any summits as it wends its way over the passes skirting the mountains of Sanchet, Ponoch and Puig Campaña to reach the 'Alpine' town of Finestrat, just a few kilometres from the Mediterranean. This doesn't mean that those with boundless energy are precluded from climbing to the summits, but all the ascents are extremely rough and, whilst the summits are certainly worth the effort, they will add considerably to the overall time for the section and turn a relatively easy last day into another 9 or 10 hours of walking. Waymarking is an indication that the authorities are at last waking up to the potential of their mountain areas for recreation.

Making a Start – to La Carrasca

Leave the hospitality of the restaurants on the Polop to Benimantell road (CV70) and at Km.7, near a small villa on the right, retrace your Day 2 route from the road along an unsurfaced road leading south-east, passing a water *deposito*, the *Fuente* and the villa Quatro Vientos before turning off right at a junction (road ahead chained). Within a few metres, at the head of a small *barranco* and a very sharp bend, seek out a very narrow track which goes off left in a south-easterly direction. The track can at times be very overgrown (recent fires have cleared it a little). Below is the road leading to Casa de Dios and you are aiming for a prominent pinnacle with a detached flake. The path has recently been waymarked in white and yellow. Ignore paths which lead off left until you are under the pinnacle. *1hr*

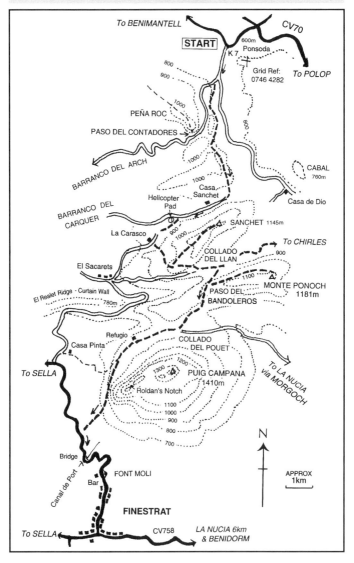

You are now at the base of some steep crags, and the path has acquired some yellow and white markers that indicate the best route. It is, in fact, a large amphitheatre, and the route traverses under the crags and then around a semicircle of old terraces until a path climbs towards a little rock gateway, under another impressive pinnacle. You can now pick out the towns of Callosa d'Ensarria and Altea la Vieja to the east, with the Bernia Ridge in the distance. Behind can still be seen the group of restaurants at the start of the section. Once over a small col you can see the twin peaks of Cabal.   *1hr 30mins*

You are now under another semicircle of cliffs. Traverse below them to join a decayed Mozarabic trail which zig-zags upwards to yet another col with some overhanging cliffs which at times are running with water. A stream (now piped) is crossed, and the route goes round the head of a small *barranco* to a little rock gateway, from which to take the last view of the restaurants at the start of the walk. *1hr 45mins*

The route is now in a high valley, well cultivated, and a good track leads between almond groves to a *finca* (Casa Sanchet). Above on the left-hand side are the impressive crags of Sanchet. Pass to the left of the old *finca* and follow a good wide road which climbs to a broad col, where a helicopter pad has been cleared and marked with white stones. This is a reminder of the extensive search which was carried out for over 20 days for a climber, missing on Peña Divino in 1991. Turn off left 30m before the helicopter pad on a path which was cleared by volunteers, and views appear to the west of Val de Arch with Peña Divino and Sella and, in the distance, Aitana. If you look carefully you can identify the headquarters of the hang-gliding enthusiast who, quite by chance, discovered the missing climber's body in a crevasse after all the efforts of the official search parties had failed.   *2hrs*

Below, on the right, is a remote valley whose *fincas* are said to house a group of Buddhists, Barranco de Carquer. The route climbs to another col, where walkers get views to the south of the jagged, curved ridge of El Realet (the Shark's Teeth), the shapely peaks of Cabeza d'Oro, near Busot, and of course Puig Campaña. To the north in the far distance is Monte Cabrer near Alcoy. You will now observe that the twin ridges of Sanchet have a trough between them. The main peak is the right (south).

Below you, at the very end of the Sanchet Ridge, can be seen the extensive *Finca* of La Carrasca, the next objective. Follow a good track which drops down a little then climbs up to the old *finca*, with its two *era* (threshing floor) stones still in place.   *2hrs 30mins*

To Collado de Llan

From the *finca* leave the road just beyond the south corner of the *finca*, and at a white rock take to a good track, still marked yellow and white, which starts to climb round the end of Sanchet. As you round the end of the mountain you get views of a track coming up from Finestrat, via the extensive *finca*, El Sacarets, seen below; this is the point where those who wish to climb Sanchet leave the main route.   *2hrs 50mins*

Ascent of Sanchet

There is no path to help you as you climb over very rough rocky ground, generally north-east just below the crest of the ridge on the south side, until you can safely gain the crest for the last section to the impressive summit. The earlier views are now extended to the mountain's neighbour, Ponoch, below whose summit on the eastern side can be seen Paso del Bandoleros, the col over which the route will later pass. Alicante and Benidorm are visible to the south-west and south. Allow 2 hours 30 minutes for this visit and add 3km to your route. Continue now east high above a *barranco* and the track coming up from Finestrat. The track is in reasonable condition and recently had acquired some white and yellow waymarkers. Eventually you come to the broad expanse of Collado de Llan with its exposed slabs. The track continues on to lead down to Chirles via Casa de Dios. *3hrs*

To Paso del Bandoleros

There is now, of all things, a fingerpost on the col and even little white and yellow posts by courtesy of the provincial authority. Head now for this obvious col in a south-east direction and you will find a path to help you once you have negotiated the slabs. From the col there are good views down to Collado de Pouet and the great north face of Puig Campaña. Look to the col between the main summit and the south-west ridge and it is possible to pick out the steep scree run used in our circuit of the Puig (Route 7). On your left, to the north-east, a rocky arête leads invitingly towards the summit of Ponoch.   *3hrs 30mins*

Ascent of Ponoch

Just like Sanchet, Ponoch will not yield easily. For those skilled in rock work, the arête is good sport and a direct route to the summit, except that at the very end you must descend from the ridge as a deep gully separates it from the summit. For walkers there is an indifferent path, often across scree, on the northern side of the arête. There may be some red markers to help you find the least inconvenient route. On reaching the great gully scramble up the last rocks to the cairn and trig point on the summit.

This is a delightful spot with lots to see: the great rock of Peñon d'Ifach at Calpe and Montgo at Javea, to the north; to the south, Santa Barbara Castle on its rock in the provincial capital, Alicante. The grassy summit invites you to walk further east to stand on the head of the 'Sleeping Lion', the name given to the Eastern Buttress, and look down on Polop, but this diversion would lose you 300 metres and put another 2km on the route. Allow 2 hours for this diversion and add 2.5km to your route.

Down to Collado Del Pouet

Leave the col and use a well-worn path between pinnacles and under the crags, dropping generally south-west, passing a cave in some red crags, until you can see the broad col below you and the large flat rock alongside the broad road which has come up from La Nucia via Morgoch (an extensive *finca*, now abandoned). You are now right between Ponoch and the mighty Puig which dominates the southern side of the col.

To the Refugio Vera Catadral

Follow the road west for about half an hour and the road ends to become a waymarked track which in turn leads to Refugio Vera Catadral. This is a rather grand name for a spartan tin hut (with tin beds as well), but it is no doubt most welcome to the rock climbers who have spent a hard day on the Puig and have made a direct descent to the hut via the North Scree from the col between the main summit and the south-west ridge, where most of the rock climbing routes are to be found.

I would like to be able to offer a direct route to the summit of the Puig for those enthusiasts who would like to finish the walk by visiting it. Sadly, I know of no decent route, and if one is eventually found it will be a scramble and not a walk. No one in their right mind would think of reversing the descent route of the North Scree, as it is very steep and loose, fine for the scree runner but not at all pleasant as an ascent route. *4hrs 15mins*

Down to Finestrat

The well-worn and waymarked track (red and white) descends gently under the northern crags of the Puig and you will have ample opportunity to admire the many pinnacles and the great notch (a fault) which the giant Roldan (who held the freehold) carved in the ridge and hurled into the sea as Benidorm Island (See Route 7 for more information). You are now high above the valley of the Rio Anchero which lies between the Puig and the castellated ridge of El Realet, with views towards Cabeza d'Oro and Amadorio. In about 15 minutes, a track leads off down into the valley towards the extensive *finca* Casa del Pintart. This is another route to climb Ponoch (see Route 6). Watch out, as the waymarkers are a bit thin on the ground here. Finally you descend to a good, surfaced road leading from Finestrat to Sella and turn left over a small bridge (Canal de Port) and down to the attractive spring Font Moli, with its gushing spouts of fresh mountain water. Don't be at all surprised to see lots of folk filling the boots of their cars with bottles of the stuff – it is much prized for its quality. In another 10 minutes you are in the interesting town of Finestrat with its many restaurants and friendly bars, after completing the Aitana Way. *6hrs*

Ascents of Sanchet and Ponoch 11hrs

Total for the Aitana Way 16hrs 30mins

Including the summits of Sanchet and Ponoch 21hrs 30mins

Val de Arc

11: PEÑA DIVINO and ALTO DE LA PEÑA SELLA

Grade:	moderate
Distance:	13.5km
Time:	5hrs 30mins
Ascent:	360m
Map:	Villajoyosa 847 (29–33)

The attractive mountain village of Sella, 17km inland from the coast at Villajoyosa, has towering cliffs, which protect it from northerly winds. They are, in fact, the end of a long ridge which runs east to west, parallel with the highest mountain, Alto de la Peña Sella, named after the village. The ridge continues east as an attractive peak, Peña Divino. The ridge separates two lovely valleys, Barranco Tagarina and Baranco del Arc, both of which can be admired during a traverse of the ridge.

Getting There

Sella lies on the CV770, which leads over the Aitana Ridge at Puerto Tudons and thence to Alcolecha and Alcoy. The village is worth a visit with its well-placed castle and *ermita*. It is extremely popular, and coachloads arrive daily from the coast to visit its excellent restaurants. There are good views down onto a river, reservoir and sierra, which all carry the name Amadorio. Most of the village houses have been bought as weekend retreats.

Making a Start

Drive first along the main road, the A170, towards Alcoy, then at Km.4.5 turn off right onto a good, unsurfaced road, with a sign *Remonta* Alemana, leading to the Barranco Tagarina. The road is

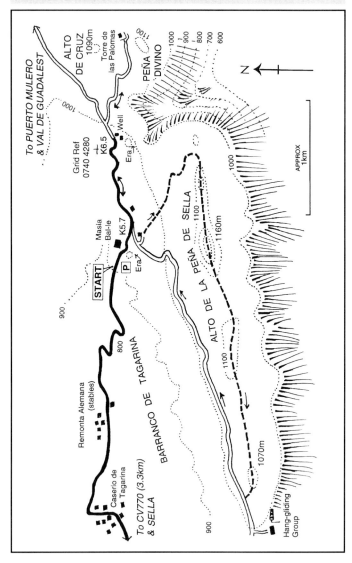

narrow, surfaced and leads past the *remonta* (stables) to a parking place on the left, an old *era* (threshing floor) with the *finca* on the other side of the road (5.5km from the main road). Across the valley you can admire the ridge of Alto de la Peña Sella, and behind you can be seen the aerials on the summit of Aitana.

To Peña Divino

Continue for another kilometre as the road becomes unsurfaced at a well on the right. This road continues north-east and will eventually lead to Puerto Mulero and then down into the Guadalest Valley. This is in fact the final section of the long-distance walk the Costa Blanca Mountain Way, from Villalonga to Sella. Just past the *finca*, on a bend, a road comes down from the right. This is both the route up to the summit of the Peña Sella and the return route. For the present your sights are set on Peña Divino and so continue upwards, passing a welcome *fuente* on the right.   *30mins*

When you arrive at a fork in the road take the right-hand way which leads to an old *finca*, with its *era* (threshing floor), and dramatic views down into the cleft between the two Peñas. Now go left up a rocky path to the left of the *finca* and find another road. Turn right to reach another old *finca*, El Torre, with a tall tower of fairly recent construction.   *1hr 15mins*

The tower is, in fact, a pigeon loft with a spiral staircase to give access to the boxes. It is too remote to have been used to rear the birds, and could have been used for a local sport in which the birds have their tails plucked to ensure erratic flight, which tests the skills of the marksman. Climb up the rocks to the south and a treat awaits you, the summit of Peña Divina. Look down into the deep cleft between Peña Sella and marvel that *bancals* have been constructed in it. Probably its southern aspect and sheltered position made it suitable for cultivation, despite its situation. To the south-west can be seen the village of Sella at the end of the beautiful Barranca del Arc.

There is a road running in the bottom of this remote valley which leads over Puerto del Contadores to the Polop road near Vipas Restaurant. Beyond are the Busot mountains with shapely Cabeza D'Oro. Further south stands the rock with the castle of Santa Barbara in the centre of Alicante. To the right of this, note the Amadorio Reservoir with the Sierra Amadorio behind it. To the south-east is the jagged ridge of El Realet, called by the locals 'the Shark's Teeth' (not a bad description), behind which stand Puig Campaña (the second-highest mountain) and its companion Ponoch. Finally you can now see the route over the Peña de Sella, but a direct approach via the cleft is not to be recommended. Remember that these crags have claimed many lives, especially those who sought a short cut.

To Alto De La Peña De Sella

Follow the road from El Torre back to the forestry road over to Puerto Mulero and turn left down the valley; just past the *fuente*, turn left again onto another road, but only for a very short while, taking the first available track left to a casita. Climb south-east on a good track at first, heading for a col between two of Peña Sella's summits. Finally a narrow path zig-zags upwards to gain the ridge. Views are much the same, with the addition, of course, of Peña Divino.   *2h 15min*

Traverse of the Ridge

You now have the pleasant task of a 3km traverse on this easy ridge over three summits in all. On the traverse you will be able to admire the steep and rocky face of the mountain, and even pick out Monte Cabrer, near Alcoy, until in about 2 hours the mountain loses its rocky crest and descends to a surfaced road.   *4h*

It is worth turning left along the road to an old *finca*, right on the edge of the cliffs, from which intrepid 'bird men' launch themselves into space at weekends and fiestas.   *4h 30min*

Back Down to the Valley

All that remains now is to descend on the good road back to the valley, enjoying the excellent views of the Barranca Tagarina with mighty Aitana to be admired across the valley.

There is lots of hospitality available at Sella, well able to satisfy mountain appetites.   *5h 30min*

12: SELLA TO BENIMANTELL

Grade:	moderate
Distance:	16km
Time:	7hrs
Ascent:	500m
Maps:	Alcoy 821 (29–32), Villajoyosa 847 (29–33)

The little mountain village of Sella, 16km from the coast at Villajoyosa, is organised to welcome tourists, with its many good restaurants and more modest bars. Many of the houses have been converted to weekend homes, and above the village is the ancient Castillo de Santa Barbara, with the village church, a lovely viewpoint. From Villajoyosa take the CV770 north and park in the village.

The walk is very straightforward, following the valley of the Arch in a north-easterly direction, all on good, unsurfaced roads, mostly free of traffic. The route crosses the eastern ridge of Aitana by one of the two passes, which are the only weaknesses in this rocky part of the mountain.

The route described leads to Benimantell, in the Guadalest Valley, where there is accommodation available, if you have not arranged to be picked up at the end of the walk. There are other options available: you can turn back from the Paso del Contadores and enjoy the views down the valley as you return to Sella, or, by far the best, you can stay the night at the Trestellador (check first if it is open, Tel: 588 52 21) and walk back to Sella the next day, using Stage 6 of the Costa Blanca Mountain Way and the Val de Tagarena (see 'Costa Blanca Mountain Way, Stage 6). Whichever route is chosen, you are in for a lovely day (or days) amongst the high mountains, but with very modest effort involved.

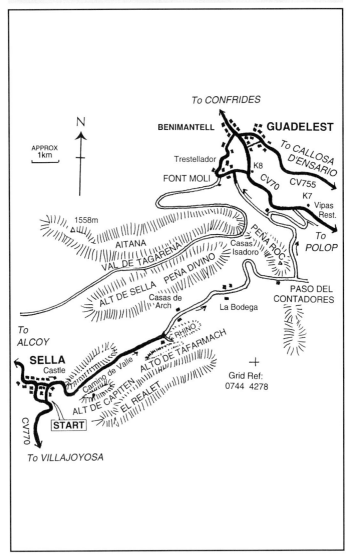

Up the Val de Arc to Paso del Contadores

On the last bend (Km.16.2) before the main road climbs up into the village, a surfaced road leads off to the right and heads north into the valley. There is a notice pointing the way to the Refugio Font de l'Arc.

First you pass a 'Alcazar' type mansion on the right, then the road settles down to follow the left-hand side of the valley, north-east, with views over your shoulder of the castle and church dominating the village. This part of the walk is especially beautiful in the wintertime, when many deciduous trees display their autumn tints, not a common sight on the Costa. At the head of the valley is the craggy mountain of Peña Roc, which is passed by, and on our left, north, are the heights of Peña de Sella and the Peñon Divino, whilst on the other side of the valley is Alto de la Capitania, La Alcantara and Alto de Tafarmach. In 1km fork left, keeping to the surfaced road, with old ruined *finca*s on the left and then on the right.
1hr

Puig Campaña with Roldan's Notch, seen from Culo de Rhino

Pass a new villa on the left, then an old *finca* on the right, as the rocks of El Rino (The Rhino) come into view on the right. This is a favourite with rock climbers. Pass first the head, with the prominent horn. Under the Cabezo de Rino two young Spanish climbers, Miguel and Nacho, have opened the very basic Refugio Font de l'Arc. There is a cheerful welcome awaiting you and probably refreshments, even a meal, if you have given notice. Sleeping accommodation is provided on the upper floor, above the common room, on mattresses (Tel: 0034 65941019 or 0034 65972106). *1hr 30mins*

To Paso del Contadores

At the *refugio* the road forks; take the one to the left (the other road, to the right, leads to Finestrat) as the road loses its surface and starts to climb. Pass some more ruins, Casas de Arch, and arrive directly under the summit of Peña Divino to the north, as Cula de Rino (the Rhino's Tail) is passed on the right of the road. In another kilometre, pas an old ruin and a pumping station. The road is now climbing steadily and reaches some extensive ruins at La Bodega. *3hrs*

At some more ruins, Cases Isadoro, fork right and start the steep climb up to the col, heading almost east, under the crags of Peña Roc, until you reach Paso del Contadores, the col and one of the only weaknesses in the eastern ridge of Aitana. *5hrs*

From the pass take a last look down the Val de Arch, with Aitana now on the right, and if you pick out the tall stone tower on Peña Divino it is in fact a dovecote (see Route 11). You can also see El Realet, the rocky arête under Puig Campaña.

Down to Font Moli

Pass through the rock gateway of the pass, and the road now starts to descend in an easy gradient to the north-west, under the crags of Peña Roc. There are extensive views now to the north, with the Guadalest Valley dominating the foreground and the mountains of Serrella, Aixorta and Bernia, with the coastal peaks of Montgo and Toix. Pass a quarry on the left and keep straight on when you reach a small casita, El Pi (the right-hand road leads down to the restaurants at Km.7 on the CV 70 Polop to Benichembla road). In about 2km the road becomes surfaced, and at a junction turn left to reach the lovely little hamlet of Font Moli (Font Ondara on the map), with its water mill and spring well equipped for picnics. Continue along the road to the north-west as it drops towards Benimantell, and the Pension Trestellador is on the right. Another kilometre and you reach the village with its many bars and restaurants. *7hrs*

Benidorm Area –
Sierra Helada/Sierras de Cortina

13: TRAVERSE OF SIERRA HELADA
FROM BENIDORM

Grade:	strenuous
Distance:	10km
Time:	4hrs
Ascent:	1000m
Map:	Altea 848 (30–33)

Sierra Helada is Benidorm's very own mountain. The mountain looks impressive, but seen from inland it presents a benign sight, looking much like a Lakeland fell, with what appear to be some gentle undulations along its crest. In reality these are five deep gullies, which you will have to negotiate on your way to the summit overlooking Albir; in total they add up to 1000m (over 3000ft) of ascent (and, of course, descent). It is, however, a most spectacular expedition, and the best cliff walk on the Costa Blanca. There are not only extensive mountain views, but in addition the attraction of walking high above the sea, on the edge of the impressive cliffs which drop a sheer 1100ft down to the beach and, at times, even overhang the vertical.

The route is not only obvious but well waymarked for most of the way in red. The steep paths are reasonable, but at times eroded and loose, needing great care, especially in windy or wet conditions. The walk cannot be recommend in such dangerous conditions.

I have always preferred to walk the route from Benidorm to Albir, but there is no reason why it should not be just as enjoyable, and equally demanding, the other way round.

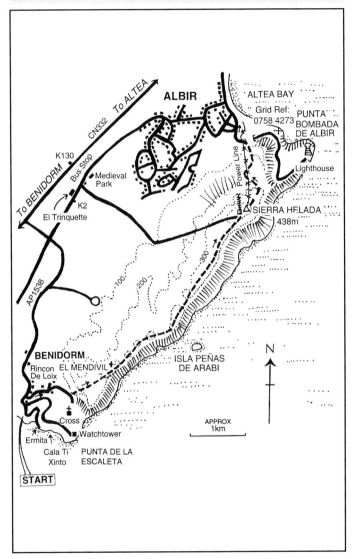

Ideally you should arrange for some transport back from Albir, although you can either risk the erratic bus service or take a taxi back to Benidorm. You can also follow the service road from the summit to the Benidorm road.

Getting There

Leave the CN 332, Alicante to Valencia road, and find parking as near to the eastern end of Benidorm's Levante Beach as local regulations allow.

To El Mendivil

Follow the route to the cross on El Mendivil by walking along the surfaced road which leads to the watchtower and the *ermita* on Punta de la Escaleta. Just past the Restaurant Pergola take the road on the left, signposted Calle Dorata, until it ends just below the cross, and then follow the white posts up onto the col, with the cross to the south.

30mins

Now the route tackles the first summit as it follows red markers to the north and heads for the top of El Mendivil on reasonable paths, passing the head of a gully with a final steep pull up to a cairn.   *1hr*

Already, on your first summit there are panoramic views. Below, on the coast, is the 17th-century watchtower at the end of Punta de la Escalada and Benidorm Island. To the south, beyond the cross at the end of the ridge, there is Alicante, with the castle of Santa Barbara on its rock, and beyond the city is Punta de Santa Pola, with the mountains of Crevillente to the west. Moving further west are the mountains of Cabezo d'Oro, Puig Campaña, Ponoch, Sanchet and the end of the Aitana Ridge. To the west stretch the wide *heurtos* of the Guadalest and Algar valleys, with the Serrella and the Bernia mountains beyond. Ahead, to the north, the ridge leads on to the distant summit of our mountain, with its antennae, overlooking Albir.

The Ridge

The traverse starts with a fairly level section, and there will not be many of these for the next couple of hours. It is, of course, prudent throughout this section to keep fairly well away from the cliff edge, but do, at regular intervals, have a peep over the edge to gaze downwards and appreciate the horrific drop to the rocky beach, at least 1100ft below you.

All too soon this gentle introduction is over and you start the first steep descent, with the tiny islet of Peñas de Arabi below, close to the beach. After about 10 minutes reach the stunted, wind tormented pines in the gully bottom and prepare yourself for the next ascent.

1hr 15mins

There are about five such gullies into which it is necessary to descend. Then follows a short, steep climb to the second summit with its cairn, and an escape route leads off to the west (left) down to near Residencia Ciudad Patricia.

1hr 30mins

There is another twenty minutes of steep descent now, with Albir in view straight ahead, whilst below to the west is the discreetly situated plant dealing with Benidorm's waste products. Arrive in the dip to find a small concrete manhole, probably something to do with the outfall from this plant.

Ahead is a deep gully, with quite a long climb back up onto the ridge again, and there are some bands of exposed strata leading upwards from the gully bottom to the ridge. The route will keep heading to the right, aiming for the spot where the strata meet the ridge, where a short scramble leads to a small shelter on the ridge again.

2hrs 20mins

As the route continues to the north, the Peñon de Ifach comes into view and you renew acquaintance with your objective, the summit – still, however, a long way off.

Now start the descent into another deep and quite impressive gully, at the bottom of which walk along the bare rocks on the cliff edge, with a chance to take some good photographs to exemplify the vertigo.

Now start the last real challenge, the strenuous scramble to regain the ridge again. You will no doubt take plenty of opportunities to rest and gaze back to try and pick out the path and marvel at the precipitous descent route which you have just followed.

There is level walking now for a short time, heading for a lonely pine tree along a much improved track up and down some minor undulations, with the main summit now much nearer, as the surfaced service road up to the transmitting station appears below you, on the left. Those impatient for a better surface to walk on will succumb to the temptation offered by a path which leads off to the left, down to this road; others will keep on until the ridge is again broken by a broad,

Rock table at the Collado del Pouet (Walks 6, 10)

Monte Ponoch and Sanchet (Walks 6, 7)

Approaching the summit of Puig Campaña (Walk 7)

In the Val de Arch, Peña Divino (Walk 12)

deep gully on the right-hand side and take the sensible decision to step off to the left to walk the last few metres up the road to the transmitting station, with the trig point on the rocky summit above it. *3hrs 30mins*

Summit Views

In addition to the views to the south and west which have been enjoyed throughout the walk, there are now unrestricted views to the north, with the whole of the Bernia Ridge, leading down to Mascarat and Morro de Toix, and finally in the distance is the Peñon de Ifach and Moraira, with its castle on the headland. Below is the Punta Bombarda de Albir, with its lighthouse, and the whole sweep of the Bay of Altea, with the old white town and the blue-domed church on high ground behind it. In clear conditions you can see Ibiza to the east.

Descents

*   **To Albir.** Leave the summit and descend the concrete steps at the side of the transmitting station, then follow the chain-link fence to the north across rocks until waymarkers show the track, which descends, zig-zagging, generally in line with the power cables, roughly in a northerly direction. On the lower slopes there are a number of other paths which cross your route, but there are plenty of waymarkings to help until, finally, you come down on to the road leading to the lighthouse to follow the surfaced road, again north, to the little resort of Albir.

*   **To El Trinquette.** If you have left transport at El Trinquette, a large sports centre to the west of the AP 1535, Albir to Benidorm road, at Km.1.8, then a pleasant descent can be made by following the surfaced service road down from the transmitters, generally west for about 2km, normally in about an hour. If you have no transport at El Trinquette and the bus does not turn up, it is a walk of only 25 minutes north to Albir, and somewhat longer along the very busy road to Benidorm (take great care, as for most of the way there is no footpath).

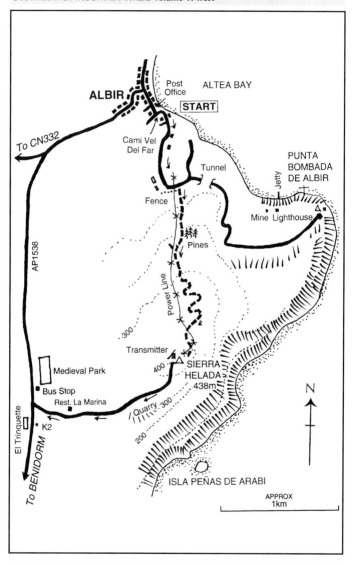

ALBIR

Post Office

ALTEA BAY

START

To CN332

Cami Vel Del Far

Tunnel

PUNTA BOMBADA DE ALBIR

Fence

Jetty

Mine Lighthouse

Pines

AP1538

Power Line

300

Transmitter

400

SIERRA HELADA 438m

Medieval Park

Bus Stop

Rest. La Marina

N

El Trinquette

K2

Quarry 300

200

To BENIDORM

ISLA PEÑAS DE ARABI

APPROX 1km

14: SIERRA HELADA FROM ALBIR

Grade:	moderate
Distance:	7km
Time:	3hrs
Ascent:	438m
Map:	Altea 848 (30–33)

Sierra Helada (the Frosty Mountain) is a 10km coastal ridge between Albir in the north and Benidorm in the south, and has some of the finest cliffs in this area. This ascent to the main summit of the mountain is as straightforward a route as you can get, you just head straight for the summit, with its transmitting masts, right from the start, and the route is well waymarked.

Getting There

Get to Albir by leaving the CN 332 between Altea and Benidorm and find parking near to the beach.

The Ascent

Leave the beach and walk back into the town to find, within a few metres, the Post Office on the right hand and a surfaced road, Cami Vel Del Far, on the left. Follow this road, past the Restaurant Riviera, through villas and apartment blocks until you get a good view of your objective, the summit, ahead. Pass a bandstand on the left, and as the houses end you will find a chain-link fence and a notice 'Punta Albir'. Follow the fence left until it ends, and there is the first red waymarker.

To Punta Bomada de Albir (diversion). To follow the road ahead will take you in just under an hour to the lighthouse, passing old abandoned ochre mines on the way. As the rough but well-marked track starts to ascend there are excellent wider views of Puig Campaña, Sanchet, Ponoch and the end of the Aitana Ridge, as well as the end of the Serrella Aixorta Ridge. A rough guide to the route are the pylons which carry the power lines which lead directly to the transmitting station on the summit. This, however, is a more gentle route following the track as it zig-zags upwards. There are a number of other tracks which cross ours on the lower section; just keep going up on the waymarks, sometimes through pines.

Benidorm, with its headlands, comes into view as you gain height and get a first view of the summit. The path leaves the power lines and moves left (east) for a little while to gain a viewpoint from which there are fantastic views down to Punto Bombarda de Albir, with its lighthouse, of the sheer south cliffs of Sierra Helada and of the vast huertos of the Guadalest and Algar rivers, with a backdrop of the mountains and the coast as far as Moraira Fort.

Pass under the power cables again and make the last steep and rough ascent over rocks to gain the fence around the transmitters, which you pass on the right (eastern) side to climb some steps to the trig point on the summit. What a view – in addition to those already seen. Now you can look south along the long ridge towards Punta de la Escalida at Benidorm, but if you want to go ahead you must allow at least three hours to get to Benidorm. Beyond the ridge is Alicante and its Santa Barbara Castle, with Punto del Santa Pola to the left and the Crevillente mountains on the right. Cabeza d'Oro, near Busot, is to the left of Puig Campaña. On a clear day you can make out the nearest Balearic Island, Ibiza, to the east, with Isla Peños de Arabi below the cliffs.   *1hr 45mins*

Descents

If you have left your transport at Albir, you can reverse the ascent route. If, however, you have been prudent enough to leave transport at El Trinquette (Km.3 on the Benidorm road) or are prepared to risk the bus timetable not being a work of fiction, you can walk down the service road beneath the summit and in less than an hour reach the main road. The road is surfaced but is rather steep in one section, and as it nears the main road there is a restaurant for refreshments, the Rivierra. If you find that the bus does not arrive, don't worry: it is only 25 minutes' walking back to Albir.

15: SIERRAS DE CORTINA

Grade:	easy
Distance:	7km
Time:	2hrs 30mins
Ascent:	170m
Maps:	Altea 848 (30–33), Villajoyosa 847 (29–33)

What is generally referred to as the Sierras de Cortina is a minia-
ture range of mountains which stretches from Puig Campaña
(1406m) to the coast at Benidorm. They rise only to 500m and
are dwarfed by their neighbour, the second highest peak in
Alicante province, but despite their modest height display true
mountain form and are worthy of any mountaineer's attention.
They have a distinct advantage over other higher peaks in that
they are near the coast and a good number of excellent restau-
rants. There are in fact five summits. It is possible to walk along
the one which carries the name Cortina on the maps. Next there
are Tapiada (556m) and Amanellas (520m), a real little
Matterhorn, then two unnamed summits right up against the
flank of the Puig. This stroll takes you along the long ridge of
the Cortina, the nearest peak to Benidorm, and seldom are such
extensive mountain views available for so little effort. The walk
can even be contemplated on a hot summer's day.

Getting There

It is possible to approach the mountain from the north, where the
CV758 from La Nucia to Finestrat crosses a pass at Km.3.9 at a height
of over 300m (a very crafty move!). This road is not shown on old maps,
but leaves the CV70 just north of the Benidorm bypass. As you drive
up the pass note the end of Cortina (The Prow, 440m) on your left and
the other peaks on your right. Turn off left to park outside the campsite
which occupies the broad area at the top of the pass.

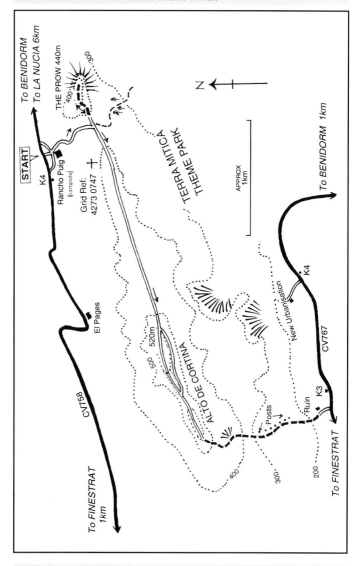

Making a Start – to the Ridge

Follow a good broad track upwards alongside the buildings in a south-east direction, and, believe it or not, in 10 minutes you are on the ridge at a broad col with The Prow on your left and the long ridge of Cortina stretching invitingly to the south-west. To the south the broad view is of Benidorm with its island and the vast theme park of Terra Mitica, Sierra Helada and Peñon d'Ifach. The northern views are of mighty Puig Campaña and Ponoch with Cortina's brothers and Amanellas.

The Ridge

Turn right to follow an excellent unsurfaced road which follows the ridge to its south-west summit and no further. There are no buildings except a shepherd's shelter. The track now offers at least an hour's gentle stroll with hardly any ascent and with expanding views in all directions. Note that it passes above two deep rocky coombes or hollows, and that below are signs of Benidorm's new prestige golf course and urbanisation.

As you walk you gain height, and looking back you can now see the two villages of Altea (old and new), Sierra Toix, above Calpe, and, behind the Bernia Ridge, Olta and even Col de Rates. You now have to climb a little to reach the highest point (520m). Below, on the right-hand side (north), can be seen El Pages restaurant and a *remonta* (stables) with a small bull ring with a wooden bull in the centre.

Summit Views

The little village of Finestrat has a magnificent setting with mountains all around it. Note the little church set on a red spur of rock with the casas colgades (hanging houses) clinging to the cliff face below. Most of your attention will, no doubt, be claimed by the shapely peak of the Puig behind the town, the only Jurassic outcrop in the area. The geological fault which causes the square notch in the south-east ridge has given rise to a number of legends concerning the giant Roldan (Roland) who occupied the mountain (See Route 7).

Most weekends there are climbers on the mountain and each year Finestrat is host to a Climbing Fiesta attended by climbers from all over Spain.

To the left of the Puig is another shapely mountain, El Realet, with its beautiful arête which is called locally 'the Shark's Teeth'. In the distance the radar domes help you identify the highest mountain, Aitana, whilst to the south is Cabeza d'Oro, near Busot, and on the coast Alicante, with its castle of Santa Barbara, can be seen.

To the End of the Ridge

From the highest point you can descend a little and continue your walk for another quarter of an hour to the cairn at the end of the ridge. From there you can only descend, cross-country, to the Benidorm road (CV767) near Km.3. It is now time for you to retrace your steps to the broad col, enjoying the views missed on the outward journey.

To the Summit of The Prow

A rough, steep track will take you in 15 minutes to the rocky summit of The Prow. The effort is well worthwhile as there are extensive views over the rich huerta of the Algar and Guadalest valleys, the Bernia with Peñon d'Ifach in the distance, and the towns of Callosa, Altea, La Nucia and Polop.

Hospitality is available 1km towards Finestrat at El Pages, and in the town itself there are a number of good restaurants and bars. On the Benidorm road, just half a kilometre from the village, is the El Alcazar, which provides satisfying fare in most pleasing surroundings at a very modest price.

Sierra Serrella/Aixorta

16: SERRELLA SUMMITS AND PLA DE LA CASA

Grade:	strenuous
Distance:	13km
Time:	7hrs 45mins
Ascent:	600m
Map:	Alcoy 821 (29–32)

The Cordillera de la Serrella is the 12km ridge which runs parallel with, and to the north of, the Aitana Ridge in a west-to-east direction from near Benisau in the west to Peñon de Castillo in the east, above the Guadalest Reservoir. Its main peaks are the twin Serrellas which are both credited with 1359m (although many do not agree that they are of equal height), Pla de la Casa (1379m), Malla del Llop (1361m), Peñon de Castillo (1120m) and, finally, the outlying ridge of Borrell (1250m), which is immediately above the road, just below Puerto Confrides. On this walk the first three summits are tackled in a circular walk, starting from the Puerto Confrides at the head of the Guadalest Valley.

Making a Start

Park your transport as near to the Puerto (pass) as possible, at about Km.26 on the CV/0 beyond Confrides. It might be convenient to make arrangements with the proprietor of the Rincon del Olvido Restaurant, just below the pass, to have a meal at the end of the walk, in which case your vehicle will be welcome in his car park. Start by taking the road which leads north from the highway near a culvert and a fire precaution sign, and continue to climb upwards under the cliffs, with good views of the road twisting and turning downwards from the pass towards Alcoy. You now have good views of the northern cliffs and the

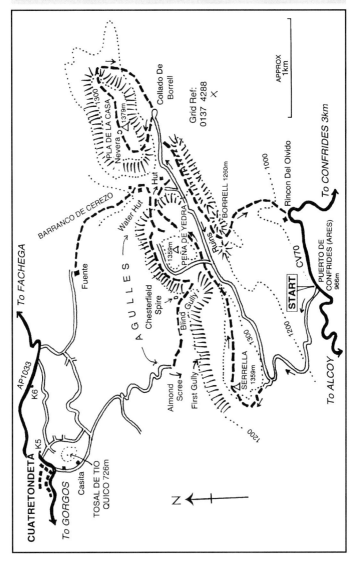

summit of Aitana, along with the high plateau beneath them. To the west, Monte Cabrer and the heights of Plans are visible. Go through a small gateway, and the path can be seen zig-zagging upwards under the Serrella peaks. *30mins*

You will only be going part-way along this road, and leave it on a bend going left on another good track going west through young pines. The objective is the western ridge of the Serrella, and when the pines give out climb up through the terraces, then the broken ground, and finally onto the rocks which lead to the ridge. The village of Alcolecha now appears below. To the east the Bernia is seen end on, looking like the Matterhorn, with Peña Severino below it, and to the south-west Benicadell, Cocentaina and Alcoy appear. *1hr*

To the West Summit

Finally, as you struggle up the steep slope, Guadalest and its castle come into view as you gain the ridge and move east towards the summit, with the forestry road visible in a trough below to the south. Take to the north side of the ridge for a while, and find a broad forestry road which traverses under the main summit to a col, from which the West Summit can be reached in 10 minutes. *1hr 45mins*

To the East Summit

Return to the forestry road and carry on to a crossroads; go straight on in an easterly direction on a faint track, and reach the East Summit in about 15 minutes. Now the shapely pinnacles of Pla de la Casa are ahead, and to the left, across another trough, are the rocks from the top of the Pinnacle Route. *2h 15mins*

Cross yet another forestry road in order to continue your traverse of the ridge, and note that you can see to the right (south) below you the Rincon del Olvido Restaurant (Forgotten Corner). To the north is the remote village of Cuatretondeta in the Ceta Valley. Guadalest Reservoir is now in full view, as well as the rest of the Serrella Ridge, Malla del Llop and Serrella Castle. Finally is the Barranco de Borrell, the deep gorge separating you from your next objective, the Pla de la Casa. To the south are the distant peaks of Jijona, Peña Roja and Mignol. *2h 55mins*

Leaving the Ridge

You now have to descend to the col before tackling the next peak. There is no path, and the scree and rocks are unstable and need care. Below you can be seen a large flat area with a small shepherd's hut, which is your next objective.   *3h 20mins*

Cross this flat area, drop down to a forestry road and head east towards Pla de la Casa and the Collado de Borell, which is a good place to stop to study your line of ascent of the next peak. Where the forestry road ends, a small cairned track leads off north through the scree at the western end of Pla de la Casa. The track zig-zags upwards through the rocks and gains the ridge.   *4hrs*

Ascent of Pla de la Casa

Follow the route already described in the last paragraph. If in doubt, keep moving left a little to find red markers, which will lead you to the top of the western buttress of the mountain. Once the ridge has been achieved, move east towards the summit, and you will see how the mountain got its name. *Pla* means a level area, and whilst the top of the mountain is no bowling green, it is more gently undulating than most. Keep going east, and when you meet a small hill, go round it to the right, and you will find the rocky arête and the pinnacles of the summit to your right. Beneath the summit is another large flat area, which in spring is covered with prickly blue hedgehog broom (*Erinacea anthyllis*), and in the centre of which is the largest and deepest *nevera* (ice-pit) that I have ever seen.   *4hrs 30mins*

It will take only 10 minutes of an easy rock scramble to gain the highest point, an elegant pinnacle with a cross and a letter-box installed by the Callosa de Segura Mountaineering Club. As might be expected, both foreground and distant views are sensational. Note to the north in the far distance the mountain of Almisira and the Forada Ridge near Pego.

The Return to Collado De Borrell

The descent is far from pleasant, as the path which goes right off the eastern end of the buttress soon disappears into scree and rocks which are extremely unstable. Keep going down until you can see below you a large crag set in the middle of the scree slope, and make this your first objective. From the crag, move further south, avoiding any temptation to use tracks which go in any other direction, as they will surely lead you into the depths of Barranco del Moro, on the wrong side of the ridge. Eventually, when Aitana comes into view, set a course for the array of aerials and domes on its summit. Take your last look at the coast, with Altea and Sierra Helada, and find a narrow track leading south-west towards Collado de Borrell. *5hrs 30mins*

You will have to negotiate the head of a small barranca, descend a little to pass under some slabs and, finally, pass through a boulder field to reach a small rise, from which, at a cairn, another track leads left down towards the Guadalest Valley. Ignore this track, and rejoin your morning route under the screes of Pla de la Casa.   *6hrs 15mins*

To the Puerto Del Contadores

A sensible route, after such a demanding day, is to follow the forestry road west as it descends a little into a hollow, then climbs up a little (bearing left at a junction) to traverse under the summits of the Serrella back to the shepherd's hut on the flat area which we visited earlier. 6hrs 45mins

Keep on the forestry road until another flat area with extensive ruins of *fincas* is reached. Go south down through the ruins, and climb to a small gap in the rocks between the summit of Borrell and the rest of the ridge. This is the Puerto del Contadores, which leads down to the Rincon del Olvido Restaurant, which can now be seen below you. *Contadores* means the counting place for sheep and goats.   *7hrs*

Ascent of Borrell (diversion)

Those with inexhaustible energy and a spirit of adventure will ignore the sensible route and head for the base of the Borrell Ridge to the south. There is a well-defined goat track which leads directly to the Puerto del Contadores, but there is one small problem: as goats do not tend to reach a height of more than a metre, climbers over this height will impale themselves regularly on the spiky vegetation. In 25 minutes, after passing some sheep folds built against the crags, you will note a tempting rake which leads upwards to the right and leads to the summit ridge. It is quite an exposed rock scramble, and once on the ridge you will have to share it with the wild mountain goats, who are the sitting tenants and much given to posing artistically in impossible situations on the pinnacles. When you tire of this diversion, return to the track and join the walkers' route at the Puerto.

Down to the Rincon Del Olvido

There is no continuous track down the steep slopes to the road and the restaurant which can be seen below you. Try to keep moving east as you descend in order to avoid the crags and the depths of a *barranco*. A useful marker is a small crag with two large boulders on top, which you should pass on the upper side. Eventually below you appears a large flattish area, from which a reasonable track descends to the road. The restaurant is a most welcome sight at the end of such a full and satisfying day, and it has a well-earned reputation for Valencian cuisine.

7hrs 45mins

17: AGULLES DE LA SERRELLA

Grade:	scramble
Distance:	7.5km
Time:	6hrs
Ascent:	759m
Map:	Alcoy 821 (29–32)

The Serrella Massif, which stretches from Puerto de Confrides in the west to the Paso del Castillo in the east, has many attractive features. There are six summits over 1000m, the largest, highest and deepest nevera, and the highest and most magnificently placed castle in the area. On its northern flank, between the villages of Fachega and Cuatretondeta, overlooking the Ceta Valley, stand the Agulles. These rocky pinnacles stand in serried ranks high up on the scree slopes beneath the northern cliffs, of which they were once part. It is sometimes difficult to pick them out, as they tend to merge with the cliffs behind them, but in clear conditions and with oblique lighting they present a unique sight in these mountains.

The main expedition is for experienced mountaineers only, used

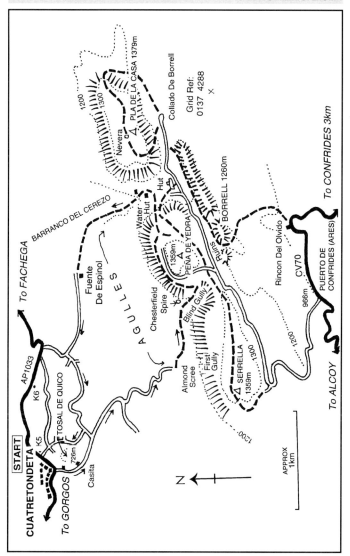

to rock climbing and crossing difficult terrain. For such people, it will be a long but exhilarating day. For those who feel unable to tackle the rocks, the good tracks through the cultivated terraces beneath the pinnacles will prove to be a memorable walk in magnificent surroundings. Hardy walkers should have no difficulty in reaching the Chesterfield Spire at the bottom of the scramble, and following tracks which descend to the nearest road.

Getting There

From the coast, leave the Jalon Valley and continue past Castell de Castells on the CV720. After passing through Fachega, turn left onto CV754 to Cuatretondeta to find parking at Km.4.5 near to the Jardi de Raphael Perez Perez. Carrer Pais Valencia leads up into the town, passing Els Fares, an excellent restaurant with the more basic Bar Canares above the main square.

The Scramblers' Route – Country Walk

Leave the gardens and walk south along a good concrete road which climbs steadily, passing a *fuente* and a casita on your left, until you can see the pinnacles ahead. Ignore a broad road leading off left until the road loses its surface and you eventually arrive at a grove of olives flourishing in the inhospitable scree beneath a gully (First Gully on map) and more intimate views of the pinnacles.   *30mins*

To the Chesterfield Spire

This is the end of good tracks for the next 5 hours, as you leave the stony grove to find a rough track going upwards, then traversing east across the scree shoot. How these scree paths survive, I cannot guess, as there are now very few goats in the hills. It may be the hunters who tread out the paths each year after the winter rains. After crossing the first scree, the path continues between scrub and rocks towards Blind Gully, keeping fairly level. When you reach the second scree shoot, it is easier to ascend the right-hand side, where the vegetation and rocks give you something to hold on to. When you reach the base of the cliffs another rough track appears, going east, and leads into the pinnacles, which are now visible ahead. You will pass a narrow fissure on the right-hand side (Willie's Folly), which separates a tooth of rock from the rock wall on the west side of Blind Gully. This fissure always seems to attract walkers, but after struggling through it you will only emerge higher up on the great stone shoot of the gully. It is better to keep straight on until you reach an elegant but leaning spire of rock – Chesterfield Spire. *1hr 30mins*

This is as far as the prudent walker should go. The views down the valley towards Cocentaina and Muro de Alcoy are impressive when seen against the foreground of the pinnacles. It is also possible to explore the pinnacles to the east, although there are no reliable paths, and it is also possible, with luck, to join the scramblers' return route near the *fuente*.

Hancliff's Route (for scramblers only)

This route is the only civilised way to the top of the Serrella Ridge. The alternative is by way of the wide gully filled with unstable rocks and scree, which after half an hour is blocked by a rock wall. The gully continues to the east, becoming even steeper and more unstable. By comparison, this scramblers' route is on rock, sometimes vegetated, but sound, and gives intimate views of the pinnacles, which become even more dramatic when seen from above. Red markers have been placed, and the route takes about one and a half hours to complete.

Start your climb above the tooth of rock next to the Chesterfield Spire, climb a modest rock wall between two pinnacles, and cross some scree towards a prominent crag, which is passed on the right-hand side. Now ascend by slabs and a groove to a rocky staircase. The sound rock gradually deteriorates into scree and scrub as the summit of the Serrella appears to the west. Below you can be seen the wall blocking Blind Gully. Keep going up until you find yourself on a nice little arête, which leads to a small shelter at the top of the climb. You now have time to take in the extensive views of the Ceta Valley as far as Gorga, and you should be able to see your car parked along the valley road. *3hrs*

Across the Serrella Ridge

Ahead of you to the east the ridge continues towards the beautiful peak of Pla de la Casa, and to the south the aerials on Aitana are visible. You are also made aware of the complex structure of the Serrella, which is, in fact, made up of three separate ridges with forestry roads in the valleys between them. To the west can be seen the main summit of Serrella, with its triangulation pillar. Continue going east and you will come to a grassy col at the end of one of these forestry roads. From here I recommend that you climb south to gain the top of some crags on Peña de Yedra, which gives excellent views down into the Guadalest Valley.   *3hrs 30mins*

Down into the Barranco Del Cerezo

Return to the col, and head east in the direction of Pla de la Casa to descend the end of the ridge. There is no path, but head for a lower col where some tracks cross at the Puerto del Cerezo between the two mountains. This is somewhat difficult to find in poor visibility.   *4hrs*

Now turn left (north) down the ravine, which will eventually lead to the Ceta Valley below, and in a few minutes arrive at a small hut used to collect drinking water for the villages below. It is tempting to follow the partially buried water pipe as a guide to the valley, but beware, the pipe does some pretty desperate things when it encounters crags. Climb instead up behind the little hut to find a higher path, which passes through a small rock gateway and then across some scree to another rock gateway, where a well-engineered path zig-zags down and finally ends in an almond grove and a *fuente*, Font Espinol.   *5hrs*

Second Country Walk

A good unsurfaced road now leads west from the almond grove, descending all the time, until you bear left and left again at junctions (yellow marker), passing to the south of Tosal de Tio Quico to regain the concrete road back into the village.   *6hrs*

18: PLA DE LA CASA FROM FACHEGA

Grade:	strenuous
Distance:	12km
Time:	5hrs 45mins
Ascent:	614m
Map:	Alcoy 821 (29–32)

The Sierra de Serrella is a 12km ridge which runs in a shallow arc from Puerto Confrides in the west to the Castillo de Serrella in the east, where the ridge becomes Sierra Aixorta. These two ranges form the northern side of the popular Guadalest Valley. The Serrella, most of which is over 1300m, and Aixorta get the most of any snow that falls here, and due to their height hold it long after snow elsewhere has disappeared. Though the route described is a circular one, climbing the mountain on its northern side from Fachega, with a surprise awaiting on the summit, the northern side is increasingly overgrown and it is recommended that you ascend via the descent route by the Barranco del Moro.

Getting There

Follow the CV720 road from Castell de Castells west towards Gorga and Alcoy, over the Puerto de Famorca, and park your transport in the village of Fachega (Km.14) near the Bar Avenida, close to the church. The bar, which also is a *hostal*, is run by the local slaughterman and can supply an excellent menu as well as other refreshments. As you pull on your boots you can examine the north face of Pla De La Casa from the terrace, and a beautiful sight it is.

Making a Start – Ascent of the North Face

Follow the motor road west to the end of the village and take the left-hand fork, signposted AP1033 to Cuatretondeta. Just before you reach the sports centre turn off left along a surfaced road, heading south-west, and in just over a kilometre reach a ruined casita where the road ends.

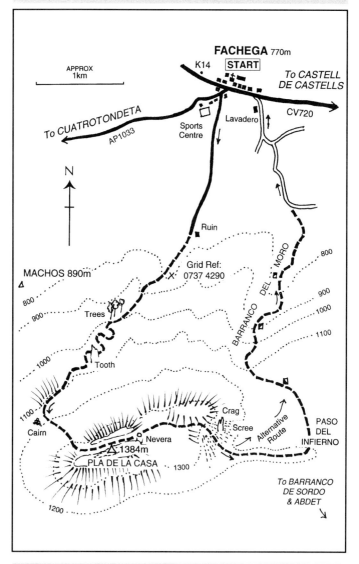

FACHEGA 770m

K14 START

To CASTELL DE CASTELLS

CV720

To CUATROTONDETA

AP1033

Sports Centre

Lavadero

APPROX
1km

N

Ruin

Grid Ref:
0737 4290

MACHOS 890m

BARRANCO DEL MORO

800

900

1000

1100

Trees

800

900

1000

Tooth

Crag

Scree

Alternative Route

PASO DEL INFIERNO

Cairn

Nevera

1384m

PLA DE LA CASA

1300

1200

To BARRANCO DE SORDO & ABDET

Above you, just below the skyline, is a large tooth of rock set in scree, which you should aim for, heading just west of south. This first section is an unremitting slog with your nose into the mountain, but there are rewards to come. Start by climbing a gully and then an indistinct track through scrub towards a group of trees and a fan-shaped scree slope. Still making for the tooth, reach the trees, still heading west of south, through some terraces and a faint path, and pass the tooth on the right. Look down for good views of Fachega, with its Calvary on the slopes of Alfaro, which is behind the village. To the east is the Caballo Verde Ridge with Penon Roch at the eastern end. *30 mins*

There is now a better path leading up to the skyline and a prominent crag, which marks the edge of the summit plateau of Pla de la Casa. The path now zig-zags and you pass a cairn before reaching more level ground and views of Alcoy, Cocentaina, with its square castle, and the mountains of the Mariolas, including Monte Cabrer, the third highest peak in the province. *1hr 30mins*

The Summit Plateau

The word *pla* in Valenciano means 'a level place', and certainly after the last hours' climbing you might be forgiven for thinking that the description is apt. But level it is not, only 'relatively level', as the large summit plateau is made up of two main ridges of rock with some delightful pinnacles. The first ridge is the summit as marked on the maps, but it is not the highest point, and you pass around it to find the true summit, with its trig point and a metal cross, by heading east of south. The ground here is covered with large mounds of Hedgehog Broom (*Erinacea anthyllis*), a spiky plant which when in bloom is a mass of blue flowers, but hell if you fall into it. Be careful, too, not to fall into the largest, deepest and highest (1360m) *nevera*, which is quite a surprise to find just below the true summit.

It takes only 10 minutes of an easy, but rather exposed, rock scramble to the summit (1379m), accommodation strictly limited. The metal cross was installed by the 'Grupo Montanjero de St Joan, of Callosa de Segura', who for some reason disagreed with the Mapas Militar and have given the mountain an extra 100m (they must have had a better altimeter). A letter box and record book are provided.

To the south you can follow the whole of the Aitana Ridge from Peña Roc to the summit itself, as well as admire the Guadalest Valley.

Cabeza d'Oro and Puig Campaña are in the far distance. This is probably the best position to also study the other peaks of the Serrella, Malla De Llop to the east and the main summits, with Confrides below them, to the west. In the distance are the Alcoy mountains and Benicadell, and to the east is Peña Severino, and above it the bulk of the Bernia. Way in the distance to the north is Almisira and the Forada Ridge.   *2hrs 15mins*

Down to the Paso Del Infierno

A track leads off the summit plateau from the *nevera*, heading north-west, right off the end of the buttress into a scree-filled gully, where the path soon disappears and you head down towards a tooth of rock set in the middle of the scree, which is your first objective. To the south, from the crag you should be able to see a small white building at the bottom of some very rough ground at the head of the Barranco del Moro. This is the first water hut (a collection point supplying the valley with drinking water), and is on the descent route.

Sturdy mountaineers may head straight for this hut, but a more pleasant and enjoyable route is to head for the col and follow the high ground down to the Paso del Infierno, the watershed between the Barranco del Morro and Barranco de Sordo, which leads down to Abdet at the head of the Guadalest Valley. The route was once a mule track used by the ice-cutters to get to the *nevera*. (In the middle of the night, with cantankerous mules to handle, no wonder they named the pass 'the Pass of Hell'.) You are now right under the soaring western crags of Malla de Llop.   *3hrs 15mins*

Down the Barranco Del Moro

Now all you have to do is to follow the old, rather decayed mule track used by the ice-cutters of old right down to Fachega, as does the water conduit which supplies the village. The water is directed into the white huts by a system of pipes. The track between the first and second water huts may prove difficult to follow as it is a little overgrown, but there is an alternative track a little to the west. You will pass a number of these huts as the path crosses and recrosses the normally dry watercourse and improves as it descends to become, eventually, a road. You can see the village and the Bar Avenida ahead, a most welcome sight.   *5hrs 15mins*

There is pleasant walking now along a good road until you reach the village *lavadero* (wash place) and *fuente*, now restored as a picnic spot, and climb up to pass under the road by a short tunnel to your refreshments in the bar.   *5hrs 45mins*

19: MALLA DE LLOP FROM FAMORCA

Grade:	strenuous
Distance:	12km
Time:	5hrs
Ascent:	669m
Map:	Alcoy 821 (29–32)

The Sierra de Serrella stretches in a shallow arc from Puerto Confrides in the west for about 12km to the Castilllo de Serrella in the east, where it changes its name to become Sierra Aixorta. It forms the whole northern side of the Guadalest Valley. Most of the sierra is over 1300m, and there are three distinct peaks in the great jumble of rocks and high valleys which make up the massif. Overlooking the Puerto de Confrides are the twin peaks of the Serrella itself (1359m); next, divided by Barranco de Moro, is the beautiful summit of Pla de la Casa (1379m). Our peak, Malla de Llop (1361m), comes next, overlooking the tiny village of Farnorca in the Ceta Valley. The eastern aspect of the mountain can be admired from Castillo de Serrella. This is no gentle walk, and there are very few reliable paths. It should not be attempted in poor visibility, not just for safety's sake but because all this effort without the benefit of some of the most majestic mountain scenery in Las Marinas is rather pointless.

Getting There

Follow the CV720 road from Castell de Castells, west, towards Gorga and Alcoy, and after you have crossed from the Jalon to the Ceta Valley at the Puerto de Famorca the village is on the left at Km.15.7. Articles in the local press have highlighted the plight of this beautifully situated

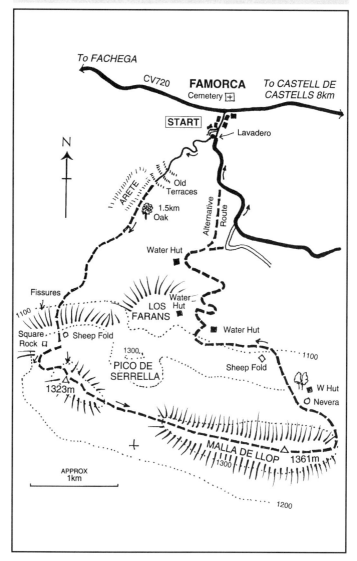

but declining village: hardly any young people, little work except the traditional cultivation of crops, and no shop. When last I was there one small bar survived, which cooked me a simple meal. If this has closed you will have to go to nearby Fachega for coffee. In Famorca there is parking in the lower village square, near to the *lavadero* (wash place) and *fuente*, both still much used by the villagers.

Making a Start

Start from the *fuente* to climb up through the village along Calle Salamanca, noting *Finca* El Cantaler, then move right along a good road heading south-west. In a few minutes leave the road to join a concrete track on the left heading south, zig-zagging as you climb for another 15 minutes until the concrete ends. You now have to come to grips with the mountain. The first marker is a flake of rock, and there is a nice little rocky arête above and on your right. Work your way up the old terraces to gain a broad ridge. You are now under the crescent-shaped lower crags of Pico de Serrella, shown on the map as Los Farans.

From this point there are no more paths for a while, and you must seek out the easiest route. There are now good views of the little village below, and you are on a level with the top arête.

There are also good views towards the coast, south-east, with Caballo Verde Ridge and, in the distance, Montgo, near Javea. *40mins*

To the Col

As we climb we can see, over to our left, another peak which is Mallaes (926m), but our objective is a broad ridge towards a band of crags. The peak of Pla de la Casa (1379m) appears on our right. In the distance, to the west, can be seen Monte Cabrer (1389m), the third highest peak in our province, near Alcoy, and eventually, high above us, is the rocky summit of Malla de Llop. *1hr*

There is still a long way to climb to reach the summit, and the route continues through a band of rocks, following wild boar tracks to go round a buttress to enter a broad valley, moving upwards, south-west, to a broad col. You negotiate loose scree and pass beautiful pinnacles and fissures, keeping close to the rocks on the right-hand side. After passing a squarish rock and a sheepfold, gain the col near to Pico de Serrella (1323m) as views open up to the north and westwards to Pla de La Casa. Now head upwards to the south for a few minutes to reach a small peak on the Serrella Ridge, with a cairn. Aitana fills the southern aspect.   *2hrs 25mins*

To the Summit

The reward for all your labours is now a pleasant traverse, eastwards, of the summit ridge, with Pla de la Casa and the water huts in the Barranco del Morro visible behind. Move now either along the rocky ridge or take advantage of a reasonable path on the north side until you reach the trig point marking the summit. This ridge is well blessed with an excellent display of crocus in the right season.   *3hrs*

The views from this summit might be easier to describe by listing the peaks which do not appear (notably Peñon d'Ifach). From the coast to the far west and north, you can pick out most of the mountains in Las Marinas, and more. This is the best point to appreciate the east face of Pla de la Casa, the mountain's nearest neighbour, and you can also look down into Barranco de la Canal between two ridges of sharp rocks which are generally known as 'the Glacier of the Serrella'. Beyond these is Serrella Castle, on its own rock, marking the end of the Serrellas as the ridge continues to Aixorta and Morro Blau.

Malla de Llop, at the head of the Barranco de Canal (Serrella Glacier), from Serrella Castle

Descent to the Nevera

A direct route is to leave the summit and descend the slope, generally northwards, to reach a shallow col at the head of a broad valley, dropping to the west. A little above the bed of the valley look left to find a faint track which leads to the *nevera*. If you fail to find this track just keep on along the valley, on the left-hand side, until you spot the water hut, and the *nevera* is 100m uphill to the south. It has tall walls and part of the roof is intact.

An alternative descent is to leave the summit and continue east for about 10 minutes and then, at the end, walk off the ridge onto a flat grassy area. Now turn left, west, keeping close to the cliffs, through a shallow col and then descend to the *nevera* and the water hut, a collecting point for Famorca's water supply.   *3hrs 40mins*

Down the Barranca

From the water hut there is a path to a small grove of birch trees (burnt) on the edge of a plateau. Just below the trees there is a sheep-fold built against a large rock. You now have to follow the water conduit down to the valley on a mule track which zig-zags and will pass a number of water huts on the side of the *barranca*. *4hrs 15mins*

At the fourth water hut it is necessary to change direction, east, into another *barranca*. Cross it, and it leads to an unsurfaced road, which in turn joins a surfaced one. Turn left (west), to reach the village square. Failure to make this turn will mean that you reach the village by a shorter route along a narrower path which drops down two terraces before reaching the surfaced road. If the village bar is not open, there is always the Bar Avenida, at Fachega, just over a kilo-metre away, or the bars at Castell de Castells on the way back to the coast.   *5hrs*

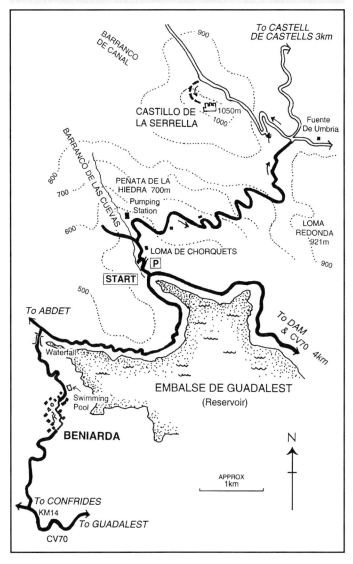

20: SERRELLA CASTLE FROM BERNIARDA

Grade:	easy
Distance:	9km
Time:	3hrs 30mins
Ascent:	650m
Map:	Alcoy 821 (29–32)

The Moors occupied this part of Spain for over seven centuries, and the remains of watch towers and castles are still to be found throughout the region on many strategically situated crags, and certainly add interest to a day in the mountains.

Serrella Castle, the highest in the region, is right on top of a sheer crag overlooking the northern side of the Guadalest Valley forming part of the Sierra de Serrella. This range runs in a shallow arc from east to west, and excellent views of the range can be had from Guadalest and the C3313. The zig-zags of the forestry road can be seen crossing the front of the castle crag and disappear over a col to the right of the crag. At the bottom left of the zig-zags a small red building marks the pumping station. The castle is not marked on the military maps, but its water supply is Pozo de Castellet.

The Route

The route follows surfaced forestry roads except for the final climb to the castle ruins, which necessitates some easy, if exposed, scrambling. Forestry vehicles and Jeep Safaris also use this road, so be prepared to share it with them! Make a start from the road along the northern side of the Guadalest Reservoir, where a very tight bend negotiates an arm of the reservoir formed by the rocky bed of the Rio Cuervos (2km from the western end, and 4km from the dam). There are some red marks on the wall, and the surfaced road leads north-west following the dry bed of the Rio Cuervos for the first half-hour. After 5 minutes ignore a track on the right, and shortly afterwards, when the road forks, keep to the right, following the water-pipes until the pumping station is reached (30 minutes). Your road now bends right to move north-east across the base of the castle crag on a well-engineered road (mostly surfaced) which zig-zags upwards in order to gain the col. Some of the gradients are very steep, so take your time, stopping to admire the views. Above you are the ruins of the castle. After 20 minutes, you pass a prominent crag to the right. Here is a good place to stop for excellent views of the Guadalest Valley (first views of Confrides at the western end) and, behind you, the Barranco de Canal, which in most of the guidebooks is called the 'glacier' of the Serrella. Whilst it has none of the characteristics of a true glacier, the twin jagged ridges somehow suggest it. Thankfully, the gradient now eases a little, and shortly afterwards you reach a broad col with a crossroads, Puerto del Castillo.

The Broad Col

You now have extensive views to the northern side of the Serrella range – not a village to be seen, only the mountains in all their glory dominate everything, from Malla del Llop (1361m) to the west to the Sierra Aixorta to the east. To the north-west is Corral de Alt and Paso Tancat with its rocky gorge. From the col, the road straight ahead goes down to Castell de Castells, and the road to the right (east) leads in 10 minutes to the Fuente de Umbria (on the left, blue sign on tree). Your way goes left (west) to zig-zag upwards towards the base of the crag. After 10 minutes, at a lone pine tree, look back to get your first view of Castell de Castells below in its lonely valley. Some rocky pinnacles are passed, and then a second col is reached. *1hr 35min*

The road (constructed 1987) continues to the edge of the glacier ridge, then dips down to the Castell de Castells–Alcoy road west of the village. Up to the left can be seen the castle ruins, which can be reached in 10 minutes by following a well-worn path – first to the right of a *deposito* (still containing water) then to the right until the rocky ridge is reached, then traverse back left to enter the castle ruins.

The Castle

Despite the neglect of nearly five centuries the ruins are impressive and the views of the surrounding mountains even more so. The Guadalest Valley, with all its many villages, is probably here seen from its most attractive viewpoint. The old 'glacier' dominates the western aspect, with Malla del Llop beyond. Altea and the coast are in the distance to the south-east, and Aitana is to the south with another Moorish castle, El Castellet, on its flank, a few degrees right of Benifato village and the transmitting station on the summit. To the north, range upon range of mountains lead to the distant horizon.

The Descent

Those with kind friends or chauffeurs can now look forward to a comfortable walk down to Castell de Castells by either of the forestry roads. Most, however, will have to retrace their steps down to the Guadalest Valley, reflecting on a day spent in some of the most magnificent mountain scenery of Alicante province. There is a bar and an excellent restaurant, the Mustique, in the village of Beniarda.

3hrs 30mins

21: SERRELLA CASTLE FROM CASTELL DE CASTELLS

Grade:	moderate
Distance:	11.5km
Time:	4hrs
Ascent:	400m
Map:	Alcoy 821 (29–32)

Serrella Castle played an important part during the Moorish occupation, as it protected the northern approaches to the small kingdom of the Guadalest Valley. It occupies a strategic position on a blade of rock which forms the most eastern end of Sierra Serrella. Here, it not only commanded all the land to the north, but also the only route over the mountains at Puerto del Castillo, where the Sierra Aixorta begins. A forestry road now follows the track used by the Moors and links the Jalon Valley to that of Guadalest. The castle is not shown on any of the military maps. While the ascent from the Guadalest Valley is described in Route 20, this route approaches from the north, from Castell de Castells. The walk is all on good forestry roads, except for a bit of scrambling up to the ruins themselves. Those with indulgent chauffeurs can, of course, combine the two

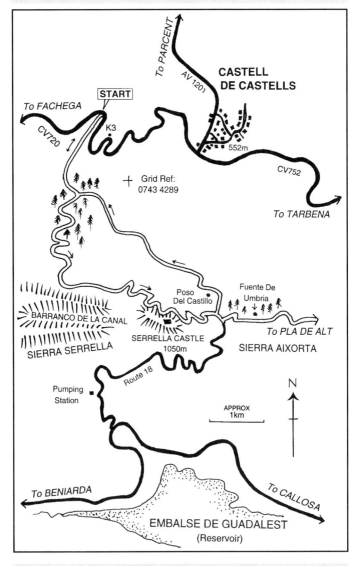

Puig Campaña with Roldan's Notch (Walk 7) from Val de Arc (Walk 12)

Punta Bombarda de Albir and Peñon de Ifach from Helada (Walks 13, 14)

routes; others, with friends to whom they are prepared to trust their vehicles, can form two parties, one from the north and the other from the south and exchange car keys at the castle. (It has been done.)

Getting There

The isolated little village of Castell de Castells lies at the very head of the Jalon Valley at the base of the pass over to Fachega and the Ceta Valley, and is completely surrounded by high mountains. You will get your first sight of the castle as you round the last bend on the AV1201 from Parcent, 1km from the village. There are two bars on the main road and one in the village centre, near the church. There is comfortable accommodation at Pension Castells, in Calle St, Vincente (Tel: 551 82 54).

Purists will want to leave their cars at the lovely Font de la Bota, at the river bridge on the outskirts of the village, especially as it has now been beautifully landscaped and provided with a *glorieta* and seating. To succumb to this attraction will, however, commit you to an hour's uphill slog to the starting point, which is just by Km.20 on the road to Fachega, where a forestry road leads off left, north-east, and there is some parking available.

Making a Start

The road is fairly level for a while, with good views down into Castell de Castells, and in a short time you will get a good, distant view of your objective, the castle. Below it can clearly be seen another forestry road, cutting across the mountain below it; this is your return route. You will also see a broad wooded gully ahead, with another road zig-zagging upwards, and this is your first objective.

To the Castle

High above you are the crags of Malla de Llop, the first of the Serrella summits, 1361m. In five minutes drop down a little to go round the head of a small *barranco,* and in another 15 minutes enter a forest and immediately turn off right uphill. The other road will be your return route. *25mins*

For the next half hour your only views will be to the north as you gain height, climbing under the ridge of the Serrella until at last you gain its ridge, and extensive views open up to the south and east.

50mins

Extensive Views

To the east rises the great crag on which stand the castle ruins, with a col below it on the northern side. To the west is the summit of Malla de Llop, and below to the south the rare sight of the waters of the reservoir in the Guadalest Valley and all its old Moorish villages, with the exception of Abdet, which remains hidden. The King's Castle dominates the fortress of Guadalest with its two attendant castles, and further to the west, on a spur of Aitana (1558m), the province's highest peak, Confrides Castle comes into view as you continue east along a good road.

Descend a little, and then there is a steep pull up to the col beneath the crags of the castle.

On top of Serrella Castle

Ascent to the Castle Ruins

Now you must scramble for a few minutes to gain the castle. Climb up to the right on a clear path to pass to the right of a large, ancient cistern, which still retains water and in which toads breed. Still moving to the right along a shelf, come to a decayed archway and here start to zig-zag upwards to gain the bare rock of the ridge. You now move left to enter the castle ruins, with a small building on the left. The ruins are in quite good shape considering that they have not been maintained for nearly four centuries. Down towards the coast can be seen Sierra Helada at Albir, Ponoch above Polop, and Puig Campaña (1410m), the province's second highest peak, near Finestrat. To the west are magnificent views of the twin jagged ridges of rock which form the Barranco de Canal, leading towards Malla de Llop, in Spanish guidebooks erroneously called 'the Glacier of the Serrella'. *1hr 25mins*

Down to Puerto Del Castillo

Back at the col beneath the castle, continue along the good road under the crags, with the western ridge of Aixorta ahead of you, and with another tree-lined road, which leads to *Fuente* Umbria and on to Pla de Alt, contouring under its northern crags. You now reach a crossroads which is the Puerta (pass) de Castillo. The right-hand road crosses the pass and descends to the side of the reservoir a few kilometres from Beniarda. The road ahead continues to *Fuente* Umbria, a nice walk (*allow 40 minutes return*). *2hrs 45mins*

Back Down to Castell De Castells

Your road is to the left and descends a little, then contours under your previous route to rejoin it amongst the pine trees. *4hrs*

These times are, of course, only walking times. You must add at least 30 minutes to ascend the castle, and it will be difficult to resist spending at least an hour there.

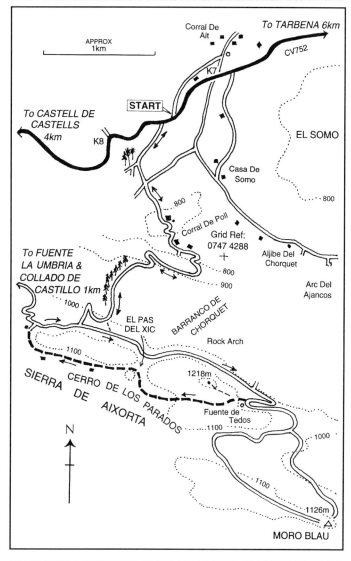

22: SIERRA AIXORTA CIRCUIT

Grade:	moderate
Distance:	15km
Time:	5hrs
Ascent:	418m
Maps:	Alcoy 821 (29–32), Benisa 822 (30–32)

Sierra Aixorta is not a well-known mountain, and unless you know the area well you may have some difficulty in identifying its summit. It is, in fact, a continuation of the same ridge as Sierra Serrella and runs from the Puerto del Castillo in the west right down to its terminal peaks of Morro Blau and Sierra de Oro, overlooking Callosa de Ensarria. You will no doubt notice these shapely mountains as you cross the huerto from Altea, and beyond Callosa, towards Guadalest, Aixorta's rocky cliffs form the north side of the valley. The summit is better studied from the high pasture of Corral de Alt, above Castell de Castells on the road to Tarbena; here the mountain dominates the views to the south, and it is from here that the mountain may best be ascended. On good forestry roads or tracks, except for the final scramble to the summit, this is a most enjoyable walk with views changing as you cross from the north to the south side of the ridge.

Getting There

Thanks to the new road, CV752 from Castell de Castells to Tarbena, the Corral de Alt can be easily reached. The only trouble is that the road is not yet shown on the map, but at least signposts have been erected. From Tarbena leave the Parcent road just above the village, and in Castells, as you leave the village on the way to Fachega, turn off by the river and the new *glorieta*. Park your vehicle on the side road leading to the well, near Km.7.5, and as you put on your boots you can appreciate your mountain away to the south.

To Fuente De Tedos

From the motor road take a good track on the southern side, in a south-westerly direction, and pass some pines on your right and an old ruin. In ten minutes the track divides. Take the left side, still heading for Aixorta, and at a crossroads go straight ahead, heading for a prominent crag, which is your objective. Above you on the flank of Aixorta can be seen the forestry road, traversing the northern slope of the mountain, which is also on your route.

Reach the ruins of an old *finca* on the left with a well and zig-zag downwards, passing a little casita on the left and ignoring a road on the right, until you reach another casita, and at a junction go right (east of south). Ahead is the Ferrer Ridge, the impressive cliffs which bound the defile of Paso Tancat and Rates. You next join a substantial forestry road, turn right (west) and start to climb a little. Ahead can be seen the 'Glacier of the Serrella' and there are pines on the edge of the track. This road will take you to Serrella Castle via *Fuente* La Umbria, but the route leaves it soon. After a number of zig-zags, turn left at a junction to contour south-east along a delightful stretch under the crags of Sierra Aixorta.   *1hr*

Look back on this section to see a *forat* (hole in the rock) and down into the valley for a view of the natural arch Arc del Aticos. There are good views across to the Paso Tancat, Bolulla and Tarbena castles, the Ferrer and Bernia ridges and Olta, near Calpe. Eventually, after a few bends, reach the *Fuente* de Tedos on the right of the track. The road ahead will take you to the summit of Morro Blau, but here we leave the road to climb up to the *fuente*. In the distance Montgo and Cabo Nao, near Javea, come into view.   *1hr 45mins*

To the Summit

From the *fuente* pass to the left of a prominent boulder and seek out a goat track leading upwards to a col. You are now on the ridge with the advantage of views to the south including Aitana and Ponoch.   *2hrs*

From the col there is a track which contours the southern side of the summit crags and which is the return route. First, however, scramble up over broken rocky ground to reach the summit with its cairn (1218m). Down the ridge to the south-east is Morro Blau, lower in height but sporting its triangulation (survey) pillar. There are views in all directions: Gandia in the north, Altea and Benidorm in the east, and the whole of the Guadalest Valley spread out below you. To the north-west are visible Confrides, the Serrella and Malla de Llop. A wonderful place to use your map and compass.   *2hrs 30mins*

Southern Traverse

Return to the col and have a pleasant traverse, west, for about an hour high above the Guadalest Valley. Try not to lose height, and head at first for the summit of Aitana with its array of radar domes. Pass on your left a substantial *finca* with an *era* (threshing floor), complete with its *era* stones, and now follow an old mule track in the general direction of the Serrella 'glacier' (two parallel rocky ridges). Where there is another col (Pas de Xic) you will have to climb a little to avoid losing ground. At this point, if you look above you on the ridge, you will see the same *forat* which you passed on the Northern Traverse. *3hrs*

You should still be in line with the 'glacier' as you drop a little to find a good level path towards a substantial *finca* and gain a little col with Serrella Castle straight ahead of you. There is a small hollow of cultivated land and a small casita as you join the track, which leads to *Fuente* la Umbria, and recross back to the northern side of the mountain.   *4hrs*

Back down to Corral De Alt

All that now remains is to turn right onto the forestry road and walk west for a short while, not forgetting to bear left at the first junction (otherwise you will repeat the circuit!) and back down to the start. Sadly there is no hospitality available, but there are handy bars and restaurants not too far away at Tarbena and Castells.   *5hrs*

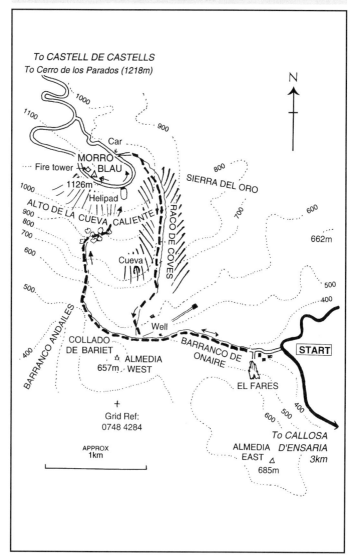

23: MORRO BLAU FROM CALLOSA D'ENSARIA

Grade:	**strenuous**
Distance:	**12km**
Time:	**6hrs**
Ascent:	**750m**
Maps:	**Benisa 822 (30–32), Altea 848 (30–35)**

Morro Blau (1126m), along with the lower peaks of Sierra del Oro and Almedia, forms the southern end of the 17km Serrella/Aixorta ridge, from the pass of Confrides to the interesting town of Callosa D'Ensaria. Other routes on the ridge are included in Routes 16 to 22. This circular route concentrates on the mountain itself. It is partly waymarked, and on tracks of variable reliability. The ascent is unremittingly steep.

Getting There

The town of Callosa d'Ensaria is built above the crossroads where the CV755 to Guadalest from the coast crosses the CV715 from Benidorm to Pego. The main town is to the north of the Placa de Quatre Caminos, and is signposted to the centre of the town and the health centre (*centro salud*), your essential marker. Your passengers may be lucky enough to catch the street name. Your route is north along Av Jaumie 1, right into C. Calvarie Convent into C. Fonteta, with Placa del Llaurador with its trees on your right. At Placa Mare Amalla abandon the signs for the health centre to keep going north into C. Clara Dels Pobres. Go along a lovely country road, Cami de Font de Onaera, with the entrance to Urbanisation Almedia on your left. After 3km the surface deteriorates near some water tanks, but with care you can take your vehicle just a little further and park at the bottom of Barranco De Onaire, with the detached pinnacle of rock known as El Fares on the left of the *barranco*.

This approach to the walk makes an excellent stroll in itself, amongst beautiful scenery, but to start the walk in the town would add two hours' road walking to what will, in any respect, be a challenging day.

Making a Start – to Col De Bariet

Follow the steep, if sometimes deeply eroded, path which ascends through trees the right-hand (north) side of the barranca. You are heading west and at times there are waymarkers, many of which seem to have been obliterated. There are now good views ahead of the summit, with a cave, Cueva Calliente, to the right of some crags which form a false summit. Above is a ruined *finca*, with its millstone, which you will pass below. Stop to give a backward glance to the Bernia, which looks superbly alpine from this angle, with its outriders Ovenga and Severino. The steep crags which drop down to the Algar and Paso del Bandoleros are also impressive. Morro Blau is to the south-west, but you need to cross another ridge before you can come to grips with it.

Now, thankfully, the gradient eases. There is a little well on the right of the track as you approach the Col de Bariet, where you join a broad forestry road and turn left. To the right the road continues north-east towards a casita and goes on down to Bolulla.   *40 mins*

On Towards Morro Blau

From here you can now see the highest point of the Aixorta Ridge, Cerro de los Parados (1218m), and on the first few steps along this road note the cairns marking a route off to the right. This is your return route from the summit.

The route lies to the north to ascend a pathless shoulder, keeping to the right of the crags of Alt Coca Calenta (a new name, it seems, for the crags to the west of Cova Calliente). To the left (south) the highest point of Almedia can be seen.

Along a Good Path

From the col a decent track continues north-west, and views open up ahead. There are exceptional views now down to the Guadalest Valley and the whole of the Aitana Massif from Ponoch to the main summit, Chirles and the high ground to Benimantell.

Turn left on the broad road for a while (north-west) then leave the road to descend into a gully bottom and scramble up easy rocks for a short while to gain a narrow track going uphill to another col overlooking Almedia and the Guadalest Valley. Avoid the *barranco* bottom as it is over-vegetated with spiky plants. You are heading for a small copse of trees on the skyline; tracks are somewhat vague but cairns are being built to help you.

Arrive thankfully at the trees to enjoy the views south-east towards the sea, Helada and Benidorm island, with majestic Puig Campaña inland. North-east you can see Montgo in the distance, with Tancat Pass and the Bernia across the valley.   *1hr 15mins*

Upwards Towards the Crags

Once through the trees the hard work starts, avoiding the main crags by passing them on the right. There are some vague tracks, but some most artistic and helpful cairns. Soon you are amongst the outcropping limestone.

As if by magic you breast the last rise to find a level area (probably a helicopter pad), and you thankfully walk along it to join the broad forestry road, north-west, for the last 15 minutes towards the fire lookout point installed on the summit of Morro Blau.   *2hrs 45mins*

There is lots to see as you identify the surrounding mountains from the most advantageous viewpoint. It might be more fun to find which are missing, notably Peñon De Ifach, although Calpe's castle is there, or rather the one remaining wall of it! New mountains are the Alcoy ones, Almisira, Azafor, Benicadell and to the north-west the highest point of Aixorta, Cerro de Parados and, of course, the whole Aitana Ridge. Below the summit is a wooden waymarker, which announces that you are on the right summit and also on PRV150 footpath.

Descent of Raco de les Coves

Leave the summit with its trig point and fire hut to retrace your steps, passing the helicopter pad and walking for a while west along the broad forestry road which eventually leads to Font de la Teja (see Route 22). There are high crags on the left, but to the right the land slopes down towards Raco de les Coves, a forbidding gully. A narrower track now leads off to the right just as the main road starts to rise. For how long I know not, the junction has been marked by an old car!
3hrs 25mins

You are heading now straight in line, with Paso Tancat and Rates Peak to the east for a while, until you encounter an old bath tub, an improvised trough for the goats, where cairns show a change of direction left for a while until you find an indistinct path on the right and change course to south.

Into the Unbelievable Gully (Raco de les Coves)

The next 45 minutes will be rough, tough and loose, so do take great care. Again, devoted mountaineers are building cairns to guide the way and to replace waymarking, most of which has been painted out. Thankfully you eventually gain the bottom of the gully, where you should turn round and approve its unofficial name.   *4hrs 15mins*

The Traverse

Now a nearly level, comfortable path contours around a hollow with bancales, rising slightly towards the skyline; a little *finca* nestles in the hollow.

You now join an old Mozarabic trail, eroded and overgrown, but still easy to follow as you get views to the south with the sea and Benidorm and Albir. Below also is the little casita on the road you crossed on the ascent, then that road itself and you have come full circle and have regained the Collada de Bariet.   *5hrs 20mins*

Walk now left for only a few metres to the cairns which mark the ascent route up the Barranco de Oniare, and reverse the ascent route. If this last section is done in the evening, and especially in good winter weather, the setting sun makes Bernia and Ferrer Peaks look even more majestic as the southern crags glow golden, whilst the northern ones are deep blue to purple, and the contrast sharp enough to satisfy any photographer.

No more route-finding to do: just follow the good track down into the trees and your waiting transport. There are refreshments at Callosa, and do not despair, you will eventually find parking.   *6hrs*

Val De Algar

24: BOLULLA CASTLE

Grade:	easy
Distance:	9km
Time:	4hrs
Ascent:	480m
Map:	Benisa 822 (30–32)

Bolulla is an old-world, unspoiled village 7km north of Callosa d'Ensarria on the CV715 to Pego, 3km past the Algar Falls, a great tourist attraction with many restaurants. There is at present no restaurant in the village, only a bar which can be rather late in opening in the morning. Opposite the bar lives an old gentleman who once took tourists on his donkey to the castle and still likes to offer his burro for photo calls. In May, like all villages in the valley of the Algar, it is the nisperus harvest, and if you look through the large barn doors of these old village houses you will see the ladies preparing the fruit for the Cooperativea at Callosa. The Cooperativas canning plant sends the fruit as far as Japan, and at the height of the harvest hundreds of pickers from Andalucia throng the town, causing an accommodation problem.

Approaching the village you will notice the groves of nisperus and oranges, and these orchards continue throughout the walk following the valley of the Rio Negro towards the village's main attraction, its Moorish castle. All on good tracks, except for the actual ascent of the castle ruins, which is a rock scramble.

Leave your transport at Bolulla and walk up Calle St Joseph, north, until on the edge of the village an unsurfaced road leads off left. In a short while enter a very small rocky gorge where the concrete surface

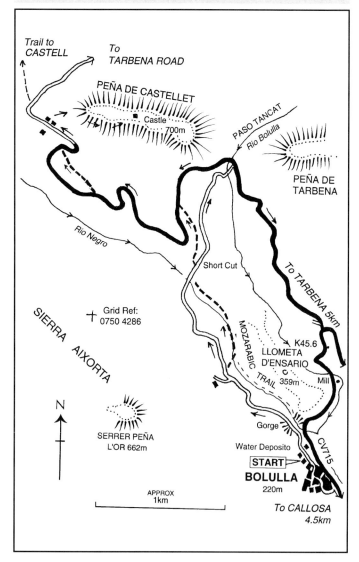

Trail to
CASTELL

To
TARBENA ROAD

PEÑA DE CASTELLET

Castle
700m

PASO TANCAT

Rio Bolulla

PEÑA DE
TARBENA

Rio Negro

Short Cut

To TARBENA 5km

SIERRA AIXORTA

Grid Ref:
0750 4286

MOZARABIC TRAIL

K45.6

LLOMETA
D'ENSARIO

359m

Mill

N

SERRER PEÑA
L'OR 662m

Gorge

Water Deposito

CV715

START
BOLULLA
220m

To CALLOSA
4.5km

APPROX
1km

is a reminder of the winter floods which rush through this narrow place. Note, on the right, some steps which lead to an old Mozarabic trail, the original way to the castle and on to Castell de Castells. This trail keeps to the *barranco* of the Rio Negro, and as a result has suffered from erosion. It is used in parts and is waymarked yellow/white. This makes a useful alternative to the road.

Ignore a road which climbs to the left and the road levels off. Stop, as always, to appreciate the views of Sierra Bernia and Peña Severino behind you.

Cross the *barranco* and note the alternative Mozarabic trail coming in on the right. Over a rise, where the neighbouring valley comes into view, the Mozarabic trail goes off left. This is a pleasant short cut and will save at least 15 minutes. Otherwise continue along the rough road.

50mins

You are now approaching the great Castle Crag, with the dark defile of Paso Tancat (closed pass) on its right. It really is closed, as you would have to be a very dedicated rock-climber to get more than half an hour into its dark depths. Now join a surfaced road coming up from the motor road to Tarbena and turn left to cross a bridge over the *barranco* of the Rio Bolulla.

1hr 15mins

Climb now on the broad surfaced road, which in about an hour takes you to a col (as described below) from which the ascent of the castle can be made.

The road changes direction (south-west) to cross under the crag, and zig-zag upwards towards the col. After 30 minutes, another track from the village (following the Rio Negro) joins on the left. Look out for the Mozarabic trail on the right to alternate the road walk. The road surface ends within sight of the col, and then the remains of an extensive *finca* just below the col is reached. This is known by the locals as 'the old village', and within living memory was inhabited by some local families during the summer months when supplies were brought up by pack mule. The *finca* buildings are still used, and you will note that there is much dressed stone in them, which could indicate Moorish origins or that the castle ruins were used for building materials. The old *era* (threshing floor) is near to the road, with a number of rollers still in situ – please do not disturb! The col is reached in 5 minutes.

2h 15mins

The era (threshing floor) at the old village below Bolulla Castle

The Col

An attraction of this walk is that, from here, there are a number of pleasant short excursions you can make before having lunch.

1. The Ascent to the Castle Ruins – Rock Scramble

Allow 1 hour return. Start either from the *finca* or the col by keeping just below the rock ridge on the southern side. Unless you are a rock-climber, do not keep to the crest, as in 10 minutes it will lead to a gap with some exposed moves. After 10 minutes, descend a little to a fir tree, cross a scree run, and head straight for a gap in the outer defensive wall. Aim upwards towards the right-hand edge of the ruins, then enter the inner wall, and head left to enter the tower. As you might expect, the views are extensive and impressive. If you can bear to look over the edge, it is now clear why the Moorish builders went no higher along the ridge. Take great care here – the walls lack maintenance! Only to the north is the view restricted by higher ground.

2. Walk Along the Trail to Castells

Allow 1 hour return. Continue over the col on the same track for 100m, and at some red way-markers go up left along the old mule track towards Castell de Castells, following the red markers, until you turn round to get good views of the dramatic crags of the Paso Tancat Gorge.

3. Walk to the Valley of Paso Tancat

Allow half an hour return. You can now explore the old settlements in this remote valley.

Descent (Allow 1hr 30mins)

Return by the same route until you reach the road junction near to the Barranco Bolulla, where instead of turning right to follow the morning's route, you keep straight on above the valley of the Rio Bolulla, descending gently to join the main road near Km.37.

Turn right down towards Bolulla, remembering , of course, to face the traffic which can be heavy in summer. The Rio Bolulla is on the right at first, and then cross a bridge over it. Note the ruins of a really substantial water-mill on the left which must in years gone by have had a very reliable source of water. Note also an unusual sight in the dry sierras, the many large willow trees by the stream. If you follow this route in winter the whole of the left-hand side of the valley is alive with the sound of small streams plunging down to join the river.

By now the bar in the village will surely be open and you can take refreshments and make the little burro's day.

Bernia from Bolulla Castle

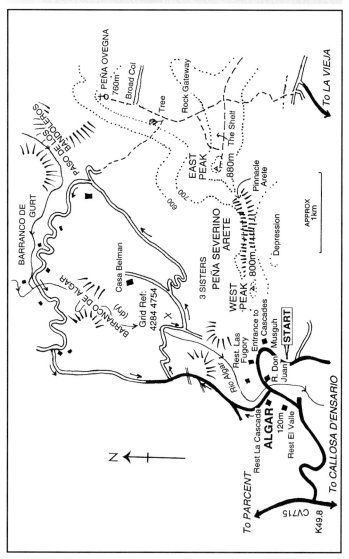

25: ALGAR VALLEY WALK

Grade:	easy
Distance:	11.5km
Time:	4hrs
Ascent:	150m
Maps:	**Altea 848 (30–33), Benisa 822 (30–32)**

The tiny hamlet of Fonts de L'Algar lies just over 2km north-east of Callosa de Ensarria, on the CV715 road to Parcent. Above the village, to the north, a confluence of five rivers passes through a narrow gorge in cascades and pools, providing a site of natural beauty which the inhabitants, encouraged by the local authority at Callossa, seek to exploit. Although agriculture still flourishes in the valley, it now seems as if the whole hamlet has been taken over by restaurants, bars, souvenir shops, museums and car parks. At this point, too, the Bolulla river joins with the Rio Algar and flows to meet the Rio Guadalest to water the vast huerto which stretches right down to the coast, the lower valley. The upper valley starts at Col de Rates. The route covers the middle section of the valley, above the cascades, and ends near the Paso De Los Bandoleros. Walking is all on good forestry roads.

Getting There

Leave the CV715 at Km.49.8 and fork right with signs to Fonts de L'Algar. There is an information kiosk by the side of the road. The road descends steeply for about a kilometre to a bridge over the Rio Algar, where the walk starts. Those residents who are not in the catering trade are actively engaged in organising car parking, none of which is free. The small park near to the entrance to the cascades is the most expensive, whilst most restaurants will either waive a fee if you patronise them or give you a discount.

Along the River Towards the Upper Valley

Turn from the road west along the southern bank of Rio Algar, passing the Restaurant La Cascada, a pleasant start to the walk, with the freely flowing river cascading over weirs and flowing between willows and bamboos, with lots of wild flowers. The flow of the river is controlled upstream by a dam, so that the precious water can be pumped back up to the Guadalest reservoir, and this means that even in a summer drought there is flowing water.

Leaving the river the road starts to climb steeply to the north and another road joins from the left. Take time to look over your shoulder and enjoy the views to the south of the coast, with Sierra Helada, the Cortinas, Ponoch, Sanchet and Peña Roc on the Aitana Ridge. Nearer is Sierra Aixorta.

In half an hour pass a sign 'Traversia Severino PR36 route 3', heading now west of north on the eastern side of the valley. There is now a rough track on the right and there are good views to the north west of Bolulla, with Aitana in the distance. Across the valley, to the north-east, can be seen Peña Severino and the summit of Sierra Bernia, whilst further to the north is the detached summit of Peña Ovenga, overlooking the Paso de los Bandoleros, with the jagged ridge of Sierra Ferrer beyond.

At a junction take the right-hand road and later, at a crossroads, turn off to the right, down towards the dry river bed of the Algar, whilst across on the eastern side of the valley the route can be picked out. Now leave the surfaced road at a marker on an irrigation control box to descend to the right on an unsurfaced road, heading for the valley bottom.   *30mins*

Down to the right can be seen the cleft in the rocks carved by the river in ancient times and from whence its waters issue into the dam and cascades. The road now leads south towards this gorge, but soon turn off left, in a northerly direction, to cross and recross the dry river bed. First go straight ahead at a crossroads, then leave this road, which leads to a substantial *finca*, Casa Belman, and take a right-hand fork; the road starts to climb upwards in zig-zags.   *1hr*

Eventually the road levels out for a long section, heading basically north towards the great cleft of the Paso de los Bandoleros and the ruins of an extensive *finca* set artistically on a small knoll. This is your next objective. On this section, look backwards to enjoy the view of the distant mountains of Puig Campaña and Ponoch, framed between the crags of the gorge which leads to the cascades. You pass now under the crags of the Severino which tower above. First you can identify the sheer northern face of the arête which joins the two summits, whilst ahead can be seen equally attractive arêtes, on the ridge of Sierra Ferrer. Eventually, to the north you can identify Rates Peak, overlooking the Col de Rates, and even the little white restaurant on the col as the route approaches the old *finca* under the eastern peak of Severino, with the detached peak of Peña Ovenga overlooking the Paso de los Bandoleros. After passing a small building with Riu Raus, you arrive at the ruins, and even though the climb has only been some 150m there are excellent views in all directions. For those who wish to follow the Severino Circuit (described in Volume 2), there is the chance to glance upward to the south to try to identify the route of your descent, by means of the steep rocky gully which leads up to the col on the Bernia.

1hr 30mins

Algar Valley walk, photo by Bob Stansfield

Down to the Valley Bottom

All too soon it is time to leave this delightful spot and continue along the road; the track which leads off to the right is the route leading to col between the Bernia and Severino. The road now drops down between *fincas* and *casitas*, a number of which are being restored, and the road zig-zags towards the valley bottom, swinging west and heading for an old ruin with a cypress tree still flourishing close to the wall. Cross the dry river bed and head south now, under some cliffs, and the route starts to climb again.   *2hrs 15mins*

Back to Fonts De L'Algar

It would be nice to be able to follow the river back to the village, but the gradient steepens and the road swings from side to side to gain height. Soon you can see the reason for your exertions, as the valley route is blocked by a high rocky spur, which the river avoids by entering yet another small gorge. Eventually you reach a small ruined casita, where a road turns invitingly to the south, but ignore it as it only leads to more ruins and a well. Your route continues north past another ruin on the left, and in only a few metres turn off left on another unsurfaced road marked on a wall with a purple spot. The other road is heading for Tarbena and Col de Rates.

You now follow a gently descending road with good views of the distant mountains ahead and, across the valley, Peña Severino, with your lunch stop at the old *finca* still visible. In parts this road is very eroded; pass one crossroad and continue south-west until a substantial *finca* appears above you on the right and the road gains a surface.   *3hrs*

Yellow and white markers now appear again, and you can see Casa Belman below on the left in the valley bottom and should be able to pick out our morning's route on the other side of the valley. In a few minutes the road again loses its surface and you ignore a track leading down to the left. When the junction with your morning route is reached, the road soon gains a surface again and you retrace your steps down into Fonts de L'Algar, with its extensive choice of bars and restaurants.   *4hrs*

26: EL SOMO CIRCUIT

Grade:	moderate
Distance:	18km
Time:	5hrs
Ascent:	600m
Map:	Benisa 822 (30–32)

Perhaps this walk could be called 'A walk around El Somo', because in the course of it you do just that, moving anti-clockwise around that undistinguished hill. You will enjoy five hours amongst majestic mountain scenery, visit a beautiful natural rock arch, a castle and a dramatic gorge. Mostly on excellent tracks, only one small section is badly worn and overgrown. Remember that the last section is a climb of some 400m, so save some energy for it!

Getting There

Since the new road from Tarbena to Castell de Castells, the CV752, was opened, you can approach the start of this walk, at the Collado de Bichauca (Km.6), from either direction. The road may not be shown on your map, so leave the CV715 at Km.30.5, just above the village of Tarbena. From Castells, leave the main road at the river bridge (Km.12).

Making A Start

Start by walking west down the road towards Castells, with views of Sierra Serrella and Mala del Llop in the distance. Below is the well-watered area Corralles de Alt, now farmed from Castells, with its well down to the right, looking for all the world like an inverted pudding basin. Beyond the well are views of the dramatic escarpment of Cocoll, and the little pointed peak Tosal del Vaquero. Now turn off, left, at Km.7 onto a broad forestry road and head south-west.

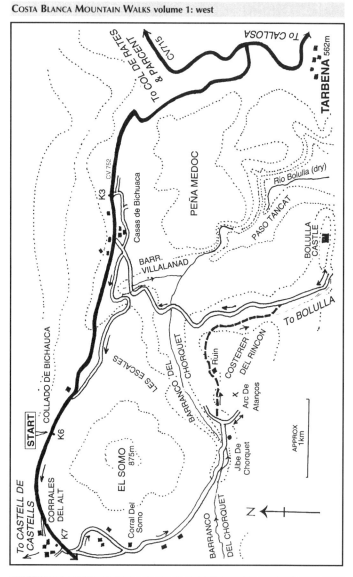

To The Chorquet Well

Change direction over what is normally very wet ground on a broad road which turns a little before climbing the south-west flank of El Somo to Corral del Somo, passing an old *finca* below on the right. At the top of a rise are the ruins of Corral del Somo at a junction where you descend left in a south-east direction. **1hr 25mins**

Pause for a moment to enjoy views of the western mountains, with Malla del Llop (north-west) and Serrella Castle to the left of it. If you look carefully in the distance, ahead and slightly to the right of the track, and high up on the flank of the Aixorta, you will see a gully. On the left-hand side of this gully try to pick out the lovely natural rock arch, Arc de Atancos. The arch is 12m across and 10m high, and is well worth a visit.

The track continues to descend, passing two casitas, until it reaches a stony *barranco* and, on the right of the track, a well built into a wall. This is Jibe del Chorquet and has excellent water, despite the fact that you must use a rusty can to have a drink. Please close the door when you have finished.

Visit to the Arc de Atancos

A few metres further along the track from the well where the track bends to the left, find a track on the right, which in 10 minutes leads to the base of the Arc. There is no track from here, and the ground is rocky and overgrown, but the effort involved in climbing to the Arc is well worth it. Allow an hour for this diversion.

On to Bolulla Castle

Your route now continues and for a short time dips gently, following the Barranco del Chorquet, but this is not your destination. Keep a sharp eye out for a small cairn and a red marker as your route turns right to traverse south-east towards Bolulla Castle. At first, the narrow track is indistinct and overgrown, but seek out the red markers which will guide you over this difficult section. After about half an hour, note a large cave on the opposite wall of the *barranco* (north-east). **2hrs**

Now, still following the red markers, cross a shallow valley with terraces and maintain height up to a holly oak. Shortly after this you reach a ruined *finca*, which you pass on the left. Cross a terrace with some dead trees to climb up the last section before you get your first views of the Paso Tancat (closed valley) with its abandoned settlement below on the left.

Step by step the views ahead become more extensive and dramatic as the path slowly climbs and the impressive cliffs of the Paso Tancat are revealed. Eventually the Sierra Bernia comes into view, then Bolulla Castle perched on its rocky outcrop, and finally the coast at Albir and the Sierra Helada. This last section of track down to the Col at Bolulla Castle is badly worn and overgrown (hell in shorts!) but eventually you gain a broad road which has come up from Bolulla.   *4hrs 10mins*

If you have the energy, turn right and continue about 100m to the col, either to admire the coastal views or to climb to the castle ruins. There is no real track to the castle, but keep away from the ridge rocks, and on the southern side make your way by means of an easy rock scramble to the ruins in about 20 minutes.

Down into the Paso Tancat
Go left on a broad track (north), climbing a little at first but eventually winding down to the Barranco del Chorquet, where it joins the Barranco de Villalanao to enter the gorge, and go into the jaws of the Paso Tancat. Cross the dry bed of the river, and start the long, slow climb (400m) back up to the Collada de Bichauca.   *4hrs 40mins*

In five minutes pass a *casita* on your left, and a short section of concrete road follows before you reach a *fuente* with bowls for the animals. Now, above you to the east, can be seen a small *casita*, Casa de Bichauca, which is on the road. Watch out for another road, on your left, which switches back in a westerly direction following the northern side of Barranco de Villalanao (changed to Cova Roja on 1:25,000 maps). Follow this good track to the head of the *barranco*, cross over to the other side and head for the col, with the road for company on the right-hand side. A short way from the col, join the road near an old *casita* on the right-hand side, and walk up it to your starting point, Collado de Bichauca.   *5hrs*

You will have to drive either to Tarbena or Castell de Castells to find a bar or restaurant.

Val de Gallinera

27: FORADA RIDGE

Grade:	moderate
Distance:	17.5km
Time:	6hrs 15mins
Ascent:	600m
Map:	Alcoy 29–32

This ridge walk is mostly trackless, so you need to be well shod and capable of picking a good route. It is difficult to imagine a route with so much interest. It starts at an ancient wash-house and the remains of a water mill, then visits an ancient monastery, the ruins of an Iberian settlement and an interesting cave-dwelling. The eastern summit has a large forat, a natural hole in the rock, and even more Iberian ruins. The final peak has an unusual iron cross, and the walk ends at a Moorish king's castle with a modern mountain refuge installed.

Getting There

Leave Pego on the CV700 to Cocentaina, along the beautiful Gallinera Valley, and start the day at the village square of Benisiva, Km.43, where the Bar Placeta will provide refreshments and food. There are also good bars at Beniali. It is worth first making a small detour along the road to the west, where you will find, on the right-hand side of the road, the village fountain and wash-house, and the remains of an ancient water-mill.

To the Monastery

Across the road from the square is the village bakery, and a set of concrete steps by the side of a steep road leads up through the pretty sister village of Benitaya. Walk through the village houses until in 10 minutes an impressive new gateway is passed on the right. The remains of the old monastery are within the walled area to the right of the gate,

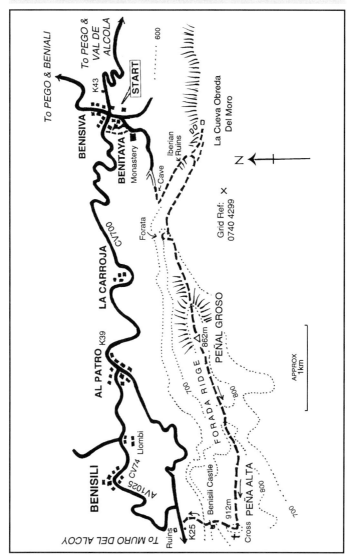

which is planted with pines. El Convento de la Gallinera was founded in 1611 by Franciscans under the patronage of the Duke of Gandia. It is said that the spot chosen for the monastery is where the sun shines through the *forat* on the Forada on the saint's day. The area is now private property, but if you walk through the gates and along the new road for a few metres you will find the old spring opposite a new reservoir. The Font de L'Hort de Mengual bears the date 1741. The old ladies in the village can still remember the monastery bell being rung to announce the distribution of food to the needy. Back on the road continue through orchards (yellow/white waymarks), up zig-zags to a right turn onto a partly concreted rough track. Follow this to a concreted left fork which becomes an old mule track.   *30mins*

To the Ruins and Cave House

This old Mozarabic trail is much decayed, and you have good views ahead of you of the *forat* on the eastern summit. After passing a water-worn cave on the left side, the track changes direction towards the east. The cave was once a spring, and legend has it that such was the flow of water that a bale of hay which fell from a passing donkey was found 5km away in the valley bottom. Ahead, just below the skyline, can be seen the remaining stones of the old Iberian settlement which you pass through.   *1hr*

Looking out of Cave House to the Forat

Up above can be seen the large caves in the cliff face, which were walled in by the Moors to form dwellings (La Cueva Obreda Del Moro), and in a further 10 minutes you reach the broad ridge. To visit the caves turn left (east) towards a large ruined *finca*. On entering the *finca*, you find a large cave with a domed roof and sockets in the walls, no doubt to provide for a second floor to accommodate the shepherd above his flock.

To the Forat

You now start your traverse of the Forada Ridge, and will be travelling west for the rest of the day. A good path leads to the eastern summit, with its graceful rock arch. You will have to scramble through the rocks to reach the arch, from which you get excellent views of Benisili Castle and, in the far north-west, the distinctive peak of Benicadell near Muro del Alcoy.   *1hr 45mins*

To Peñal Groso

The main peak of the ridge at 862m can be seen ahead with its white triangulation pillar. For the rest of the ridge traverse, there are no reliable tracks, so some route-finding is necessary. First descend to a col, and then strike upwards, passing some distinctive crags, one of which bears a strong resemblance to Kilnsey Crag in the Yorkshire Dales. After passing an intermediate summit, you arrive at the main summit.   *2hrs 40mins*

To Peña Alta

The way ahead can now be seen clearly, with your objective, Peña Alta, identifiable by its metal cross, and below it, to the north, the beautifully situated ruins of the final objective, Benisili Castle (Castillo de Alcala). Across the valley can be seen Lorcha Castle in the Serpis Valley, and there are magnificent views east down the whole length of the Val de Gallinera. To the south are extensive views of the wild wastes of the Val d'Alcala. Between you and your objective, however, are a number of undulations which it is necessary to avoid. At the first depression, with a small almond grove, avoid rocks by traversing a little left.   *3hrs 30mins*

Avoid a broad barranca at a cairn with a hunting sign by traversing left (south) to avoid losing height, and make for a large boulder, on which the owner of the hunting rights has staked his claim in paint.
                                                                        4hrs 15min

The Forat

At the top of a shallow valley, move right a little to follow a short rocky arête, which gives access to the final ascent to the cross. The unusual metal cross on the summit has recently been vandalised by some mindless persons, however they cannot destroy the beautiful views across the Val d'Alcala and the southern mountains. *4hrs 50mins*

To Benisili Castle

It is now necessary to leave the main ridge and descend the spur to the north, which leads to the castle seen below. There are two tracks, one on each side of the rocky arête, before you reach the grassy plateau on which the beautiful ruins stand. There is a *fuente* at the end of a small path to the west of the arête. The castle is strategically placed to command the whole valley, as far as Beniarrama Castle, clearly seen 10km to the east. Benisili Castle is of Moorish origin, having been built by Al Azarach, the Moorish king. It passed to Jaime I in 1258, and he in turn gave it to his heir, Pedro. The castle therefore has right royal connections, but these failed to save it in the disastrous earthquake of 1644. If you climb the parapet, you will find a small bunk-house built into a turret on the northern side, equipped as a refuge by local mountaineers. The first-aid kit is very basic, but included a full bottle of brandy when last I visited this hut! *5hrs 40mins*

Back to the Road

There is an old mule track which zig-zags down to the north to reach the road near Km.24. The track was always difficult to follow until in 1990 an extensive forest fire removed all the vegetation and it was rediscovered. The nearest reliable refreshment place is Benisiva. *6hrs 15mins*

28: ALMISIRA VIA ALTO DE CHAP

Grade:	scramble
Distance:	14km
Time:	5hrs
Ascent:	457m
Map:	Alcoy 821 (29–32)

Almisira (757m) is easily recognised by its array of antennae, which occupy the summit. On approaching Pego from Vergel there is a particularly attractive view of this mountain, and as you drive towards Adsubia to enter the beautiful gorge which leads to the Val de Gallinera you can admire its bold northern crags. To the north of the summit on a small lower spur is the ancient Castillo de Gallinera. Beyond the gorge lies the unspoilt and fruitful Val de Gallinera, famous for its cherry orchards, which are a mass of blossom in spring.

The route described here is only for those hardy souls who can climb steep rocks, undeterred by spiky undergrowth. During the ascent of Alto de Chap it is necessary to endure these conditions for about an hour. Thereafter, once the high plateau is reached, there are good tracks all the way.

Those who seek a more gentle route should reverse the descent route via the castle. There is little need for route-finding to reach Pla de Almisira in about 2 hours. Start from the school in Beniarrama and go down the lane. Head towards the castle for a short while, but at the first junction bear right to contour round a large barranca.

Malla de Llop with the Barranco de Canal (the 'glacier') (Walk 19)

Serrella Castle (Walk 20)

Sierra Bernia from Bolulla Castle (Walk 24)

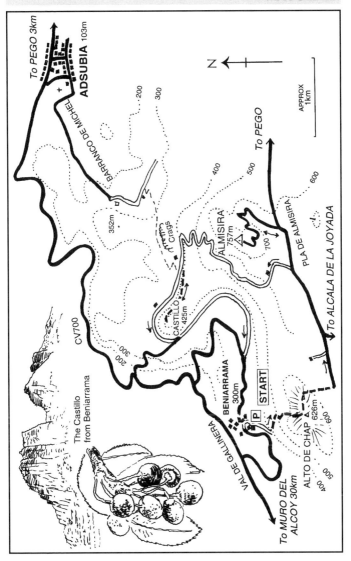

To PEGO 3km

ADSUBIA 103m

BARRANCO DE MICHEL

N

APPROX 1km

To PEGO

200

300

352m

Crags

400

500

600

ALMISIRA 757m

700

PLA DE ALMISIRA

CASTILLO 425m

To ALCALA DE LA JOYADA

CV700

300

200

300

BENIARRAMA 300m

START

P

The Castillo from Beniarrama

VAL DE GALLINERA

ALTO DE CHAP

626m

600

500

400

To MURO DEL ALCOY 30km

Making a Start

From the isolated, unspoilt village of Beniarrama (school, shop and restaurant all closed 1993), look upwards to the south where the skyline is dominated by a line of crags, Alto de Chap (626m). It is, in fact, part of the Forada Ridge, which forms the southern side of the Val de Gallinera. From the village the cliffs seem impregnable, but there is one noticeable weakness. By making for a prominent buttress, which is passed on the west side, it is possible to climb through the crags to reach the top of the escarpment.

Start from the Calle Almassera in the west end of the village, and take the small concrete road leading to the cemetery and then an unsurfaced track past the Stations of the Cross with their ceramic pictures. Ignore a track leading to the left, even though your track seems to be heading away from the buttress. After a few zig-zags, in about 15 minutes turn off left (red marker), heading straight for the castle. The way is level at first, then climbs a little on a good track. Finally on a bend, the track ends in a cherry grove.   *30mins*

Scree Grove to Lower Combe

The trees are growing in scree, and the *campesino* has made a rough mule track which goes upwards through the trees. But it can only be detected only by those with a well-developed imagination and supreme optimism: mule droppings confirm the route. The next section is rather difficult.

When the almond trees end there is still a vague track up to the base of the buttress, beyond which the track is extremely overgrown and difficult to find. In 10 minutes reach the wall of the buttress. Turn right (west) in order to get round it. For the next 10 minutes you will have some misgivings, but the track is there, under all the shrubbery. Persist in trying to find it, as the terrain on either side is even more difficult. (Secateurs, pangas, gloves and thorn-proof clothing are a distinct advantage here.) Eventually, a track emerges from the undergrowth, over scree and then rock, to reach the lower combe with its pine trees.   *50mins*

To Peter's Rake

Move upwards onto a narrow path which goes left (north-east), aiming for a narrow cleft between the buttress and the main cliffs above. At the cleft, you find yourself in the upper combe. Climb upwards through the pines towards the crags, bearing just a little to the right, to find a narrow rock staircase which leads to the rake (red markers). You have a short rock scramble upwards towards the top of the cliffs, ending in a short groove, which leads to a cairn on the summit of Alto de Chap.

1hr 30mins

To Almisira

There are extensive views to the south across the broad expanse of Val de Alcala. To the west is the Forada Ridge, and to the east your ultimate goal, the summit of Almisira. Below lies the road from Pego. Go straight down to the road (south-east), taking great care, as the terrain is broken limestone pavement, to reach the surfaced road and turn left (east).

1hr 45mins

Pass a small casita on the left, and a junction where the road comes up from Val de Alcala, to reach Pla de Almisira. On the way, note the yellow/white markers, which indicate the unsurfaced road on the left, leading back to the village via the Castillo de Gallinera. This road is your return route. At the Pla, a surfaced road leads upwards to the summit.

2hrs 40mins

The Summit

From this vantage point, you can spend some time identifying the peaks which can be seen in every direction. To the south are Peñon Roch and the Cavallo Verde Ridge, with Serrella Castle beyond and Peña Mulero in the distance. To the north, beyond Villalonga, can be seen the serried ridges of three Sierras – Zafor, Gallinera and Almirante.

The Castle

Much is known of the history of the extensive castle which once crowned this strategic mountain, but only a few stones remain. Moorish in origin, its governor was Abdalla Marhop. In 1243, it fell to Nicolas Scals. The castle probably suffered in the earthquake of 1644, but it is more likely that what little remained was scattered when the road to the transmitting station was constructed. A forestry lookout cabin has been newly installed on the summit and is manned during high fire-risk periods. Just below the cabin, on the north side, is a small section of wall with a cement coping. Some say that the wall is one of the remains of the Moorish castle, others claim that it is even more ancient, being of the Iberian period.

Looking over Gallinera Castle to Gandia and the sea

Descent to Castillo de Gallinera

Retrace your steps to the road and turn right, and in a few minutes turn off again to the right (north) at the yellow/white markers. Pass a small casita, and in 15 minutes, at the top of a small rise,there is a magnificent view of the picturesque castle below. The road starts to deteriorate, and it is hard to believe that until the late 1980s it was passable with care by motor traffic. Pass under the impressive northern cliffs of Almisira until you reach a small casita, beyond which a red marker shows the rough track to the castle itself. Several years ago, the owner of the castle installed a gate to prevent access. (Apparently everyone just walks round the gate, but to be very careful as the ruins are dangerous, especially the deep, open cistern.)   *3hrs 40mins*

    Carry on down the unsurfaced road, passing Casa de la Pradera, around the castle, to head for Beniarrama, eventually joining a surfaced road. Turn left to arrive at the village. Bar Roca is to be found in Calle Almassera.   *5hrs*

29: FORNA TO VILLALONGA

Grade:	moderate
Distance:	10km
Time:	5hrs
Ascent:	200m
Map:	Jativa 795 (29–31)

This is a lovely walk between two ancient castles, crossing a modest sierra with views of the remote valley of the Rio Serpis. It is mainly on good tracks.

Getting There

To get to the beautiful little village of Forna, leave Pego on the CV700 towards Cocentaina, and near Km.51.6 turn north on the CV717 for 4km. As you reach the top of a small hill, just before entering the village, park your car and walk up a good track to the right (east) to visit Forna Castle. The castle is in a good state of preservation and is Moorish in origin, having belonged to Al Azadrach, a Moorish king. In 1262 it belonged to Don Bernardo de Guillen, whose six sons were known as Los Caballeros de Panacho Negro (Knights of the Black Plume). Notable features of the castle are its well-preserved entrance and the four towers facing north, the water cisterns (or are they dungeons?) and the arrow slits. Unlike other castles in the Gallinera Valley, it survived the great earthquake of 1644. Agile and slender readers will be able to squeeze between the locked portals, others will have to obtain a key from the town hall in Adsubia. As you ascend you get good views, and to the north you can pick out the first section of this walk, the steep concrete road.

Making a Start

Start near the Calle *Fuente* and go north up a steep concrete road between new villas. In 10 minutes the road ends and you take to a very eroded mule track which zig-zags upwards on the west side of a barranca. As you climb, look back for lovely views of the village and castle, with Sierra Negre behind them. The track now contours round a

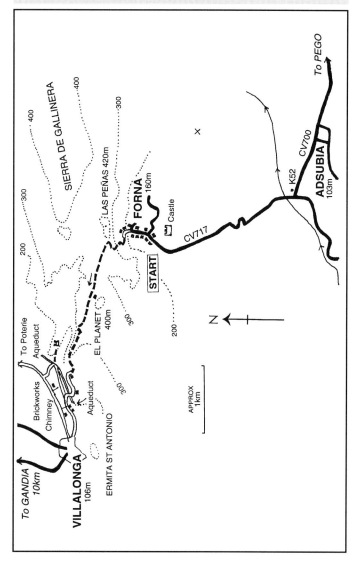

broad gully and crosses easier ground. Look back and you catch a glimpse of Almisira, with its transmitters on the summit. At the highest point you pass an occupied casita on your left.   *45mins*

Down the Barranco del Castillo

Just past the little *casita* views start to open up to the north, first down into the *barranco*, then of the towns of Patria and Gandia, and finally the ruins of Villalonga Castle at the northern end of the ridge on the other side of the *barranco*. In the distance can be seen Sierra Ador. Now the track starts to descend quite steeply through pines until the large town of Villalonga appears, with the Serpis Valley behind it.
1hr 20mins

During the descent there are lovely views of the Sierra Ador mountain range behind the town. On a little hill just outside the town is the picturesque hermita of San Antonio, with a calvary leading to it.

To Villalonga Castle

At a newly constructed villa join an unsurfaced road which leads down through other villas and will eventually lead to the town. Move north-east and watch out for a small aqueduct. Your route is to descend the road until you reach the villa with the name Belater Lolita (just above the brick-works) on the right, then follow a road moving north-east until you reach the aqueduct. Now go south up a rocky stream bed under high walls on the right which support orange groves, and enter the Barranco del Castillo. A reasonable path traverses the slope upwards towards the castle ruins, which are clearly visible. The last few metres into the ruins is much eroded and needs care.

2hrs 30mins

From the castle the Serpis Valley can be seen behind the town leading to Alcoy through the Val de Infierno gorge. Only a railway occupied this valley, but it closed 30 years ago. Happily, the abandoned track is preserved as an unsurfaced road, which gives access to walkers who can enjoy the majestic scenery, the waterfalls and rapids of the beautiful Rio Serpis, and the varied wildlife, which includes kingfishers, herons and exceedingly large trout (see Route 33). Behind Gandia, near the coast, can be seen the Sierras of Bota and Faconera.

Villalonga (the Long Village) is of Roman origin, established by *colonia*, retired soldiers of the Roman army who took their pensions in

Spain and were given land to farm. They built their villas in a line, probably along a reliable water supply. The castle is of Moorish origin, but by 1240 was in the possession of King Jaime I of Aragon.

Sadly, there is as yet no alternative route to offer back to Forna, but it is always interesting to reverse a route, simply because the views are totally different from the outward journey.   *(5hrs)*

There is a good restaurant, The Nautilus, at Forna.

30: VAL DE ENCANTADA
AND ERMITA DEL SANTO CRISTO

Grade:	moderate
Distance;	11.5km
Time:	4hrs 30mins
Ascent:	210m
Map:	Alcoy 821 (29–32)

Planes lies some 40km inland from the coast and is about the limit for a day walk, especially for those who are travelling from the south of the region. It lies on the western side of the Pass of Benisili at the head of the Val de Gallinera, with the town of Muro de Alcoy only 6km away. It is on the Rio Hondo, surrounded by mountains in a most peaceful situation. The town is well worth exploring, with its quiet streets, but it was not always such a backwater. In the 13th century it was designated the Baronia de Plane by King Jaime I, and was the administrative centre for a large area. The ruins of the 11th-century castle indicate its importance during the Moorish period. The town seems totally unaffected by its loss of status and boasts three patrons: the Mother of Christ of the Roses, Sant Roc and Santissimo Cristo de la Villa. The patronal festival and Moors and Christian parades are in early October.

Getting There

From the coast, via Pego, follow the CV700 through the beautiful, unspoiled Val de Gallinera, famous for its cherry orchards and a

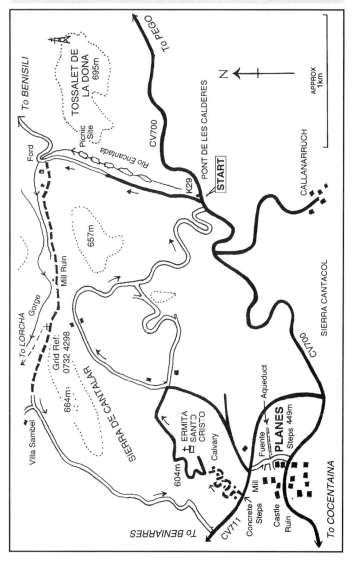

wonderful introduction to the area. After passing through Adsubia, you enter a small gorge, with the Rio Gallinera tumbling over its rocky bed in rapids and cascades and with the fairy-tale castle of Beniarrama perched on its crag above you on the left. In the cliff on the right-hand side is a small cave which until a few years ago contained a comprehensive collection of prehistoric cave paintings. Sadly some have been removed illegally by collectors, and, rather late in the day, a protective fence now protects what is left.

Pass through some of the eight Moorish villages, some prosperous, others such as Llombo deserted, with the last and highest one, Benisili, verging on extinction. Climb to the pass named after this village, with the ruins of Al Azarac's Castle (the last Moorish leader) on the left, to drop down past the road to Margarida on the left, and at Km.29 cross the Rio Encantada by the Pont de le Claderes and park on the western side, where a surfaced road leads north into the valley (Cami de l'Almadec).

To Moli De Encantada

The little Rio Encantada rises in the Sierra Cantacol not far from the village of Margarida and runs for only 8km to join the broad Rio Serpis, which flows out of the Beniarres Reservoir, meeting it at a beautiful collection of lagoons to the south west of Lorcha. Its short length is, however, full of interest and beauty, as it first follows a valley, then passes through a rocky gorge.

Follow the surfaced road, which is signposted to the picnic area, north-east, noting a steep track climbing up the left-hand side of the valley which is our return route. The river is on your right, and soon the impermeable strata allows small pools to develop with some pretty cascades and rapids. The deepest and most attractive pool has been developed as a picnic site, with a small waterfall issuing from crags on the far side. If you can resist an early break, continue down until you reach a level area, Pla de Encantada, where there is another picnic site, but do not cross the river by the ford. The hill on the right (with the transmitters) is Tossalet de la Donna (611m) whilst ahead, to the north, Sierra de l'Albureca rises to 767m. The Gallinera Way (31/Day 3) joins us for a while, having come down from the Benisilli Pass via Barranca del Llombo (Relanches).

On your left at a newly restored villa turn off to the left to follow the fence on the southern side of the villa and pick up a narrow track which follows above the river, on its western bank. Pass the gateway of Villa Monica, head for a ruin and then drop down to the river level at the remains of an old water mill, Moli de Encantada.   *1hr*

To Villa Sarabel

Now leave the level of the river to climb towards another ruin on the right-hand side. On this section, you get lovely views of the river flowing through rocks, with cascades below you, as it enters the narrow gorge, where we, sadly, cannot follow.

Climb now towards the skyline and some pines until you reach a road and get wide views to the north of Benicadell, a very shapely mountain, with the white *ermita* of Beniarres on its slopes and the vast waters of the reservoir in the foreground.   *2hrs*

The road to the right leads only to a private house, Villa Sarabel. You leave the Gallinera Way and turn left to follow the broad road as it descends, south-west, to join the motor road CV711. On this section you have extensive views of Planes with the Mariolas beyond.
2hrs 30mins

To Ermita Del Santo Cristo

Turn left (south-east) for about 400m until you find some concrete steps on the left, the start of the Calvary.

The stations of the cross are marked, in the usual style, by small shrines with ceramic decoration, and as you gain height the views to the south-west extend over the impressive remains of the castle and the lovely little town to the Mariolas, Monte Cabrer, with the white keep of Cocentaina Castle, and finally to Benicadell. To the south-east is Sierra de Cantacuc, with the tiny hamlet of Catamaruch, above the Val de Encantada.

If you are counting the stations of the cross it is at Station 10 that the *ermita* appears above you, and you then join the motor road and walk up to this magnificent shrine, an excellent viewpoint. To the east, beyond the pass of Benisilli, guarded by its castle, is the last peak of the Forada Ridge, Tossal de la Crue (912m). To the north is the vast extent of Beniarres Reservoir and the prominent *ermita* above the town of the same name, under the slopes of Benicadell.

The *ermita* is dated 1850, but unless you have sought out the verger in the town you will not be able to see much of the interior, except when mass is celebrated on the patronal festival (October).

3hrs

To the Collado

To the west looms the great summit of Azafor, above the Serpis Valley, and it is in this direction that you follow the road as it descends from the ermita until a crossroads is reached. The road to the right leads down into Planes and the road ahead is a short cut.   *3hrs 45mins*

Turn left, north-east, climbing again to reach the highest part of the road at the col, where it changes direction to the east. From this point those with lots of energy can scramble to the highest part of Sierra Cantalar (664m) through the terraces, whilst others admire the views to the north down into the Val de Encantada and beyond to the Forada. The road levels and passes a casita on the right and a ruin, Corral de Collado, on the left. It finally swings round to the south-east and starts to descend, with Tossalet de la Dona ahead and the first section of your route below. Right ahead is Sierra Cantacuc, the source of the Rio Encantada, and the tiny hamlet of Callamarruch as, with one final, very tight hair-pin bend, the road leads to Pont de les Calderes. There are plenty of refreshments up the hill in Planes.   *4hrs 30mins*

Gallinera Way

31/DAY 1: BENIARRAMA TO BENISIVA

Grade:	moderate
Distance:	17km
Time:	5hrs 30mins
Ascent:	300m
Maps:	Jativa 795 (29–31), Alcoy 821 (29–32)
Sketch map:	See page 13 for the Gallinera Way

Getting Started

From the coast, leave the N332 at Vergel, taking the CV700 to Pego then, with signs for Cocentaina, via Adsubia. On this approach Almisira, your first mountain, then Beniarrama Castle will appear on the skyline. Adsubia is your last chance to buy supplies and obtain refreshments before starting the walk, as Beniarrama has no facilities. Follow the Rio Gallinera as it follows the road through a picturesque rocky gorge where there seems to be little room for both road and river. In winter there will be the added attraction of the rushing water, whilst in summer the dry river bed is full of pink oleanders.

Once out of the gorge with its towering cliffs, Beniarrama (Gallinera) Castle appears high up on your left and then the village itself, perched high over the road. Near Km.46.5 note an old *finca* and a road leading off to the right to a ford over the dry river bed (it is running underground). This is the end of the last stage. Turn off up the hill to the village and start your walk near the school at the eastern end. s172

To Beniarrama (Gallinera) Castle

Drop down a little on a good unsurfaced road in line with the castle, seen high ahead on a spur of rock. The high banks are a riot of colour in spring with lots of wild flowers, especially flax and acanthus. In about 10 minutes, as the road starts to rise, pass an old *finca* on the left and take the road which forks right around a barranca and under the walls of the castle.

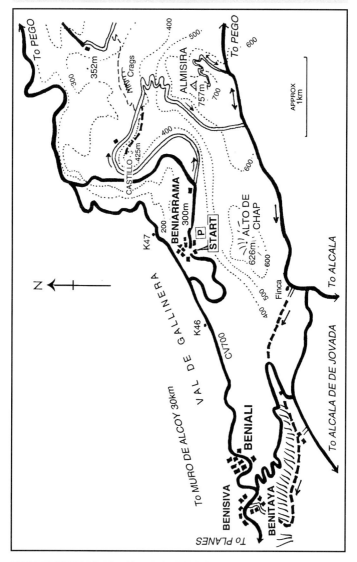

Pass under the castle, fork right at a junction and then swing completely around the castle to find a little casita (Casa de la Pradera). Continue for five minutes and a red marker shows the way off to the right to ascend the castle. The castle is Moorish and was captured by the Christians in 1250. It was, however, badly damaged in the earthquake of 1644, but is still an interesting ruin with its water cistern and one of its towers intact. The castle, however, is privately owned, and a few years ago the owner placed a gate across the entrance so that observers are forced to admire it from afar (very unusual for Spain). Most people avoid the gate by walking around it, but to take great care not to fall into the deep water cistern, which is dangerous as it has no cover!   *1hr*

To Almisira

Continue to climb in a southerly direction towards the towering crags of Almisira and then pass underneath them. It is hard to imagine, as the road deteriorates, that in 1982 it was possible for motor vehicles to use this road. Such is the power of nature over the works of puny man that even the farmers' tractors cannot use it now. As you climb there are extensive views of the Vall de Gallinera, with its tiny villages, and to the south-west the Forada Ridge, with Monte Cabrer, the third highest peak in the province, beyond. Across the valley is Sierra del Almirante, which is the last mountain to be crossed on the last stage. When you are well up on this road, look down for the finest view of the fairy-tale castle, which no owner can take away. The strategic position of this fortress is clear, guarding the entrance to the valley. You will visit its sister castle, Alcala, which guards the upper entrance to the valley, at the end of the next stage. Finally the coast and the Mediterranean appear with views of Gandia.

Ahead Sierra Carrasca now appears on the skyline and you pass an old ruin on the left and reach a surfaced road. Turn left (east) along the road and in five minutes reach a col, Pla de Almisira, where another surfaced road zig-zags up to the summit of your mountain, which you reach in another 20 minutes.   *2hrs*

On this, your first summit, you can spend a happy time plotting the various mountain ranges. To the south is Peñon Roc and Caballo Verde ridge. Beyond is Sierra Serrella and Peña Mulero on the Aitana Ridge. To the north are the Sierras of Almirante, Azafor and Gallinera – all on the final stage of the Costa Blanca Mountain Way.

Much may be known of the history of the castle which once crowned this summit, but little remains to be seen. Some years ago a transmitting station was constructed and a road made to the summit, which must have demolished what little remained after the earthquake of 1644. It is of the Moorish period and we know that Abdalla Marhop was governor. In 1243 it fell to the Christians under Nicolas Scals. Its fame is that it was the scene for the signing of an important treaty which bears its name. There is now a forestry observation point also on the summit, and just below this a low wall with a concrete cap was pointed out to me as the only remains of the Moorish castle. Some time later this was also identified to me as part of an Iberian hill fort. To the west and south-west is a vast, sparsely populated area with only two villages. It is the Val de Alcala. The views to the east take in a vast sweep of the Mediterranean from Gandia to the jagged ridge of the Segaria.

Almisira to Benisiva via Forada Ridge

Leave the summit and return down the road to Pla de Almisira, then turn right (south-west) along the surfaced road, passing the road up from the valley which you used earlier. Continue for 1.5km along the road, now passing a road on the left which leads to Val de Alcala, and then look for a *finca* on the right, where we turn off onto a track which is chained and marked in red. The track leads west through olive and almond groves which turn into terraces. It is now necessary to traverse across one of the terraces (markers) and to follow the right-hand side of a small valley which is terraced, still heading west towards trees on the skyline until a track appears. Now your views are of the Forada Ridge and summit ahead, with the Alcoy mountains behind them. To the south-west across the Val de Alcala is Monte Cabrer.

There is now a broad unsurfaced road which heads towards the ruins of an old corral, passes through it, and in a few minutes gains the motor road down to Beniali, just as it starts to drop down in dramatic hairpin bends to the valley below. From this point you have excellent views of the whole valley laid out below you.   *3hrs*

There are two routes available on this next section. The first starts as a narrow track some 20m to the south-west, along the motor road, and soon gains the edge of the escarpment, where the track disappears. This is the direct route; it is unmarked and very time consuming due to the rocky nature of the ground. A more civilised route is to continue along the motor road for about another 1km, turning right where you

meet another road, and you will soon see a small group of large *fincas* on the right-hand side of the road. Red markers show the broad track which heads north, passing one large ruined *finca* from which you can plot your course, still basically north to the edge of the escarpment. There is a small col to aim for, with a ruin on its left. Most of the time you are in line with the summit of Forada. There are one or two tracks, but it is mainly cross-country work, and red markers have been provided on this section. Reach the cliff edge overlooking the valley.
4hrs 30mins

Head west on an old Mozarabic trail which leads down into the valley, eventually joining a broad road which leads to the tiny village of Benitaya. Pass through the village and continue down to the main road (CV700) at the village of Benisiva. Refreshments and meals are available at the only bar, Placeta, next to the small square. The *patrona* has also indicated that she could possibly find accommodation for a small party in private houses.   *5hrs 30mins*

Benisiva

31/DAY 2: THE FORADA RIDGE

Grade:	moderate
Distance:	17.5km
Time:	6hrs 15mins
Ascent:	500m
Map:	Alcoy 821 (29–32)

This ridge walk is mostly trackless, so you need to be well shod and capable of picking a good route. It is difficult to imagine a route with so much interest. It starts with an ancient wash-house and the remains of a water-mill, then visits an ancient monastery, ruins of an Iberian settlement and an interesting cave-dwelling. The eastern summit has a large forat, a natural hole in the rock and even more Iberian ruins. The final peak has an unusual iron cross, and the walk ends at a Moorish king's castle with a modern mountain refuge installed. Start the day at the village square of Benisiva, where the Bar Placeta will provide refreshments and food (there are also good bars at Beniali). It is worth first making a small detour along the road to the west, where you will find on the right-hand side of the road the village fountain, wash-house and the remains of an ancient water-mill.

To the Monastery

(See map for Route 27.) Now cross the road to the village bakery, Panadero Alphonso, and climb a set of concrete steps by the side of a steep road which takes you up through the pretty sister village of Benitaya. Walk through the village, until in 10 minutes an impressive new gateway is passed on the right. The remains of the old monastery are within the walled area to the right of the gate which is is planted with pine trees. It is said that the spot chosen for El Convento de la Gallinera, which was founded by Franciscans under the patronage of the Duke of Gandia in 1611, was where the sun shone through the *forat* on the ridge on a particular saint's day. If you walk through the gates you can visit the Font de L'Hort de Mangual, an old spring, all that remains of the monastery, with its date stone showing 1741. Some old ladies in the village can still remember the monastery bell being rung to announce the distribution of food to the needy. Back on the road, keep going upwards, through orchards, up zig-zags to a right turn onto a partly concreted rough track. Follow this to a concreted left fork which becomes an old mule track with yellow/white waymarks.

30mins

To the Ruins and Cave House

This old Mozarabic trail is much decayed, and you have good views ahead of you of the *forat* on the eastern summit. After passing a water-worn cave on the left side, the track changes direction towards the east, and ahead of you, just below the skyline, can be seen the remaining stones of the old Iberian settlement, through which you pass.

1hr

Ahead of you now can be seen the large caves in the cliff face which have been walled up to form dwellings (La Cueva Obreda del Moro), and in a further 10 minutes you gain the broad ridge and turn east towards a large ruined *finca*. On entering the *finca*, you will find a large cave with a domed roof and sockets in the walls, no doubt to provide for a second floor.

To The Forat

You now start your traverse of the Forada Ridge and will be travelling west for the rest of the day. There are no reliable tracks, so some route-finding is necessary as you head for the eastern summit, with its graceful rock arch. You will have to scramble through the rocks to gain the arch, from which you get excellent views of Benisili Castle and, in the far distance to the north-west, the distinctive peak of Benicadell near Muro de Alcoy.

1hr 45mins

To Peñal Groso

You are now heading for the main peak of the ridge at 862m, and it can be seen ahead with its white triangulation pillar. You first have to descend to a col and then strike upwards, passing some distinctive crags, one of which resembles Kilnsey Crag in the Yorkshire Dales, beloved of rock-climbers because of its challenging overhang. After passing an intermediate summit, arrive at the main summit.

2hrs 40mins

To Peña Alta

The way ahead can now be clearly seen, with your objective, Peña Alta, identifiable by its metal cross, and below it, to the north, the beautifully situated ruins of your final objective, Benisili Castle. Across the valley can be seen Lorcha Castle in the Serpis Valley, and there are magnificent views east down the whole length of the Val de Gallinera. To the south are extensive views of the wild wastes of the Val d'Alcala. Between you and your objective, however, are a number of undulations which it is necessary to avoid. At the first depression, with a small almond grove, avoid the rocks by traversing a little left.   *3hrs 30mins*

Avoid a broad barranca at a cairn with a hunting sign by traversing left (south) to avoid losing height, and make for a large boulder, on which the owner of the hunting rights has staked his claim in paint.

4hrs 15mins

At the top of a shallow valley, move right a little to follow a short rocky arête, which gives access to the final ascent to the cross. The unusual metal cross on the summit has recently been vandalised by some mindless persons; however, they cannot destroy the beautiful views across the Val d'Alcala and the southern mountains. *4hrs 50mins*

To Benisili Castle

It is now necessary to leave the main ridge and descend the spur to the north, which leads to the castle seen below you. There are two tracks, one on each side of the rocky arête, before you reach the grassy plateau on which the beautiful ruins stand. There is a *fuente* at the end of a small path to the west of the arête. The castle is strategically placed to command the whole valley as far as Beniarrama Castle, clearly seen 10km to the east. Benisili Castle is of Moorish origin, having been built by Al Azarach, the Moorish king. It passed to Jaime I in 1258, and he in turn gave it to his heir, Pedro. The castle, therefore, has right royal connections, but these failed to save it in the disastrous earthquake of 1644. If you climb the parapet, you will find a small bunk-house built into a turret on the northern side, equipped as a refuge by local mountaineers. The first-aid kit was very basic, but included a full bottle of brandy when last I visited this hut!   *5hrs 40mins*

Back to the Road

There is an old mule track which zig-zags down to the north to gain the road near Km.24. The track was always difficult to follow until in 1990 an extensive forest fire removed all the vegetation and it was rediscovered. The penalty you pay for having such a clear path is to soil your clothing on the burnt bushes. The nearest reliable refreshment place is Benisiva.

6hrs 15mins

31/DAY 3: BENISILI TO LORCHA

Grade:	**moderate**
Distance:	**20km**
Time:	**6hrs**
Ascent:	**250m**
Maps:	**Alcoy 821 (29–32), Jativa (29–31)**

The first two stages of the way have been spent in magnificent scenery high on the ridge of the Forada. The scenery in the next stage is totally different as you walk through an Enchanted Valley and by the Rio Serpis with the sound of rushing water in your ears. The first section, to the Villa Saribel, and the final section to Lorcha are all on excellent tracks. The middle section is rough, cross-country walking, but with the benefit of magnificent views of the high mountains and the deep waters of a large reservoir (another novelty for a Costa Blanca mountain walk). In bad visibility this section would be most difficult to follow even with a compass. On the last section, too, you visit lakes, follow an old railway track and climb to a beautiful castle. Those with energy still to spare may enter a gorge called Hell (Barranco del Infierno). What a day!

Down into the Enchanted Valley

The last stage ended on the motor road (CV701) right under the turrets of Benisili Castle, near to Collado de Benisili, the watershed between the Gallinera and the Serpis valleys. This one starts a few metres west

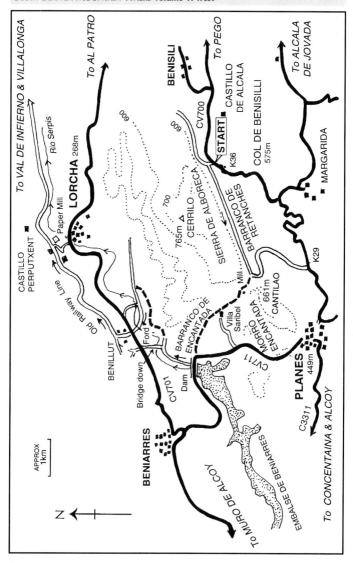

near Km.26, where a surfaced road leads off right (north). Only a few metres along this road an unsurfaced road drops down left to the north-west, and we follow it down into the Barranco de Encantada (the Enchanted Valley). Below on the right can be seen the Rio Encantada and behind it, across the valley, Sierra de Albufeca. The heights ahead are the Sierra Cantalar, and in a gap between two of the peaks can be seen the unmistakable castle at Cocentaina. The road zig-zags a little at first then heads down the side of the valley to a ford across the Rio Encantada. It is worthwhile continuing along the road by the side of the river, upstream, until in about 5 minutes you can admire a waterfall, cross a bridge and return to the ford. *1hr*

To Morro de Encantada and Villa Saribel

Ahead can be seen a villa with a metal fence. Pass the villa on the left-hand side and then turn off right along a good track which follows the rushing waters of the Rio Encantada. Pass the gateway to Villa Monica as you head for an old ruined house and then drop down almost to the level of the river where there is another ruin, most probably a water-mill. You now have to start climbing towards yet another ruin on the skyline, which is passed on the left-hand side. On this section the views down into the narrow gorge, with its cascades and rocky pinnacles, is most impressive. Keep climbing (north-west) towards a few pine trees, still on a good path, until the beautiful rocky ridge of Benicadell can be seen ahead. A few red markers help as you move a little west around a broad barranca and leave the gorge of the Rio Encantada, which continues a few degrees to the west of your route, which is roughly north-west. In a few minutes you gain a broad track and then meet a substantial road and turn right, with the Villa Saribel ahead. *2hrs*

The town of Cocentaina, with its square castle, is at the western end of Monte Cabrer and, moving further west, an old friend, Benicadell. Whilst most of the city of Alcoy is hidden by high ground, on the slopes of the mountain, Sierra de Menechaor, behind it, if you have a good eye, you can spot the monastery of *Fuente* Roja set in the tree-clad slopes below the summit. Below, to the north-west, is a vast stretch of water, Beniarres Reservoir.

To Embalse De Beniarres

This next hour is not easy to follow as you have to walk cross-country on a bearing of north-west through thick scrub made up mainly of gorse (which has yellow flowers, spikes, is no use to anyone except bees and goats, and inflicts deep wounds) and rosemary (which has pretty blue flowers, smells refreshing, is beloved by chefs and yet still manages to scratch you fairly badly, especially if you are wearing shorts). There is a compensation for this hardship in that the views are extensive and dramatic. If you really have to do this section in poor visibility (heaven forbid), you will not only miss these views but unless you keep on course (if in doubt keep north) you stand in danger of dropping down again into the Barranco de Encantada where, as you will see later, there is no accommodation at all for walkers in its murky depths. Your route is marked to the right of the Villa Saribel, and you follow the almond terraces above the *finca* until arriving at the *nevera*. It is the smallest one I have found, and is probably an ice house for the *finca*. Normally *neveras* are to be found high on the northern slopes of mountains above 1000m and were used to make ice from snow, which was transported down to the valleys during summer nights and sold to preserve food. The industry died with the introduction of refrigeration by electricity. On the next stage you will visit a good example on the Azafor Ridge. Other good examples are to be found on Monte Cabrer and Sierra Planes.

From the nevera head for Benicadell, with the village of Beniarres below its western buttress. Keep on this route until you can again see the reservoir and the dam at its western end below you. Over on your right, a little to the west, you can see a cleft in the rocks which is the final section of the gorge of Barranca Encantada; and through the gap is your first view of the broad and fruitful valley of the Rio Serpis, your final objective at the end of this stage of the Gallinera Way.

In half an hour you arrive at a very small casita which is well provided with a bunk and a fireplace. Pass to the left of it and find a reasonable track which continues north-west to head between two ancient and rusty electric pylons, passing a neat little cairn as you go seeking out the red markers. You now pass another old ruin and then the track starts to descend through pines towards an extensive *finca*, ahead to the right. You do not visit this *finca*, but in a few minutes the pines give way to the olive groves and you meet the unsurfaced road to the finca. Turn left for a short while and join the CV701 motor road on the south bank of the reservoir. Turn right and walk towards the dam.

The dam was built in 1983, mostly used to irrigate the vast huerta on the plain of Gandia. The catchment area is vast, with tributaries coming down from the mountains which encircle it in every direction. Cross the dam by all means, and on the opposite bank is a picnic area with a memorial to two airmen who crashed into the lake. The *commandante* and *sergente* died 'in defence of our mountains' on 12 December 1980, so must have been fighting a forest fire. Parts of the aircraft are incorporated into this unusual edifice. This is a lovely place to take a break under the trees, with the breeze coming off the water to cool you after your exertions.   *3hrs 15mins*

The Side of the Rio Serpis to the Enchanted Lakes

Now there is a lovely, easy half hour to walk on a good track by the side of a broad, rushing river. There is music, too, from the shallows where the river crosses rocks, and there are deciduous trees by its banks. If you are quiet you may spot herons, kingfishers or even a dipper.

Leave the motor road just before the dam and drop down right on an unsurfaced road which leads to the river bank. Now follow the river for 2km until you can see Lorcha Castle across the valley, and pass one or two villas on the right-hand side of the road. In a few minutes the river broadens as the Rio Encantada joins the Serpis, forming lakes which at some time were developed as a picnic area, but is now a little derelict. During the winter of 1992–3 the small dam, which carries a path across the Rio Encantada, was breached. You can, however, still find a way across when the river is not in flood. There are still picnic tables under the great willow trees, an invitation for yet another break. You can also explore the narrow gorge of the Encantada, but the path only lasts for a few metres before you are confronted by the sheer sides of the gorge with access only for those with wet suits and the proper equipment. A spring gushes from the rocks above you to join the *rio*.

3hrs 30mins

Enchanted Lake to Lorcha Castle

Your next objective, not as easy as you may think, is to cross over the Rio Encantada and the Rio Serpis and head north to cross the main road (CV711) and join the track of the abandoned railway which will take you east right to the castle. Matters are complicated by two factors. One, the direct line, crossing the Rio Serpis half a kilometre upstream from the lake, is not possible as the bridge no longer exists. Two, the footpath across the Rio Encantada, on top of the small dam, disappeared when the dam was breached It is normally possible to cross the river upstream of the dam as the level is now reduced somewhat. In winter, especially after rain, it would be prudent for a recce to be carried out of this crossing, and if necessary the support party could transport the walkers to the road via Beniarres.

Cross the Rio Encantada and follow a reasonable path which follows the right-hand (south) bank, climbing as it goes until you reach a newly cleared fire break. On this section do not forget to look back for wonderful views of the buttress of Benicadell with the river in the foreground.

Cross the firebreak and you find yourself in a vineyard. Walk around the edge of it to gain a broad grass track which you follow downhill in a northerly direction through more vineyards. *3hrs 50mins*

At the end of this track join a gravel road with a 'No Pasa' sign on the right. The sign has been placed by the owner of a large villa and is of dubious legal significance as the road leads on over the mountains for 12km back to Benisili. You do not, however, need to worry about it, as you turn left to walk in a westerly direction along an avenue of willow trees before crossing a bridge over the Rio Serpis and continuing north through a small hamlet, Benillat. Climb upwards with good views of Benicadell and its *ermita* with its white tower. You are now confronted with another 'No Pasa' sign, for which there is no explanation other than the close proximity of the industrial town of Alcoy. As elsewhere, its large population no doubt rushes out into the country at weekends and fiestas leaving the inevitable piles of rubbish tied up in plastic bags. The road can be seen about 50m away and I have never been challenged when walking this stretch. However, it can be avoided by going left on a footpath which is not very stable but in 5 minutes gains another broad gravel road coming up from the river (from the broken bridge); turn north and gain the motor road (CV711) at Km.2.5. *4hrs 30mins*

Cross the road and take the left-hand, broad unsurfaced road leading north through some farm buildings to join the old railway track. *4hrs 45mins*

Turn right, east, along the track, and in an hour you will arrive at the old Lorcha Station, right under the attractive castle. *5hrs 45mins*

Visit to Lorcha Castle (allow 30mins)

The proper name for this castle is Perputxent, the name of this part of the Serpis Valley. It is another 14th-century castle built by the Moors under Al Azrequ. Climb up directly from the station. There are good views of the little town of Lorcha, Sierra Azafor (the next stage of your walk) and Sierra Ador.

To Barranca Del Infierno

For those who still have the time and the energy there can be no finer end to the day than a short exploration along the Rio Serpis to the entrance of this narrow gorge. You simply follow the old abandoned railway track as far as you wish before returning to the railway station. The scenery is spectacular, the mountains gradually close in and you first pass high above the river but in about an hour drop to the river level. On the opposite side you can see a dam which provided a head of water for a generating station with the conduit hugging the cliffs. The old railway passed over a substantial arched bridge which, sadly, was demolished when the railway closed. Across on the other side of the river are the buildings of the electricity station including the engineer's house. The road bends now down to the level of the river, where a new bridge was constructed by Army Engineers in 1988. The old turbines are still in place as are the sluices.

From this crossing you can, if you have time, continue to another bridge and the first of the short tunnels (torch required) which it is necessary to negotiate before you can continue towards Villalonga. If you have any time left at the end of the Gallinera Way, you may wish to do a full trip along the railway to Villalonga – perhaps returning by an alternative route over the mountain.

To the Village of Lorcha

From the railway station, walk down the surfaced road which passes the large paper mill until you reach the main road, CV701, near Km.7. Now cross the bridge and follow the main road up the hill until you enter the village on the right-hand side of the road.   *6hrs*

From the Barranco De Infierno Diversion

From a point half a kilometre from the railway station take a footpath which goes down to the left and passes through some allotments to gain the road bridge over the river on the main road.

There are five bars in the village, most of which will provide you with a meal.

31/DAY 4: LORCHA TO BENIARRAMA

Grade:	moderate/strenuous
Distance:	18km
Time:	8hrs 30mins
Ascent:	600m
Map:	Jativa 795 (29–31)

This stage is a traverse of a beautiful mountain, Azafor (Safor), at 1013m the highest peak on the walk. The ascent is all on good tracks, but the traverse of the eastern escarpment is track-less and very rough walking, and should never be attempted in poor visibility.

To Fuente Olbist

Leave Lorcha, where there are five bars to delay your start, and leave the main road (CV701) just higher than the beautiful *fuente*, Font Grota, where the tables are made of old mill stones. Now cross the dry river bed and take a broad unsurfaced road which will lead you to your first objective, *Fuente* de Olbist.

The road has an easy gradient and heads north-east, ending at Villalonga some 10km away. Note some old cave houses built against the cliffs on your left, and the road starts to zig-zag to gain height, with Barranca de Basiets on your right-hand side. It is surprising how soon you will be able to enjoy extensive views to the south, with Lorcha and its little calvary in the foreground, the impressive eastern buttress of Benicadell and a wide view of the Serpis Valley. An unusually large and unnecessary notice declares that the mountain is 'For Public Use'.

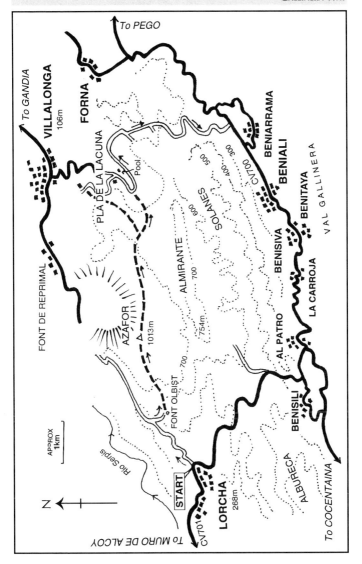

Another *barranco*, Vertiente de la Carrasco, joins from the right and you now get a view of the southern end of the Forada Ridge. The gradient now eases a little and you reach a viewpoint on the left where you can look down some 400m into the Serpis Valley, with the old abandoned railway track which you may have explored on the last stage.   *1hr*

Continue along the road, climbing gently as the bulk of Azafor's southern slopes come into view ahead. After a while you will note another deep *barranco* on our right and, across on the other side, a track and the *fuente*. This is your route and you have to go around the head of the *barranco* where there is some red shale. You reach a junction and leave the road to Villalonga, turning right onto another road, heading south-west.   *1hr 20mins*

The road now passes under some smooth slabs of rock which look like granite and seem to be glacial, then another track, which is a short cut, forks off left. You keep on and are now high enough to see, to the south, the town of Muro de Alcoy; in another few minutes, you arrive at the beautifully laid out Fuente de Olbist. In addition to the spring, there are tables and benches and a nice barbecue.   *1hr 30mins*

To the Summit of Azafor

Go up some steps at the side of the barbecue and turn right onto a narrow track which will take you on up to the summit of the mountain. There is a flourishing mountaineering club in Alcoy and a number of them in Valencia, and this mountain is a favourite walk, so be prepared to meet lots of *excursionistas* at weekends and fiestas. All this traffic means that the path is clear and well marked by cairns. At some points it is easier going to take to the exposed strata, especially where the path has eroded. Climb some zig-zags and go round a shallow *barranco* and climb up again. Below you is a view of the road to Villalonga. The views to the north expand until you can see the coast at Gandia and the Valencian mountains. Now descend into a shallow trough between two of the mountain's summits and find an old *nevera* much decayed. From the *nevera* strike straight up to the summit cairn with its triangulation point. The views are extensive in every direction, but the most impressive is to the south, where you look down on Villalonga and the Font de Reprimal which, with its restaurants, is right by the side of the Rio Serpis and at the end of the road from Lorcha via the old railway track. You can spot it just below the quarry workings.   *3hrs 15mins*

The Summit to Pla De Lacuna

It is now apparent that Azafor, whilst presenting an impressive but benign aspect from the south, presents a very different one on its northern side. The whole of the northern face is, in fact, a 6km curved escarpment, with great cliffs descending sheer to the valley of the Serpis 900m below. There are about four main buttresses with gullies in between them. The southern side is set at a gentler angle but is made up of broken limestone and scrub. Your route is to head east from the summit over two smaller summits, visiting the heads of the gullies to admire the dramatic views down into their depths. You could, of course, climb to the top of the buttresses for even more dramatic views, but this would take considerable effort and, what is more important, time. You have a long way to go to the end of the walk.

As mentioned earlier, this section of the walk demands route-finding skills over very rough ground, with no tracks to follow, and needs good visibility. Red markers have been placed to indicate the route, but remember the danger of the escarpment to the north. This section is not recommended in poor visibility.

For the next 45 minutes continue visiting the gully heads until you can see, over to the south-east, the summit of Almisira, with its distinctive array of aerials, and the road across its flank which was used at the start of the walk. *4hrs*

At this point, the escarpment curves to the north and the next buttress is Tosal Redo, which you do not visit. Across a wide *barranco* can be seen the ridge which leads to this buttress, but your objective is to keep east and find the easiest route to gain the ridge from which you can plot your course down into Pla de la Lacuna. There are red markers to help you. When you reach the ridge look to the south-east and you will see the forestry road crossing the end of Sierra Almirante from the Vall de Gallinera to Lacuna and Villalonga. *5hrs 30mins*

Down to Pla De La Lacuna

The forestry road can be seen to drop from left to right to the valley bottom and then change direction north-east. It is this point that you should aim for across the usual steep and rocky ground. (I used a ridge in line with my objective and veered to the left (north) when the ground became rather steep.) Do not be tempted to head for the bottom of the dry stream beds: they are hell. A more civilised route, if you can find it, is to aim for a ruined *finca*, to the east, from which a road leads down to the large pond by the side of the road; turn right along the road. When, thankfully, you arrive at the road, offer up a small prayer of thanksgiving that this section is over and start to climb the excellent road to the end of the walk. *7hrs*

La Lacuna is a small farming community set in a fertile basin at 500m, sheltered by the mountains and 7km from Villalonga on a reasonable, if twisting, motor road. Most of the plots are now farmed from Villalonga or used at weekends and fiestas as summer homes. There is a bar/restaurant/disco which, however, only seems to open on these occasions.

The End of the Gallinera Way – Over the Sierra Del Almirante

This is the last stage of the way and a most pleasant one. You have a good road which rises gently to the ridge and descends to the Val de Gallinera. There is room to link arms and walk abreast (if you feel like it) as you admire the views down into the Pla De La Lacuna. In half an hour the ridge is reached and the road levels out. On this section two roads which lead to villages further up the valley join from the right. You can say goodbye to the northern mountains and pick out Almisira and the Forada Ridge which you visited earlier on the Way. Eventually the road zig-zags steeply down to the ford across the Rio Gallinera and the motor road (CV700). No crowds to welcome you, not even a bar to celebrate, but hopefully your support party will whisk you swiftly to Adsubia to celebrate your achievement and to recollect the four days of walking in this beautiful and interesting area. *8hrs 30mins*

In the Val del Algar (Walk 25)

Mozarabic trail up to the Forada Ridge (Walk 27 and Gallinera Way)

Almisira from Pla de Almisira (Walk 28 and Gallinera Way)

Approaching Gallinera Castle (Walk 28 and Gallinera Way)

North-West Sierras

32: BENICADELL

Grade:	strenuous
Distance:	10km
Time:	6hrs 45mins
Maps:	Alcoy 821 (29–32)

Benicadell is a long, rocky ridge which starts modestly at the Puerto de Albaida on the CN340, Alcoy to Valencia road, with Cerro de la Cruz guarding the pass, and runs north-east for 6km to drop dramatically to the Puerto de Salem on the Beniarres to Castellon de Rugut road (CV701). From the south you may admire the long line of crags which make up the south face, but to admire the dramatic north-east buttress and Barranco del Port you should drive towards Lorcha, where the summit and the buttress look like a perfect cone, at the end of the ridge. The ridge itself forms the boundary between the provinces of Alicante and Valencia. An alternative and easier access to the summit from the north is shown on the map, from the col on the Castellon de Rugat road from Beniarres.

Getting There

Your starting point is the small, attractive village of Gayanes, at Km.5 on the CV701, Muro de Alcoy to Beniarres road. If you are coming in from the coast via Pego and the Val Gallinera, turn off at Planes towards the dam, cross it and turn left in Beniarres towards Muro del Alcoy.

Follow the street up past the church and keep on going up the Carrer de Calvaria, ignoring the blue and white arrow which indicates the traverse, until you come to a wide open area with a beautifully carved stone cross and lots of pigeon lofts. Park your cars here.

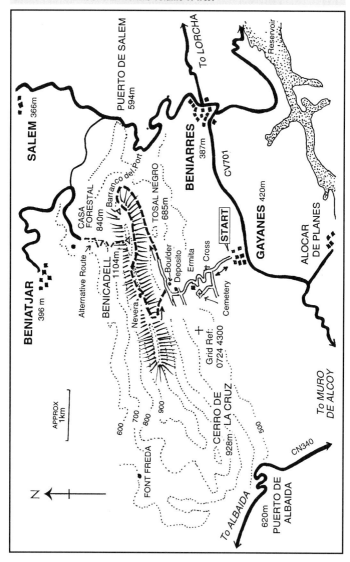

Making a Start to the Ermita de San Francisco de Padua

When I did this route I was upbraided by a local huntsman for leaving my car too low down the mountain when it could be driven uphill for a few more kilometres (the Spanish in general, and huntsmen in particular, do not subscribe to walking unnecessarily). I leave the decision to you. A metalled road climbs in zig-zags up to the little *ermita* with its spring, tables and lovely situation overlooking Beniarres Reservoir. Above the *ermita* the road loses its surface but continues to climb towards the south face, and if you look carefully you might be able to identify your route off the second summit. Views develop of the Serpis Valley and, to the south-west, Monte Cabrer. Pass now a water deposit at crossroads and go across directly.

Under the South Face to the Col

Peurto de Albaida can be seen to the west with its terminal peak of Cerro de la Cruz (928m). You now ignore a road leading off left and settle down to a north-easterly course roughly parallel to the ridge, with the little hill of Tosal Negro ahead just to the right. On the way, along a broad track, note a large boulder on your right. This is where your descent route from the second summit ends. The track now starts to become a little indistinct and drops down for a short while, but keep heading for the col between the mountain and Tosal Negro.   *1hr*

From the col, under the crags of Benicadell you can see ahead another col with a distinctive rock outcrop on its left, and it is this outcrop that you make for. There is no path at all, and at times it is easier to follow the tops of the terraces until you find an easy way to climb up for a few metres. There are views now of the village of Pego, with its transmitting antenna. When you reach the outcrop you will be able to appreciate the next stage of your climb, as you are at the bottom of the impressive Barranco del Port.   *1hr 30mins*

Barranco Del Port

This gully forms a direct route to within a few metres of the main summit, so is a classic approach to the mountain. It is, however, very rough and of unremitting steepness. There is no path, and you must use your skills to find the least uncomfortable route. Generally keep away from the base of the crags, as they can waste time as they form spurs at the bottom of the rocks. Once you gain some height, the base of the crags on the right does give you some reasonable going until, thankfully, the ground becomes easier, a path appears and you are onto a small grassy col between the summit crags and a rocky spur.   *2hrs*

Aitana (1558m), highest peak in the province, can now be seen to the south-east peeping over the Serrellas. To the east is the Forada Ridge and, in the distance, Montgo and the Segaria Ridge. Above you are the main crags of the summit, but unless you are a rock-climber the way to the summit lies across a *barranco* to a col within minutes of the top. No mountaineer likes, at this stage, to lose height, but happily you do not have to make much of a descent, only to the base of a wall, where there is a fair path which in a short while takes you to another col right on the ridge. It is now just a few minutes' scramble to the trig point on the main summit.   *3hrs*

The *views* in every direction beggar description. You are right on the northern boundary of the province of Alicante, and I found it very satisfying to look south on most of the other peaks which I had climbed since 1986 (Puig Campaña, the second highest peak remains hidden). I was glad that I had saved Benicadell to the end – it was worth it. Below you is the valley of Albaido with the little villages of Beniatja and Salem. Somewhere in the distance is the town of Jativa, supposed to have an ambience which reminds one of Tuscany, and to the south-west the rocky ridge continues to the second summit.

To the Second Summit and the Nevera

Leave the summit and return to the col and the best part of the walk, the traverse of the ridge to the second summit. There is a good path all the way first to the left then to the right of the ridge until at last you strike up left to gain the second summit with (surprise, surprise) a lovely *nevera* beneath its summit crags. The *nevera* is in good condition, with its corbelled roof intact and some 'Roman' type doorways. It is now clear why there is such an easy path to the summits from Puerto del Salem.   *3hrs 45mins*

Now you must take a decision as to whether to continue your traverse or follow my route down off the ridge. If you take the first option I am assured that you will have no difficulty on the ridge, but there could be difficulty, due to the confusing network of country lanes, in finding a direct route across the *campo* back to the village. This route will add another 45 minutes to the timing given for this walk.

Back Down to Gayanes

Carry on along the crest of the ridge for a short time and then follow a good path which starts to descend south-west off the ridge, on the south side, heading for the base of some crags at the head of a barranca. In 10 minutes you are in the barranca and there is no path to help you, only the distant track below you, which is your objective. Scramble through boulders and undergrowth then over exposed slabs until you can see a faint path to head for, which in turn leads to the good road near a boulder.   *6hrs*

Rough walking over, you now have a chance to gaze up at your ridge and savour the day's experience as you retrace the morning's route back to your transport and the hospitality of Gayanes.   *6hrs 45mins*

33: LORCHA TO VILLALONGA AND RIO SERPIS VALLEY

Grade:	moderate
Distance:	20km
Time:	7hrs 30mins
Ascent:	225m
Maps:	Jativa 795 (29–31), Villalonga 795–IV (29–31)

This walk is a little longer than usual, but the gradients are easy and it is all on good, unsurfaced roads. It is also on the edge of the usual area for walkers staying in the south of the Costa, but is easily accessible to those staying in the north, around Gandia, who can, of course, start their walk from Villalonga if they choose.

You first of all cross a spur of Azafor (1011m) and descend to La Reprimala, 2km from Villalonga. The return to Lorcha is along the old railway track, which follows the fast-flowing Rio Serpis through a most picturesque gorge, El Barranco Del

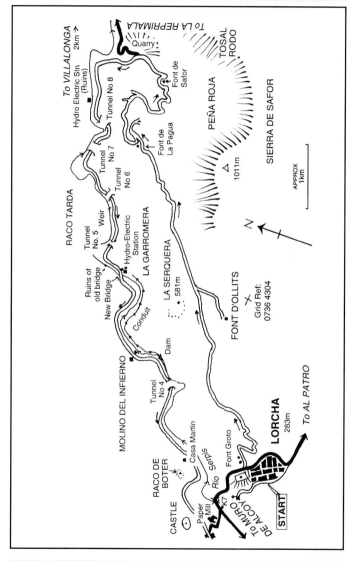

Infierno, rich in wildlife, to the ruins of the ancient Moorish castle at Lorcha. It is important to carry torches for negotiating the tunnels, especially the first one, and to make yourself visible to any traffic using the road.

Getting There

Lorcha is reached by leaving the CN332 at Vergel and following the CV700 through Pego and the Val Gallinera to Planes, where you turn off right to Beniarres via the dam, and then turn right onto the CV701 to Lorcha. There is now a narrow surfaced road from Al Patro direct to Lorcha, which shortens the journey considerably but, sadly, is not signposted.

Take the first road to the right, just after the village street, in Al Patro, and go down past the wash-house to the abandoned village of Llombay, where you turn off right towards Villalonga. At the top of a rise, in about 2km, take the first left north-west onto the new road, over Sierra de la Albureca, to Lorcha. This road is not, however, for the faint-hearted.

Villalonga is reached by leaving the CN332 1km south of Gandia, taking the VP1012, near the village of Bellrequart, and in 8km enter the town and turn right at the Guardia Civil Barracks towards the river, following signs for the Reprimala and Dos Hermanos restaurants, which you reach in a further 2km.

To Fuente de Olbist

Leave Lorcha, where there are five bars to delay your start, and leave the main road (CV701) just above the beautiful *fuente*, Font Grota, with its tables made of old millstones, cross the dry river bed and take a broad unsurfaced road which will lead to the first objective, *Fuente de Olbist*. The road is well graded and heads north-east. It ends at Villalonga, some 14km away. Note some old cave houses built against the cliffs on the left. The road now starts to zig-zag to gain height, with the Barranca de Basiets on the right-hand side. Soon there are extensive views to the south, with Lorcha and its little calvary in the foreground, the impressive eastern buttress of Benicadell, and a wide view of the Serpis Valley. An unusually large and unnecessary notice announces that the mountain is for 'Public Use'. Another *barranco*, Vertiente de la Carrasco, joins from the right and you get a view to the south of the end of the Forada Ridge. The gradient eases a little and you reach a viewpoint on the left where you can look down some 400m into the Serpis Valley, with the old abandoned railway track that will be the return route. *1hr*

Continue along the road, climbing gently as the bulk of Azafor's southern slopes come into view ahead. After a while note another deep *barranco* on the right and, across on the other side, a track and the *fuente*. This is the route, and you have to go around the head of the *barranco*, where there is some red shale. Reach a junction. Leave the road to Villalonga and take the right-hand road, changing direction to south-west. *1hr 20mins*

The road now passes under some smooth, exposed slabs which look like granite and seem to be glacial, and another track forks off to the left. This is the route for the ascent of Azafor (1011m). You are now high enough to see the town of Muro de Alcoy to the south, and in another few minutes arrive at the beautifully laid out *Fuente* del Olbist. In addition to the spring there are tables and benches and a delightful barbecue. Enjoy the extensive views down the valley of the Rio Serpis, with the western buttress of Benicadell in the distance, looking like the Matterhorn. *1hr 30mins*

Down To La Reprimala

Retrace your steps to the main forestry road and continue east along a fairly level section with magnificent views on the right of the great semi-circle of crags which form the northern escarpment of Azafor. Across the valley, to the north, are extensive views of Sierra Ador, but little can be seen of the Rio Serpis in its deep gorge below you. Eventually, the road starts to descend, and views to the east open up to show the huerto of Gandia and eventually Villalonga and the coast. After passing Font de la Pagua there is some development and you must avoid being diverted from your descent (see map). Keep left at a junction with a house with 'lumpy' walls, then right at the next junction. Reach the quarry, and the road becomes surfaced. In the quarry note a road going off to the left. This is your route, and leads in half a kilometre to the river and the old railway track. There is sometimes a signpost here! Pass through some villas and reach the old track with the old hydro-electric station on the opposite side of the river. The station, which is in ruins, was converted from a flour mill, and the old conduits can be seen above the buildings. This makes a lovely spot for lunch.

Those who demand more than a picnic can continue down the metalled road for slightly more than another kilometre to Font de la Reprimala, with its gushing fountains and its two excellent restaurants with terraces overlooking the fast-flowing Serpis.   *3hrs 30mins*

Along the Side of the Rio Serpis to Lorcha

Leave La Reprimala and retrace your steps to the quarry, where you turn off right to drop down, on an unsurfaced road, to join the old railway running beside the river and the old hydro-electric station described above.   *4h 30mins*

The railway was completed by an English company in 1893 to carry coal and other materials for the developing industries of Alcoy from the port of Gandia. No doubt influenced by the decline of coal as a fuel and the improved road systems, the line was closed and dismantled in 1969. It was quite a feat of engineering, as the track clings to the side of a deep gorge, Barranco del Infierno, and passes through eight tunnels and numerous bridges and cuttings until, at Beniarres, it becomes the main road to Alcoy. Because of the seclusion and the abundant water, wildlife and wild flowers abound. There is a wide variety of fish in the river, with trout which look more like young sharks. The track has been designated as a public road and surveyed by the highways authority. The section west of Lorcha Station has been widened and graded, but the rest of the line will present some considerable difficulties, especially the bridges and tunnels which are one train wide only. Pressure is mounting for the area to be designated as a Natural Park; meanwhile be prepared to meet some traffic, especially at weekends and fiestas – another good reason for carrying torches.

A short distance along the old track come to the first and longest tunnel (No.8), and in half a kilometre to another shorter one (No.7). The river below runs in rapids and small cascades over rocks. Cross some bridges, without the benefit of parapets. After a short cutting enter another tunnel (No.6), and on leaving it enjoy the views ahead of a wide weir stemming the river to provide water for one of the mills which once worked in this valley.

Most of the little stations and workmen's huts have disappeared, but you now pass one on the right, and shortly after this watch out ahead for your first view of the stone supports, all that remains of the bridge which carried the track to the other side of the river for the remaining 5km to Lorcha. When the railway closed, the metal spans were dismantled and a culvert constructed to cross the river lower down near the hydro-electric station. This structure was destroyed when the river was in spate in the winter of 1986. The Spanish Army Engineers constructed the more substantial bridge, which so far has resisted the flood waters. The road now leaves the line of the railway beyond the bridge supports and drops down to the old mill which is still used as a reserve generating station. This mill was called La Garromera and is worth exploring. You will find the sluice gates well greased and in working order. *5hrs 30mins*

Cross the river and in a few minutes you are back on the track. Watch out on the opposite bank for the conduit, which carried the water to power the mill from a dam 1km ahead. Pass another old station and then reach the dam across the river, still in good order due to its substantial construction.

You are now high above the river as you enter the last, short tunnel (No.4). Pass through cuttings and curve around a *barranco* with an old ruined *finca* on the right, Casa Martin. *6hrs 30mins*

Just round the bend after Casa Martin you get your first dramatic view of Lorcha Castle, high on a spur of rock. Below on the left can be seen Lorcha and the paper mill by the river. When you reach the old buildings of Lorcha Station, you turn off left (south), pass the paper mill, and reach the main road near the bridge across the Serpis. The comforts of the restaurants and bars of Lorcha are now only a few minutes away as you turn right, just past the delightful *fuente*, and walk up into the village. *7hrs 30mins*

34: PUNTA DE ALFARO AND BARRANCO DE MALAFI

Grade:	moderate
Distance:	13km
Time:	5hrs 30mins
Ascent:	500m
Map:	Benisa 822 (30–32)

The Sierra de Alfaro (El Far in Valenciano) forms 7km of high ground to the north of Sierra Serrella, with the Ceta Valley in between them, and stretches from Fachega in the west to near Pla de Petracos, about 6km west of Benichembla in the upper Jalon Valley. The summit, 1166 metres, can be ascended from Fachega; the northern boundary is the remote Barranco de Malafi. This is a rather long but very enjoyable mountain day, with a mix of good forestry roads and rough walking, especially down the last 4km of the barranco itself. If the river is in flood it will be impossible to complete this circuit, and you will either have to postpone your expedition or be satisfied with the first part, along the ridge, as only extremely tall, well-waterproofed walkers will be able to tackle the barranco in flood.

Getting There

Leave the lower Jalon Valley at Parcent and follow the CV720 along the dry upper valley, passing Benichembla (last refreshments), until at Km.28, just after you have crossed a new bridge over the river, you turn off right (north) at Villa Mercedes along a narrow surfaced road which was once signposted to Val De Ebo. The road follows the normally dry valley of the Barranco de Malafi, and the ruins on the right of the road are all that remain of the ancient Ermita de Petracos. This section of this little-used road is a lovely stroll in itself, as you pass between rocky cliffs and orchards for about 4km until the valley

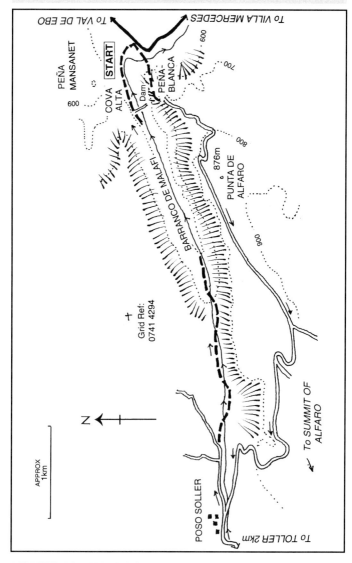

To VAL DE EBO

To VILLA MERCEDES

PEÑA MANSANET

600

START

PEÑA-BLANCA

Dam

COVA ALTA

600

700

800

876m

PUNTA DE ALFARO

900

BARRANCO DE MALAFI

Grid Ref: 0741 4294

N

APPROX 1km

To SUMMIT OF ALFARO

POSO SOLLER

To TOLLER 2km

opens out a little near Cova Alta, where you park your transport, passing ancient cave paintings on the right.

On the left of the road is your first objective, Peña Blanca, the eastern end of the Alfaro Ridge, whilst across the valley is Peña Mansanet, past which the road starts to climb over the Sierra de Cironet towards the remote village of Val de Ebo, some 6km distant.

Making a Start – Ascent of Peña Blanca

Cross the dry river bed and head south-west; with no path to guide you, tackle the steep slope as best you can. At times it is easier to keep to the rocks, and there are one or two small arêtes, which are more fun than the well-vegetated sections. Below you can be seen the return route down the Barranco de Malafi and the small flash dam at its eastern end, constructed to hold back flood waters and protect the motor road. This is the most energetic part of the walk, but it is soon over as you reach the top of Peña Blanca, with views to the south of Cocoll with Sierra Aixorta beyond. To the north is Sierra de Mediodia.

40mins

Along the Ridge to Punta De Alfaro

You will no doubt be very surprised to find a broad unsurfaced road which now follows the top of the ridge in a westerly direction, making very pleasant walking indeed. Its purpose is soon clear, as the new plantings of conifer trees appear. It is necessary for the foresters to break up the limestone rocks using heavy machines, then in a small pocket of soil plant the tiny trees which they hope will help to prevent erosion. As you gain height you can now see the villages of Benichembla, Parcent and Alcalali to the east, along with the Caballo Verde ridge, whilst in the distance can be seen the coastal mountain of Isodoro, near Benitachell.

1hr

Views to the north-west now open up to show Benicadell, near Beniarres, and on its right the Forada Ridge above the Val Gallinera. To the south-east is the Bernia with Severino, whilst due south is Puig Campaña. On slightly higher ground to the left of the road is a small shelter, which could indicate the summit of Punta de Alfaro (876m), as the road drops slightly to a road junction.

1hr 30mins

Turn right at the junction, still heading south-west, whilst to the north-west the mountain of Almisira, with its transmitting masts, near

Pego, just peeps above the horizon, as you go around a broad *barranco*. After this the road divides and you take the right-hand fork to start to climb in a series of zig-zags. On the left is a depression which shows signs of cultivation, and you pass an over-large notice proclaiming that the mountain is dedicated to the public use. Eventually the road levels a little and contours around some barrancas. There are views now of the coast to the east, including Montgo, whilst to the south are the peaks of the Serrella, Pla de La Casa and Malla de Llop. There are also dramatic views on your right down into the Barranco de Malafi and to the extensive *finca*, Pozo de Soler, in the valley bottom, which is on your route.   *2hrs 30mins*

Down to the Pozo De Soler

This is the end of your traverse of Alfaro, as the road starts to descend in very steep zig-zags until you can pick out the buildings around Pozo de Soler and join the road which has come in from the village of Tollos to the south-west. Follow the road north-east to the *fincas*, with the well and drinking troughs and corrals for sheep and goats, a lovely spot for a break and lunch.   *3hrs 30mins*

Into the Barranco De Malafi

Leave Pozo Soler and head along a good track for a short while, in a north-easterly direction, with the track crossing and recrossing the river bed until you reach the entrance to the gorge, between crags. This is a valley which is seldom visited and is rich in wildlife. The crags of Al Faro, above on the right, are a favourite haunt of the peregrine falcon and those who study them. In a very short time, however, the path disappears and you must do the best you can, finding the easiest bank of the watercourse to walk on or even in the river bed itself. Above can be seen your route along the ridge of Al Faro. It is a great relief when, at last, the dam comes into view!   *5hrs*

Pass the small dam on the left-hand side and now walk through almond groves back down to Cova Alta.   *5hrs 30mins*

Western Sierras

35: SIERRA DE LA PLANS

Grade:	**moderate**
Distance:	**6.5km**
Time:	**3hrs 30mins**
Ascent:	**431m**
Maps:	**Villajoyosa 847 (29–33)**

This walk is on the perimeter of the mountain area accessible from the coast for a day walk, but is well worth the extra travelling time, about half an hour beyond Confrides. Your efforts are rewarded by unique views, and the village of Penaguila is nearby, with its palace, Roman bridge, ornamental garden, fuente, castle and many other interesting features.

Getting There

From the coast take the CV70 through the Guadalest Valley and over the Puerto Confrides (now called Ares on the new maps) and turn off left just as you enter the village of Benasau, following signs for Villajoyosa. On the approach to Alcolecha the road forks and you take the CV780, on the right, to Penaguila and Benifallin. At Benifallin turn off onto the CV785 towards Terremanzanas and park near to Km.20 as the road climbs towards the Puerto Benifallin. The escarpment on the right, with its many buttresses, is Sierra de la Plans.

A few metres below Km.20 two unsurfaced roads lead off south. This is where you start and end your walk.

To Collado Del Plans Via Barranco Del Horts

Take the left-hand track alongside the *barranco*, heading south, with quarry workings below you. On this section you have a guide in the power cables which are also headed for the col. Across the valley you

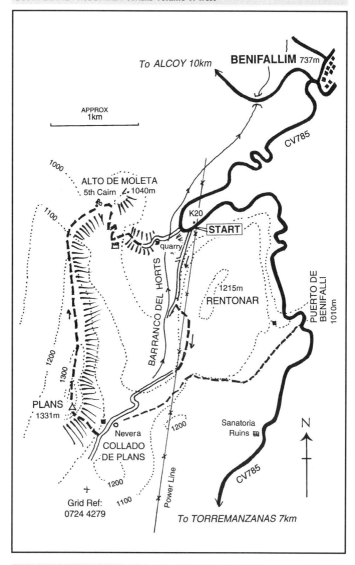

have plenty of time to admire your route along the top of the escarpment as well as the small *barranco* which leads down back to the quarry which is near your return route. The track now levels out, and you take a rougher, steeper track on the left (red marker) following the electric cables and going for a short time south-west until, just past a large pylon (red marker), you leave the power lines to join a broad track which leads to the col. *1 hr*

Collado Del Plans to the Summit

On the col you will find a lovely little *nevera*, one of the few with its roof intact. This example is of the corbelled type, where the roof was formed into a dome by reducing each course of bricks or stones. I strongly suspect that the facing stones, which finished off the roof, have been purloined to construct the little casita nearby. If you walk to the top of the col you will get distant views of Torremanzanas.

Just past the *nevera* (red marker) you strike up, north-west, for the summit of the mountain across pathless terrain, but with the joys of stopping now and then to enjoy the expanding views – even if they are restricted to the south-east for a little while. In about half an hour your labours are rewarded and you gain the ridge and a cairn. You are on the Sierra de la Plans. *1hr 40mins*

Sierra De La Plans

Pico, the esteemed Valencian mountain-guide writer, says that these views are some of the best in the province, and he should know. To the south is the valley of Xixona with the village of the same name, and beyond, in the distance, the provincial capital Alicante, with the Castle of Santa Barbara on its lofty crag. To the left of this is Cabeza d'Oro, near Busot, with Sierra de la Grana in the foreground. Then there is Peña Miojorn, and to the west El Maigmo, Le Empenydor and El Carrascal. To the west is La Peña de la Blasca, near Banares, followed by the massif of the Mariola, which includes Monte Cabrer and which rings the city of Alcoy in the distance. To the north the beautiful ridge of Benicadell dominates the scene and to the right of this Sierra Safor (Asafor). Now, moving east, Alfaro and Serrella appear, and finally Aitana and Puig Campaña near Finestrat. Within view are the three giants of the province; how many other, loftier peaks can claim this honour?

Traverse of the Ridge

You will be amazed to discover that there is an excellent track along the ridge, north, until it drops down to the Alcoy road. This flight of fancy is, however, soon demolished by the prospect of a 6km road walk back to the car.

You leave the ridge at the fifth cairn just before the track ascends the last summit of Alto de Moleta and head, slightly west, for a ruined *finca* below you. Below the ruins, descend decaying terraces until you reach a particularly broad one, whereupon you traverse to the left (north) until you reach a *barranco*; cross this to gain a surprisingly good track which will take you down, past a cave house, across the barranca and up to the main road near Km.20.   *3hrs 30mins*

There are a number of bars in Benifallin, or why not, if you have time, explore Penaguila before returning to the coast? I am sure that once you have visited this area, you, like me, will want to return time and time again.

36: CABEZA D'ORO

Grade:	moderate
Distance:	10.5km
Time:	5hrs
Ascent:	866m
Map:	Villajoyosa 847 (29–33)

The name Cabeza d'Oro (Golden Head) may relate to the colour of the rocks or be related to the minerals which were mined here many years ago, and there are still a number of old mines marked on the maps. It is a beautiful mountain from every aspect, with lots of rocky arêtes and pinnacles; and the mountain is unmistakable, as the first coastal peak which you see as you drive from Alicante north along the main road or the autopista. The ridge is 5km long, running north to south from Collado de Grana to the crags above Cuevas De Canalobre, the caves above the little mountain village of Busot which are such an attraction to tourists. This route is the favourite one to main summit via Raco de Seva.

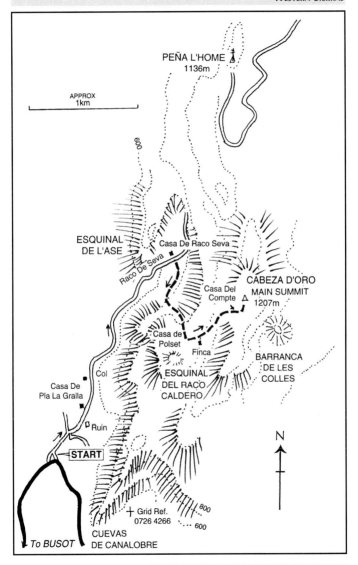

PEÑA L'HOME
1136m

APPROX
1km

600

ESQUINAL
DE L'ASE

Casa De Raco Seva

Raco De Seva

CABEZA D'ORO
MAIN SUMMIT
1207m

Casa Del
Compte

Casa de
Polset

Finca

BARRANCA
DE LES
COLLES

Col

ESQUINAL
DEL RACO
CALDERO

Casa De
Pla La Gralla

Ruin

N

START

To BUSOT

Grid Ref.
0726 4266

800

600

CUEVAS
DE CANALOBRE

211

Getting There

Start from the village of Busot, 19km from Alicante and 9km from El Campello, where there are plenty of bars and restaurants, and drive through the village on the surfaced road which is signposted to Cuevas de Canalobre. After 4km, on the last right-hand bend, 1km from the caves, park your transport on a wide space where two unsurfaced tracks join the road.

To Casa De Raco Seva

Your track runs north to slightly north-east and is waymarked all the way in yellow and white. The good track passes beneath the impressive western crags of Cabeza d'Oro and close to one gigantic detached pinnacle, Esquinal del Raco Caldero. In the distance can be seen the northern peak of the mountain, Peña d'Home, with its antenna, and ahead on the left is another pinnacle, Esquinal De l'Ase, which we shall pass close to in order to enter the Raco de Seva (a broad cleft). To the east and south-east there is a wide panorama of the broad plain of Alicante and the peak of Migjorn (1226m), above Jijona. In the far distance the peaks of Foncalent and Mitjana rise from the plain, and on the coast can be seen the city of Alicante, with Santa Barbara Castle on its rock and the island of Tabarca.

In 15 minutes you have passed the gate to a house, and then reach a ruin on your right and then, on the left, an occupied casita in a little col, probably Casa de Pla la Gralla. The track now starts to drop a little as you approach the sharp arête of Esquinal De l'Ase, and as you enter the Raco Seva, ahead can be seen a substantial *finca*, Casa de Raco Seva, where you leave the good track for rougher walking.   *30mins*

To Casa De Polset

The narrow path is, in places, badly eroded and would need care in wet conditions. Thankfully it is still waymarked, and as you climb you get more intimate views of the mighty cliffs of the western face. Ahead, you are heading for some reddish cliffs which have some small cave dwellings cut into them, high up; some enterprising rock climber has pinned a plate to one of them, no doubt to help the postman! *45mins*

In a few minutes a narrow path, marked in red, leads off right to the caves, as you continue upwards, passing them on the left. The path now levels a little and passes through pine trees. Above can be seen the main summit and the col to the right, by which you will gain the ridge. In a few more minutes the summit track joins from the left and the path widens as you approach the col with its farm and the roofless Casa de Polset. *1hr 15mins*

Enjoy the views down into the Val de Busot and the coast from this vantage point, which is supposed to have once been a lonely Guardia Civil post. Now turn back to retrace your steps to the junction with the summit path and start the steep and sometimes rough ascent to the summit.

To the Summit

Now follow the markers as you climb generally north-east through pine trees, with the northern summit, Penya l'Home, ahead. Your views extend with every step and you reach the crags which form the arête. Here there are some water-worn rocks, from which have leached chemicals, which have left coloured stains. *2hrs*

Once you have passed these rocks there is an easy rock scramble, with one or two nice moves, before you gain the ridge itself and realise the mountain has kept its secrets to the very end. In 10 minutes, walking north, you come to a small building, still roofed, Casa del Compte. The building has a deep shaft, which could have been used by miners or may be used to gain access to a cave, Coiva de la Granota, below the summit. Local climbers use it as a bivouac, but it is no place to sleepwalk! The summit has a trig point and, unbelievably, a water *deposito*, fed by carefully placed tiles. *2hrs 30mins*

The Views

The views are magnificent, and all the old favourites of Las Marinas are to be seen to the north. To the north-west are the mountains of Alcoy, Monte Cabrer (1389m), Els Plans (1330m) and Benicadell (1104m).

Further east are the mountains of Las Marinas: Aitana (1558m), the Bernia (1128m) and Puig Campaña (1406m). Also visible is the beautiful jagged ridge of El Realet, also known as Castellets and locally as the Shark's Teeth, and just above Sierra d'Orcheta is the Peñon de Ifach on the coast at Calpe.

To the north the ridge continues towards Peña l'Home, the Collado del Grana and the ridge of Sierra de la Grana, with its summit of

1095m. The views in other directions, the south and west, have already been mentioned, but this is a summit to linger on and to plan future expeditions.

Back Down to Busot

I strongly recommend that you use the same route to descend the mountain, with the chance to enjoy new aspects to the west and south. For those adventurous souls who demand a challenge in route-finding, there is an alternative descent from the Casa del Polset via Barranca de los Colles. You first cross to the old ruined *finca* next to the *casa*, and from there a reasonable unmarked path descends for a while to the head of a terraced gully, by which a rough descent can be made to the *campo* to the east of the Caves of Canalobre. You really do need a lot of luck to find the correct unsurfaced roads, not shown on the maps, which will eventually lead you west to rejoin the motor roads to the caves about 1.5km below your starting point.

If you have time you may wish to visit the caves, and there is lots of hospitality in Busot. *5hrs*

Costa Blanca
Mountain Way

The Way

The Way was proposed in 1990 to mark the fifth anniversary of the Costa Blanca Mountain Walkers. By May 1991, the route was settled, and by the end of the year it had been walked.

The Way is strictly a walkers' route, and only on Caballo Verde Ridge and on Aitana is any route-finding required, and these sections are waymarked. Most of the route uses unsurfaced forestry roads or provincial surfaced roads, constructed to allow the country people reliable access to the high pastures and crops. This brings certain benefits: not only is traffic almost non-existent on these roads, but they follow the ancient mule tracks, and the views are more enjoyable when you don't have to watch where you are putting your feet all the time.

Since the inauguration in 1991, the Way has proved popular with walkers, back-packers and a lone cyclist. Some did the crossing as a series of day walks over an extended period, whilst others walked on consecutive days. Two pensioners completed the five sections in four days. The cyclist left his wheels only for the Caballo Verde Ridge and the final ascent of Aitana.

Completion of the first five sections entitles the walker to be entered on the roll of *compañeros* (See Appendix 1). Regular updates of the route and news of new *compañeros* appear in the newsletters of the Costa Blanca Mountain Walkers. These can be obtained from the group secretary (see local press) or through Cicerone Press.

Why Walk It?

Day walks are the norm for most walkers, so the chance to 'keep on walking' has its own magic for all mountaineers. This route crosses the whole of the Las Marinas mountains, plus a few kilometres in La Safor (Valencia), from north to south. In more than 100km it is intended to introduce the walker to the varied scenery of the area.

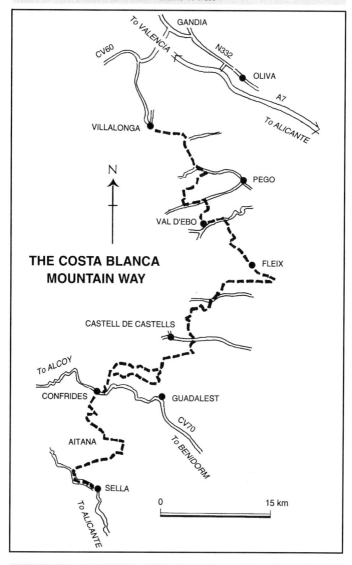

The Way starts in the lush huerta of the Rio Serpis, vast well-watered orchards spreading out to the sea. You pass your first ancient castle at Villalonga, and then go through the cherry orchards to your first peak, Almisira. North of Almisira is a vast open panorama reminiscent of Scotland as you head for the deep gorge of the Val de Infierno. Descending the gorge and ascending to Fleix in Val Laguart, you use the ancient Mozarabic trail, Camino del Jubias, passing the typical *lavadero* or village wash-house to reach Fleix. Above the village are the towering crags of Peña Roch and the Caballo Verde Ridge, scene of the 'Moor's last stand' in the 17th century.

Next the Way descends into the Val de Pop (the valley of the Rio Jalon). Lower down, the valley spreads out into a wide fertile basin totally protected on all sides by mountains, and famous for its wine, fruit and almonds. You cross the dry bed of the Rio Jalon, and climb through the Val Galistero by the Fig Tree Path over the high plateau of Val de Alt on a new forestry road, passing a notable ancient *finca*, with its oven and *era* (threshing floor). The Val de Alt is a typical high plateau, farmed from Castell de Castells, and you see ahead the long ridge of Aixorta rising to the high peaks of Serrella, with the beautiful natural rock arch of Atancos on their north face. You cross this ridge at its weakest point, which is, however, protected by probably the most picturesque of the castles, perched on a crag commanding the pass.

From the pass, you look down on to unquestionably the most popular and scenic of the valleys, Guadalest, with its numerous castles. Above the waters of the reservoir rises your final objective, Aitana itself. The last day is reserved for the ascent of the highest mountain in the province, with views now over the whole route of the walk to Alcoy, Alicante and beyond. Descending to Font Moli for the final night, you can examine an ancient *nevera*, or ice pit.

In these five glorious days, you will not only have stored up a lot of cherished memories, but will have gained a thorough appreciation of the beauties of the mountains of Las Marinas and of the Costa Blanca.

How To Walk It

The ultimate way to enjoy this walk is, I feel, to be alone, but if I had to have a companion, I cannot think of a more idyllic way to undertake this expedition than with a mule. To walk the way with a mule is, traditionally, to go at a modest pace, and in the manner for which most of the trails were constructed centuries ago, and without the burden of a rucksack. True, the conversation would be a very one-sided, but such a companion would immediately put you in tune with the countryside and the local people. To be practical, though, there a number of ways in which to organise your crossing of the Way.

The Way is 135km long and fairly steep and rough in parts. Walkers should be accustomed to such conditions, and because it is likely to be dry and hot should carry adequate water – at least a litre per day. Accommodation is available at each stage, but if there are friends who do not wish to do the walk it is a good idea to have a back-up team with car – apart from the obvious safety aspects it can make a wider choice of accommodation available.

The duties of the support party can vary from merely logging the progress of the walkers for safety purposes to transporting their gear and even setting up camp, producing a meal or making sure that the beds are aired in the overnight accommodation!

Some support teams will want to meet up with their walkers at every opportunity, and some members will even want to walk back along the route to meet them (thus logging their progress as having walked that part of the Way twice!). Others will arrange to meet their party only for the mid-day break, and at the end of the day.

The support vehicle can carry spare food and water, plus a full first aid kit, and it is recommended that it carries at least one sleeping bag. Lucky is the walker who has a support party equipped with a four-wheel drive vehicle (and, of course, a competent driver). Over half of the Way can be traversed by such a vehicle, but remember that in bad weather whole sections of the forestry road are liable to disappear, and the rest to become quagmires. The modest guide (see 'Support Party Notes') is restricted to decent surfaced roads, and is intended to make the task of the support party a little easier by supplying routes, times and mileages, and including the known accommodation available.

There can be no doubt that an attractive way to do these walks is as a back-packer with a small tent. The route for back-packers will be shorter, as they do not have to pass through all the villages seeking accommodation, and there are plenty of wonderful spots in which to camp. The back-packers' route will only pass through the villages of Forna, Fleix, Beniarda and Benifato. There will be no chance to replenish supplies on days 2 and 3 without leaving the route. One solution is to back-pack with a support party who will meet the walkers at mid-day and pitch camp for them at night, but the most civilised way to do the walk is by using overnight accommodation and a support party.

For those with insufficient time, or stamina, there is no reason why the Way cannot be enjoyed a section, or even part of a section, at a time.

The way is suitable for mountain bikes, but I would not like to carry the machine over the Caballo Verde Ridge. Horse riders will be able to use about 75% of the way. The standard times are, I feel, modest, and allow for the walker to enjoy the experience. I await with interest the first 24-hour crossing, no doubt by a fell runner.

Costa Blanca Mountain Way – timetable and distances

	km	hrs/ mins	total km	total hrs/mins	Ascent (m)
STAGE 1					
Villalonga to Forna	8	3.30	8	3.30	
Forna to Adsubia	4	1	12	4.30	
Adsubia to Castillo de Gallinera	4.5	2	16.5	6.30	
Castillo de Gallinera to Almisira	3.5	1.30	20	8	
Almisira to Val d'Ebo	9	3	29	11	1100
STAGE 2					
Val d'Ebo to Pla de Mollo	3.75	1	3.75	1	
Pla de Mollo to Rio Ebo	6.75	3	10.5	4	
Rio Ebo to Fleix	1.5	1	12	5	
To Barranco del Infierno	5	2	17	7	
To Isbert's Folly	5	2	22	9	439
STAGE 3					
Fleix to East Col	3	1	3	1	
East Col to Collado de Garga	6	2.30	9	3.30	
Collado de Garga to Km.4.5	5	2	14	5.30	
Km.4.5 to Corral del Somo	11	4	25	9.30	
Corral del Somo to Castell de Castells	4	1	29	10.30	824

	km	hrs/mins	total km	total hrs/mins	Ascent (m)
STAGE 4					
Castell de Castells to Serrella Castle	7.75	2.15	7.75	2.25	
1h allowed at Castle					
Serrella Castle to Beniarda	8.25	3.10	16	5.35	
Beniarda to Abdet	5	1.30	21	7.05	
Abdet to Confrides	4	0.55	23.5	7	884
STAGE 5					
Confrides to Fuente Arbol	6.	1.30	6	1.30	
Fuente Arbol to Partagas	4	1.20	10	2.50	
Partagas to Summit of Aitana	1	0.50	11	3.40	
Aitana to Font Moli	10	3.20	21	7	772
STAGE 6 (OPTIONAL)					
Font Moli to Puerta Mulero	6	2.30	6	2.30	
Puerta Mulero to Sella	14	4.00	20	6.30	640

Costa Blanca Mountian Way   115.5km. With Barranco de Ebo 135.5km

All 6 sections   135.5km. With Barranco de Ebo 155.5k

Ascent   4019m. 6 sections 4659m

STAGE 1: VILLALONGA TO VAL D'EBO

Overall time:	**12hrs**
Walking time:	**11hrs**
Distance:	**29km**
Ascent:	**1100m**
Maps:	**Jativa 795 (29–31), Benisa 822 (30–32)**

Getting There

The Way officially starts at Villalonga Castle, which is about 2km south-east of the town itself. There is now no accommodation in the town, but there is a vast amount available in the seaside town of Gandia, 12km to the north. From Gandia, travel south on the CN332 in the direction of Alicante, and 1km out of town turn off right (west) on to the VP1012, near to the village of Bellrequart. In 8km, enter the town of Villalonga, go down the main street heading north-east, and along Calle Levante head for the local brickworks, which has a tall chimney in line with the castle itself. Passing the brickworks on the right, look for a good unsurfaced road, Cami de Castillo, going off to the right (red marker), and after 0.5km an aqueduct marks the start of the walk.

Villalonga (Long Village) is of Roman origin, established by colonia: retired soldiers who remained in the colony to farm. Their villas were set in a line, probably along a water supply. The castle is of Moorish origin, but by the year 1240 was in the possession of King Jaime I of Aragon.

To the Castle

Walk over the aqueduct (south-east) along a concrete road, passing a gate and very high terrace walls on the right-hand side along a dry stream bed to join a well-marked track which climbs out of the *barranco* up the northern slopes of the castle ridge. The last section, to gain access to the extensive ruins, is much eroded and a bit of a scramble, but at least nowadays you do not have to face the missiles of the castle defenders. *0.5km – 20mins*

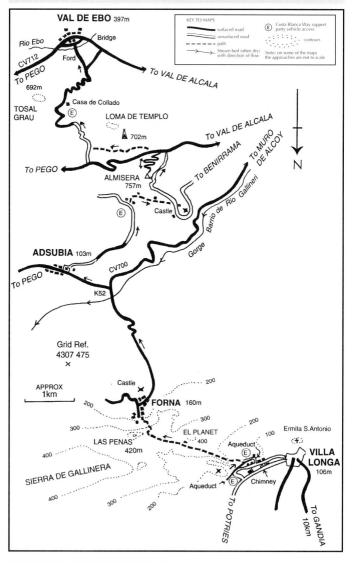

There are excellent views to the north, with the large town of Gandia on the coast (north-east), and the Sierra de Falconera behind it. North-west is the Sierra de Ador, and west the Serpis Valley, leading to Alcoy, with Sierra de Azafor (south-west). Due south are the slopes of Sierra de Gallinera, which you have to cross on your first leg towards Forna.

Descent

Leave the castle and retrace your ascent route as far as the aqueduct, then turn left onto a broad unsurfaced road. The popular short cut behind the villas has been gated.   *1km – 1hr*

This road goes west-south-west following the aqueduct until another road forks right to bring you to a more substantial road near Casa de la Belatera Lolita, just above the brickworks.   *1hr 30mins*

If you wish to avoid the castle start in the town centre and follow Calle Levante to pick up the route near Casa de la Belatera.

The Ascent of Sierra De Gallinera

Turn left up a concrete road, passing villas on the left and orange groves on the right-hand side, until the surface ends at a new villa, and you take a very rough rocky track which climbs upwards to the south-east. Sadly, this is the venue for Sunday motor-cycle trial riding by the local lads, so the track is much eroded in places. Soon the track becomes more reasonable, as you climb a parallel ridge to the one on which the castle stands across the Barranco de Castillo. You now reach the more level area between the two valleys, and say goodbye to the northern mountains as you reach a small casita with views to the south.
4.5km – 2hrs 20mins

Your views are now of the rocky ridge of Sierra de Segaria, with the headland of Llorensa, near Moraira, in the far distance. Almisira, with its TV transmitters, where you can have your lunch break, is to the south-west, with the quarries on the northern flanks of the Sierra Negra.

The track leads towards Almisira for a while, then, after contouring round a broad valley, you change direction east to descend a steep gully leading to Forna. Montgo now appears on the coast behind the Segaria Ridge.   *2hrs 50mins*

Forna

Pass through this pretty little village, through the square with a bar and the Restaurant Nautilus, passing the church, going south on a good surfaced road. Pass a ruined calvary on the right to reach a little rise with a crossroads. In 10 minutes the road on the left (east) leads to the ruins of the ancient castle, which is in reasonably good repair. Some 100m above sea level and quite extensive, it is Moorish in origin, belonging at one time to Al Azadrach, the Moorish king. In 1262, records show that it belonged to Don Bernardo de Guillen, whose six sons were known as the Caballeros del Penacho Negro (Knights of the Black Plume). Notable features of the castle are the entrance, fortified walls and four towers facing north. You will need a torch for a full exploration. Strangely, the castle survived the great earthquake of 1644, which destroyed other castles in the Gallinera Valley, including Gallinera which you will pass later in the day.   *8km – 3hrs 30mins*

To Adsubia

The road undulates and twists in between the hills, and you get a good view of your next goal, the summit of Almisira, with its antennae on top. In 15 minutes you pass a quarry on the left, and in half an hour an extensive farm on the right. In 50 minutes cross the Rio Gallinera, with no surface water in the summer but quite beautiful in winter. You now get your first view of the Castillo de Gallinera, on a rocky spur below Almisira. Turn left (east) on the main road and take care to walk facing the traffic, as there are many heavy lorries using the road due to the quarries in the area. Drop down now to the larger village of Adsubia. The new restaurant, La Moleta, is on the right of the road, and will one day have accommodation. The present proprietor will, however, put you in touch with villagers who will rent you a room for the night. This could be useful if you have had to make a late start from Villalonga.

12km – 4hrs 30mins

To Castillo De Gallinera

Pass through the village square and at the fountain turn right, passing the church (on right) up towards a cross, where you bear left to walk through lush orange groves in the Barranca de Michel for 40 minutes. You are heading for a col to the north of Almisira, and in 25 minutes bear left at a junction, climbing and zig-zagging up a little, with a casita on the left. You can now see the col just to the right of the quarry

Path running under the cliffs of Almisira (Walk 28 and Gallinera Way)

Planes, with zigzag path to Ermita del Santo Cristo (Walk 30)

Benicadell from the south (Walk 32)

Embalse de Guadalest and Aixorta (Costa Blanca Mountain Way, Day 4)

on the flank of Almisira. The road is now unsurfaced, and you pass another casita on the right; a road goes down to the left, which you ignore. As you climb more zig-zags, take time to admire the view behind you of Adsubia, Pego, the coast and the craggy ridge of Segaria. Ahead, above you, is a little white casita, which is on your route. Just before you reach the power lines going up to the summit of Almisira, turn right up a short road to the casita, and pass in front of it to find a mule track going north-east. In 10 minutes the track divides (the upper path leads to a good well) and you go down for another 10 minutes to reach a large fallen pine tree, which was once a good marker (red markers). *15.5km – 5hrs 30mins*

Looking south-west, you can pick out your next objectives. The first is a ruined building on the skyline, with crags on the left. The second is a white building between the ruins and the castle. (Red markers on this section to the castle.)

Leave the lone pine and keep level on a good path to climb up to the ruins on a small, level area. Now climb a little on a good path under some rocks to reach the unsurfaced road coming up from Beniarrama towards Almisira close to the castle. *16.5km – 6hrs 30mins*

Castillo De Gallinera

This is a beautiful castle, strategically situated to guard the entrance to the valley. Although destroyed in the earthquake of 1644, there is still much to see, including a water cistern, and the views are very rewarding. Unfortunately, it is privately owned, and recently the owner installed a new gateway, and it cannot be visited without permission. So far, I have been unable to trace the key-holder. Moorish in origin, the castle was conquered in 1259 by Jaime I, who gave it to his son in 1322. The approaches (from the south) are marked in red, but are much overgrown.

To Almisira

Turn south on the good unsurfaced road which has come up from the village of Beniarrama, and start to climb towards Almisira. The road, which now moves south-west under the cliffs of the mountain, soon starts to deteriorate into a rough track. It is hard to imagine cars using this road in the 1980s, such is the devastation caused by winter rains, showing nature's contempt for the puny works of man! On this stretch, you will be treated to extensive views of the whole of the Gallinera Valley, with its many scattered villages. It is famous for fruit growing, especially cherries, which flourish here. Bordering the valley on the southern side is the ridge of Forada, beyond which can be seen Alicante province's third-highest peak, Mont Cabrer, and next to it (north) the beautiful Benicadell. As you gain height, the Castillo de Gallinera looks like something out of a fairy tale, by far the most beautiful viewpoint from which to take photographs. Just off to the right above the village of Beniarrama are the cliffs of Alto de Chap, a sporting scramble.

Above you, the cliffs of Almisira close in, and behind you are extensive views of the coast – Gandia and eventually Cullera appear to the north-east. As you gain a small rise Sierra de la Carrasca, beyond the Val d'Ebo, appears to the south, and you pass a ruined *finca* on the left to reach the road which runs along this high plateau. This is a remote, high wilderness with no buildings, and is frequented only by foresters and shepherds.   *19km – 7hrs 30mins*

To the Summit

Turn left (east) along the road, and in 5 minutes reach the Pla de Almisira, and turn up the service road to the summit, which is reached in 20minutes.   *20km – 8hrs*

Vistas Unlimited

On this, your first summit, you can spend a happy time plotting the various mountain ranges which can now be identified. Notable amongst them are, to the south, Penon Roch and the Caballo Verde Ridge (Section 3); Castillo de Serrella, the highest point on Section 4; and finally Aitana Ridge, with Peña Mulero. Note the prominent road which leads down from Aitana summit (Section 5). The summit of Aitana, however, remains tantalisingly hidden by the intervening ridge of Carrasca, behind the Val d'Ebo, which itself is hidden in its deep valley. To the north, beyond Villalonga, can be seen the serried ridges of the Sierras of Azafor, Gallinera and Almirante.

The Castle

Much is known of the history of the extensive castle which once crowned this strategic mountain, but only a few stones remain. Moorish in origin, its governor was Abdalla Marhop. In 1243, it fell to Nicolas Scals. It was the scene of the signing of the important Treaty of Almisira between the Moors and the Christians. The castle probably suffered from the earthquake of 1644, but it is more likely that what little remained was scattered when the road to the transmitting station was constructed. A forestry lookout cabin has been newly installed on the summit, and is manned during high fire-risk periods. Just below the cabin, on the north side, is a small section of wall with a cement coping. Local people disagree about its origins, some saying that the wall is one of the remains of the Moorish castle, others claiming that it is even more ancient, and is of the Iberian period.

To Val d'Ebo

Leave the summit and descend once more to the Pla de Almisira, crossing the road and heading on a good track through some pine trees towards another transmitter on a small hill to the south. You head left (east) of the hill on a good marked track which contours its flanks. Below, you can see Pego, and the straight road leading to Vergel, the coast beyond, and Segaria Ridge to the south-east, with Montgo in the distance. At a fork go left, and now watch out for markers, as the trail forks off left down some zig-zags and passes under some small flat slabs to gain a broad ridge. From here, the track is at times indistinct, and red markers have been placed. Be prepared for the line of the path to zig-zag to lose height now and then, but generally keep heading east on the broad ridge until you can see an unsurfaced road ahead. Join it near a ruin and turn right (south).

Passing a casita on the left, top a little rise to see Tosal Grau ahead. You will cross a col to the right (west) of its summit. Look out for a well with water on the left, then start to climb again. You now have to drop to negotiate the head of a barranca, after which the road gains a surface (for how long, I know not, as the wild plants are growing through it already). Start climbing, passing some caves on the right, and gain the col at Casa de Collado with its excellent well. Look back and say farewell to the northern mountains, and start the descent to Val d'Ebo.   *25km – 10hrs*

As you cross the col, you can see the village below you, with the bulk of the Sierra de la Carrasca as a backdrop to the south. Relish now thoughts of dinner and a good night's rest as you stroll the remaining 3km down the well-engineered road through orchards of apples, pears and cherries to turn left at a junction, cross over the ford and enter the village with its bars and restaurants.   *29km – 11hrs*

Val d'Ebo is isolated but cosmopolitan, as for generations young men have sought employment in France, and at times the number of French-registered cars outnumbers the Spanish ones. The *hostal* has been closed, but the present patron of the Bar la Plaza, Juan Frau, has offered to find accommodation in the village for walkers who can dine at his bar. The bar is in the main square (Tel: 557 11 91). Alternative accommodation is to be found in Pego, 13km away.

STAGE 2: VAL D'EBO TO FLEIX

Walking time:	**to Fleix 5hrs, with diversions 9hrs**
Distance:	**to Fleix 12km, with both diversions 22km**
Ascent:	**439m**
Maps:	**Benisa 822 (30–32)**

On this stage you do not climb a mountain but descend into the deep gorge of the River Ebo. The modest mileage allows time to explore the valley of the Ebo and visit the Barranco del Infierno. The Barranco itself is strictly for rock-climbers, and I am indebted to Roger Massingham's climbing guide for this thrilling expedition (described in detail in Mountain Walks on the Costa Blanca, volume 2).

To Pla De Mollo

Leave Val d'Ebo and go down Avenida Marina Alta (east) towards the river. Just before the bridge, turn off right along a surfaced road which gives access to an unsurfaced one, which follows the south bank of the normally dry Rio Ebo. Pass the cemetery and a ford across the river; in a few minutes pass another, shallower, ford. If the river is in flood, you may have to use this ford to cross it, and then walk through apple orchards on the north bank towards Corrales de Pego, an extensive ruined *finca*, which is your first objective. Normally, you gain access to it from the road via the dry bed of the river.   *1.5km – 30mins*

Seek out an old Mozarabic trail behind the ruins of the *finca*, which climbs up the south side of a ravine, with the road on the other side.

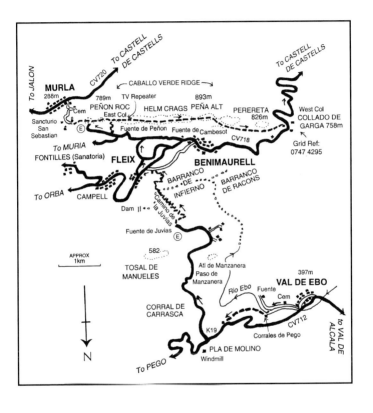

Soon the road can be seen ahead, and you reach it just below Km.9. Turn right and walk up the road to each the pass, Pla de Mollo (480m), with its old windmill, converted into a private house. On the way you get good views of Val d'Ebo and the cliffs of the Barranco del Infierno.

3.75km – 1hr

To Font De Juvias

At Km.19, turn off right (south-east) on a surfaced road towards the ridge of the Sierra de Mediodia. Ahead are the peaks of Monte Negre (649m) and Manzanera (702m), with the jagged rocks of El Castillo in the foreground. You will get a brief glimpse of the sea on your left-hand side and, to the right, in the far distance, the peaks of Monte Cabrer and Benicadell. Keep left at a junction. *5km – 1hr 30mins*

On your right, pass an extensive *finca* with a good well, Corral de Carrasca. *6km – 2hrs*

Look back over your shoulder for a last glimpse of Almisira (the lunch stop on the last stage) with Forada Ridge.

Climb up now to the modest pass of Manzanera. To the west are the Sierras de Carrasca, and below, in a depression, are a few farms on the lip of the gorge. Descend from the pass to a junction with an extensive ruin, where a good track goes down into the gorge. Keep straight on. *7km – 2hrs 20mins*

On the next section, you get good views of the gorge to your right, then the southern views of the Sierra Solana and the houses of Campell on the south side of the river valley above the gorge. The long wall across the hillside is the boundary of Fontilles, a leper colony, and Orba Castle can be seen. The twin peaks of Peña Roch at the eastern end of the Caballo Verde Ridge next appear and, finally, the church and the village of Fleix, your objective, which is on the lip of the gorge in the Val Laguart. Rushes growing by the path indicate a stream, and your good road starts to degenerate as the stream invades it, and you arrive at a flat area with a good well with five troughs, much used by shepherds. This is the Pozo de las Jubias. *8km – 2hrs 30mins*

Down The Camino De Las Jubias

The Mozarabic trail starts within a few metres of the well, under a wall, but is at present obscured by a lush growth of vegetation encouraged by the stream, which has completely taken over the path. Thankfully, within a few minutes the stream loses interest and leaves the trail, which you will follow down to the bed of the Rio Ebo.

These ancient ways were most soundly constructed and extremely well-engineered. Do not be tempted to take short cuts, because to follow these trails as they skilfully negotiate the most severe gradients is one of the great pleasures of this area. At the moment, you cannot see where the trail is going, but once you have passed a squarish boulder you start to follow the western edge of a deep rocky ravine; then, suddenly, the southern view opens out to reveal once more the deep valley of the Rio Ebo. This is not all. On the far side of the valley, on the lip of the gorge, is the little village of Fleix, and above it is the Caballo Verde Ridge, your first objective on the next stage. Note a complementary Mozarabic trail winding up from the valley floor – your twin – and half way up the route is the waterfall Cascade de Llet Tallat (Sour Milk Ghyll), which you will pass on the ascent to Fleix. In summer the waterfall is often dry, but after heavy rain or in winter it is a delight to see. Now you lose height and can see to the north-west sheer cliffs, which are the 'jaws' of the Barranco del Infierno, and the stony bed of the river, which you reach. To cross the river is usually possible, even in winter, but in extreme conditions you may have to get your feet wet.

Take a break, and perhaps have lunch before deciding what to do next as Fleix is only just beyond the top of the waterfall, one hour and 300m of ascent away.   *10.5km – 4hrs*

Possible Diversions

Barranco Del Infierno (north-west)

If weather conditions permit, a very rough walk north along the river bed will bring you in an hour to the narrowing walls of the Barranco, and the caves and rock scrambles which lead to the climbing pitches, which have some fixed ironwork of extremely dubious security. Very impressive, even in its lower stages.   *5km – 2hrs*

Isbert's Folly (south-east)

After heavy rain, you will be confronted with a lake, which will prevent this diversion. Whoever Isbert was, he certainly got it wrong! At the end of this diversion is an extremely narrow cleft in the crags, into which was built a concrete dam, which does hold water when the Gota Fria comes. The snag is that whilst this does flood the valley right up to the river crossing where you will be lunching, within a few days the precious water has percolated through subterranean channels, and the valley is dry once more! This inundation, however, encourages a lush growth of grass, which in its turn attracts not only shepherds with sheep and goats, but also herdsmen with bulls! To visit the dam, follow the river bed, or the paths on its banks, as it twists and turns between red-coloured crags with some interesting caves, and in about an hour you come to a broad area where the reservoir should have been. Now look to the right for the cleft in the crags and the old dam.   *5km – 2hrs*

Up to Fleix via the Waterfall

Start to ascend (all the way on the Mozarabic trail), first under some cliffs on the east side, then in 20 minutes cross the barranca and the stream directly under the waterfall (or, in summer, the alleged waterfall) to the other side of the valley. Ascend to a cave, pass through it, then recross the stream, and in 15 minutes pass the village wash-house (*lavadero*) of Fleix, and emerge on to the road at Km.2, just 2 minutes from the Bar Nostros, where a warm welcome awaits you. This is a simple village 'pub', with very basic decor.

You are now in the Val Laguart, a collection of three villages, and at Fontilles there is a leper sanatorium (now, thankfully, mostly engaged in research). Accommodation is now available at Benimaurell (hotel). There is a campsite at Campell.

Direct 12km – 5hrs; Barranco Del Infierno 22km – 9hrs

STAGE 3: FLEIX TO CASTELL DE CASTELLS

Overall time:	14hrs
Walking time:	10hrs 30mins – 11hrs 15mins
Distance:	29km
Ascent:	824m
Maps:	Benisa 822 (30–32)

This is a very long hard day, suitable for enthusiasts in training and for masochists. We pass through some sensational scenery and traverse a lovely 6km ridge with historical connections, ending the day at a remote mountain village.

For those not in the above categories, the walk can, if required, be shortened:

- *by shortening Stage 2 by foregoing visits to Isbert's Folly and Val de Infierno to allow for a traverse of the Caballo Verde Ridge as part of Stage 2, thus shortening Stage 3 by walking up the road direct to Collado de Garga*

- *by ending the walk at Corral de Somo, and accepting a lift into Castell de Castells, thus saving 3km and 1hr.*

The Caballo Verde Ridge is no Striding Edge, but it is composed of broken limestone and is treacherous in wet weather, difficult to navigate in bad visibility, and not to be attempted in darkness. The many grykes (fissures) are not known as ankle snappers for nothing! The rest of the route is on good surfaced or forestry roads and will accommodate sturdy vehicles. On the Fig Tree section, however, the Barranco Molino section is steep and loose, and even local farmers' vehicles have trouble in wet conditions.

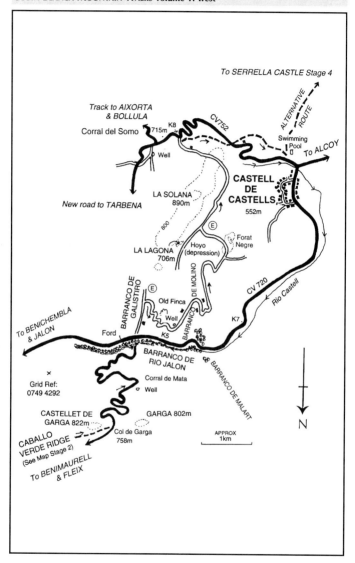

To the Western Col

Start the walk from the church at Fleix and go up a concrete road, passing a telephone kiosk and the *fuente* on your left. The route is generally south as you pass a casita (Tosalet) and admire the views ahead of the Peñon Roch and the Caballo Verde Ridge, with Helm Crags half-way along it. Climbing through orchards of cherries and apples, you can see the first objective, the col beneath Peñon Roch. In a few minutes, ignore a road off to the right, and in 12 minutes reach a level road and turn left (east), passing the *Fuente* Peña, with its analyst's report on the mineral qualities of the water.

Below you is the Val Laguart and the village of Campell. Across the valley rises Sierra Mediodia, and to the east lie the jagged ridge of Segaria and the mighty bulk of Montgo. Ignore a road on the left going down to Murla. Pass an old *finca* on the left, and reach Casita del Cerezas on the right with its pretty garden. To the left, under the crags of Peñon Roch, you can see a quarry, which is where the surfaced roads ends.   *1.5km – 30mins*

Follow the surfaced road until it ends at the quarry and continue towards the col, passing Molar Rock on your right.   *2km – 40mins*

Now turn south up towards the col. There is a waymarked path – go up through the terraces, making for the right-hand side of the slope to the col. The path keeps generally to the left of boulders and slants right to below the col. Now take to the slabs, and climb direct to the col.   *3km – 1hr*

You now have views to the south down into the Jalon Valley (Val de Pop) and of the village of Benichembla. To the east can be seen the beautiful buildings of Fontilles, the leper colony, where so much important research has taken place, which has resulted in the virtual elimination of the disease in the western world. To the south-east, Col de Rates, with Rates Peak above it, and the small white restaurant are now visible. Walk up a little, and you can see the first section of the ridge with Pudding Stone and, in the far distance, Peña Alta, the highest point (842m).

To the south, Cocoll, Sierras de Aixorta and Serrella appear, and you can pick out the Barranco de Gallistero, with the forestry road climbing over to Forat Negre – your afternoon walk. To the east-south-east are the rounded summits of Silla de Cao and Tosal de Navarro, between which runs the Greenwich Meridian. In the far distance behind Rates is the jagged ridge of the Ferrer.

Peñon Roch (793m)

This craggy summit (actually, there are two) marks the eastern end of the Caballo Verde Ridge, and on its highest summit there once stood a Moorish castle. Nothing now remains except a few dressed stones and tiles scattered over the slopes, but things were much different in the 17th century, as this ridge marks the Moors' last stand in Valencia. In 1609 a great battle occurred on this ridge as the troops of the Spanish king subdued the last remnants of the Moorish occupation (route described in volume 2).

Ascent of the Peñon (Diversion)

To reach the summit of the Peñon is a rock scramble, and to cross the two summits follow a rocky arête and ridge down to the *Ermita* San Sebastian, and then via a calvary to the village of Murla, a very rough expedition with no paths, but very rewarding. Allow 2hrs 30mins to Murla. There are orange markers on the ascent and descent of the summits only. For those experienced in rock-climbing only, start on the south side of the summit crags by crossing a maze of large boulders, well vegetated with spiky plants. If this does not put you off, perhaps the 4m wall will! The obstacle, however, has its weakness, and is the last obstacle before traversing carefully upwards towards a small belvedere. From here, strike straight up to the summit on broken ground. The small holes made by treasure-seekers, and a few broken pots and tiles, indicate that you are nearing the summit. To descend, go down a short rock climb (easy) on the north side, which is a little exposed, and traverse up to the eastern summit. From here, keep to the ridge as far as possible, passing Dog Rock on the left whilst descending slabs to gain the short but delightful Murla Arête, then make for the metal cross above the village, descending through old terraces to the *ermita*, then down to Murla on a good track.

The Ridge Walk

Start your traverse of the ridge by passing the Pudding Stone on the north side. There are yellow/white markers on the ridge itself, as there is no path, and the best advice is to keep to the rocks whenever possible. At times, however, small sections of what would pass as a footpath do appear. These have probably been trodden out by hunters. Where you do have to leave the crest to avoid pinnacles and the like it is usually easier on the southern side of the ridge. In 10 minutes you reach a TV repeater cabin which was blown over in the winter gales of 1989 and has never been repaired, and then you reach a small cairn. *3.5km – 1hr 10mins*

Overhang Rock and Helm Crags can be seen below you, which are avoided by dropping down slightly on the south side. Below Helm Crags on the northern side is a cave, and you pass a tiny rock shelter and a cairn before reaching the pinnacles at the western end of the crags. *4.5km – 1hr 50mins*

Between you and the rocky crest of Peña Alta are two intermediate summits, and in half an hour you can see Intermediate Summit and a substantial cairn, from which can be seen your final objective, Aitana (1558m), with its array of antennae, away to the south-west. With diligence you can see the Castillo de Serrella, your first objective on the next stage. *5.25km – 2hrs 20mins*

Now head for a small rock shelter on Intermediate Summit. *5.8km – 2hrs 50mins*

It is now necessary to move slightly to the right across some terraces to rejoin the ridge up to the summit of Peña Alta (842m), following a number of very small cairns. Below, to the north-west, you can see Perereta (826m), with its stone cross, and next to it Castellet de Garga (822m), beyond which is the col guarded by Garga (802m). *6.6km – 3hrs 5mins*

Below, under Perereta, is a ruined *finca*, your next objective, which is reached by descending the easy slopes of Peña Alta. The crosses mounted on crags overlooking mountain villages are to ward off both evil spirits and lightning. Obviously the villagers of Benimaurell still favour this form of protection, as the young men of the village, no doubt persuaded by the old folk, rebuilt this cross in 1952 after the old one collapsed. *7.5km – 3hrs 15mins*

On reaching the ruins of the *finca*, find a footpath which contours under Perereta to the col between this mountain and the Castellet de Garga. From here, a path leads south to the road, about 1km below the col. The way, which is now waymarked red/orange, leads on a good path to the Collado de Garga, by way of a short section of the original Mozarabic trail, passing an old *nevera* on the left. *9km – 3hrs 50mins*

The col is occupied by a number of shepherds' stone huts and usually smells strongly of goats. After admiring the view, it is probably better to drop down to the oak grove for a break. All the wells are locked to preserve the water for the animals. From the col you can see your next objective, the river culvert across the Rio Jalon on the A1210, and you can appreciate the views of the Barranco Gallistero and the Fig Tree Route across to Forat Negre, your afternoon walk.

To the Rio Jalon

As a contrast to the last four hours of rough walking, you now have 5km to walk and 500m to descend on an excellently engineered surfaced road, which leaves you free to admire the ever-changing views as you zig-zag down. In half an hour, pass an oak grove on the left, a shady resting place, and at 3km (45mins) you pass through a small collection of houses, Corral de la Mata, with a new house on the left. Just past this is a ruin with a well with water in it. Pass a house, La Hermitage, on the left, then a restaurant called Chez Pierre et Christina, where meals can only be obtained by advance telephone booking. You now cross the dry river bed to the main road and Barranco Gallistero.

12.5km – 5hrs 30mins

Where the Barranco Gallistero joins the Rio Jalon, you start the next stage of your walk. Here, a few years ago, stood a grove of old and fruitful fig trees. Sadly, the construction work has taken its toll, and only one wounded specimen survives. With your back to the road, look up a broad valley (east of south). To the left is the bulk of Cocoll (1047m). Immediately ahead is a broad track and an unnamed peak (part of La Laguna) on the right. The summit ridge ends in a rock gully, and between these points can be seen the new forestry track zig-zagging up over the ridge.

To the Barranco de Molinero

Follow the track up the Barranco de Gallistero alongside the dry river bed, passing a casita on the right and a *fuente* on the left, and in 15 minutes reach a junction. Take the right-hand fork, which leaves the valley and starts to climb in well-engineered zig-zags to the right-hand flank of Innominate Peak. As you gain height, look back to see the Caballo Verde Ridge appear to the north, and finally arrive at Innominate Crags, where you find an old *finca*. Carry on round the edge of the ridge, where there is a *fuente*.

After a short climb, around another bend, is an old, quite extensive *finca*, with a well, oven and *era* (threshing floor), a wonderful spot to rest for a while, with commanding views.   *14.5km – 6hrs 15mins*

To the north-east is Peñon Roch, the end of the Caballo Verde Ridge, and Montgo is visible. Leave the old *finca* moving south-west, and press on down a little into the Barranco de Molinero.

Below, you can see the substantial new road bridge over the Rio Jalon; seeing the river in its normally dry state, it seems hard to justify such a bridge, but when winter comes with its storms it certainly proves to be of great benefit to the people of Castell de Castells and beyond. It seems a long way down to the head of this *barranco*, and a long climb (now north-west) up to regain the height lost, but soon turn south-west again to reach another ruined *finca* and a deep roadside well on the left.   *16.5km – 8hrs*

Just past the ruins a road leads off left. You keep straight on.

Above to the right is the summit of Forat Negre (866m). Reach a high plateau with a depression below on the left, which has some dew-ponds; it has in the past been cultivated. The road now rises a little, and ahead you can see new views and a ruined casita on the left of the road, as well as another road striking off south under La Solana (890m). Reach the ruins, then turn off right (south-west) on the road which will lead to Corral del Somo.   *19.5km – 9hrs 30mins*

To Corral Del Somo

As the road climbs steadily, you get a brief glimpse of Castell de Castells below on the right. Take the opportunity on this section to look back in appreciation of the day's route, as Caballo Verde disappears from view and, on gaining a small rise, you are treated to magnificent views of Aitana and the Castillo de Serrella. Between Aitana and Alfaro in the far distance is Monte Cabrer (1389m). Ahead, the ridges of Sierra Aixorta appear, and amongst the pinnacles on its northern slopes is the beautiful natural rock arch of Arc del Atancos. *23.5km – 10hrs 15mins*

Descend now, passing a new villa, to the surfaced road at Corral del Somo. This fertile plateau, with plenty of water, is now farmed from Castell de Castells. Back-packers can now seek out a camping site for the night. Those with a support party waiting on the road will be whisked away to their accommodation; others have a pleasant walk down the valley, following the ancient Mozarabic trail from Bollula to

Castell de Castells. When only a few metres from the road watch out for a track leading off to the right which is waymarked in yellow and white. On this first fairly level section, the trail widens, but within 10 minutes it narrows again as the typical stone steps help it descend in zig-zags. Ahead you see the peak of Aixorta and Serrella Castle, which is the next stage of the walk, then the dramatic Barranco de Canal, the 'glacier' of the Serrella, and finally the first of the Serrella peaks, Mala de Llop. If you look carefully you will see a forestry road contouring across the northern slopes rising slowly towards the col to the left of the castle. Your route heads directly for the col from Castells. With persistence you will be able to see it, especially the bends.

The motor road now comes into view and you join a broader track for the last few metres. Cross over the road onto a broad track which descends gently, passing a ruin on the left, to rejoin the motor road at Km.1 on the outskirts of the village. Turn left towards Font De Bota and note the yellow and white waymarkings on the first track on the left. This is the start for Stage 4, waymarked PRV 149. The entrance to the swimming pool is next and also a signpost to Camping El Castilett.

There is now a choice of accommodation in the village at two hotels and two pensions. *29km – 10hrs 30mins*

STAGE 4: CASTELL DE CASTELLS TO CONFRIDES

Overall time:	(allowing 1hr for castle) 9hrs 40mins
Walking time:	7hrs
Distance:	23.5km
Ascent:	to castle 498m; to Confrides 386m
Map:	Alcoy 821 (29–32)

There are no rocky ridges today, only good forestry and country roads through beautiful mountain scenery. The way crosses the Sierra Serrella and reaches the highest part of the walk so far at Serrella Castle (1050m), then descends into the picturesque Guadalest Valley, with its reservoir. Accompanied by the sound of rushing water (a rare experience on the Costa), the way ascends to Abdet and Confrides for the night. Sturdy vehicles, horse riders and mountain bikes may also use this whole route.

Making a Start

Today's route starts a few metres from the Font De Bota, along the road to Trabena, where you turn up the unsurfaced road heading south after passing a surfaced road with a sign 'Camping El Castillet'. Your route is waymarked as the PRV149.

Ignore two side roads on the right as the massive northern cliffs of Aixorta come into view and see if you can spot the shapely natural rock arch, a twin to Arcos Aticus.

After 2km reach a Y-junction and take the road to the right. After just over 1km, ignore another road leading off to the right (which is the old route from Km.3 on the Fachega road) to reach a crossroads on the Puerto de Castillo. The road ahead, south, leads down to the Guadalest Valley, PRV18; the one on the left, east PRV18, leads to *Fuente* de Umbria and the Aixorta. You take the road on the right, east, PRV149, which will climb the southern flank of the castle crags which dominate the view. You zig-zag upwards, passing attractive pinnacles, to reach

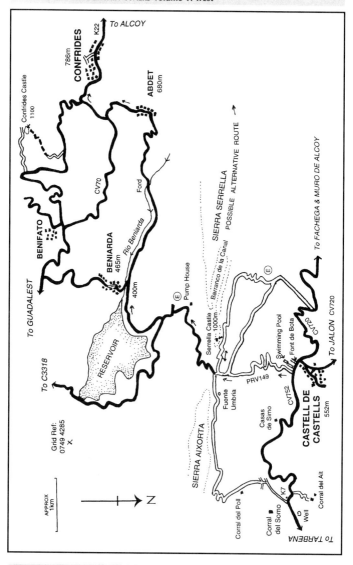

another col where views open up towards the Barranco de Canal and distant Malla de Llop.   *5.5km – 1hr 45mins*

Ascent to the Castle Ruins

Try to make this a long halt to allow for the ascent of the castle. To get to the top will only take a few minutes. Strike up to the right (north) on an indistinct path to pass to the right of a large stone water cistern. Despite the passage of many centuries, it still holds water, and toads breed in it. Still moving to the right along a shelf, at a broken arch start to zig-zag upwards to gain the rocky ridge. Now move left along the ridge to enter the extensive ruins. As might be expected, the all-round views from such a strategic situation are sensational: to the east, the sea, Sierra Helada, Ponoch and the second-highest peak in the province, Puig Campaña (1410m); to the west, the 'glacier' of the Serrella or Barranca de Canal dominates the view. (1hr allowed in timing.)

Descent to the Puerta De Castillo

Leaving Collado de Castillo, the view ahead is dominated by Sierra Aixorta as you descend a steep road under the northern crags of the castle. When you reach a lone pine tree on a bend, look down to say farewell to Castell de Castells. Ahead, on the northern flank of Aixorta, you will see a tree-lined road leading to *Fuente* Umbria. This is the back-packers' route from Corral de Somo, which will shortly join your track on the col. To the left, you get your last views of Cocoll and Forat Negre. In the far distance, the Bernia and Ferrer ranges peep over the intervening ridges as you reach a crossroads and turn right (south). In a few minutes, as if by magic, the Aitana range appears, and you look down once again on Guadalest.   *6.25km – 15mins*

Author's Note

When the Way was initially devised it was essentially a walkers' route, and in view of this the temptation to follow the Serrella Ridge in a shallow arc north-west until a descent could be made to Confrides was resisted, despite the attraction of keeping to the tops for most of the route.

Circumstances have, however, changed as paths have become forestry roads, some of them surfaced. For the rest of this stage, once walkers leave the Puerto de Castillo, they will be on concrete or macadam for most of the time until Confrides is reached.

The ridge route is now described at the end of this walk.

Down to the Reservoir and Beniarda

Descend now on a mostly broad surfaced road under the southern crags of the castle as the dam at the eastern end of the reservoir appears below. In half an hour you pass a large crag on the left and are treated to excellent views right up the 'glacier'. In 20 minutes, just after passing an old *finca* on the left, you pass a pumping station and soon join the main road around the reservoir.   *10.75km – 4hrs 10mins*

During this descent, you will have the best views of the Aitana range. Peña Roc is at the eastern end, with Peña Mulero and Peña Alba, and finally the summit of Aitana itself. On the northern flank, note the Partagas fissures and cliffs, beloved of pot-holers. Just below the summit antennae are some rock formations which many people mistake for a castle. The actual ruins of Confrides Castle are on a jagged crag detached from the mountain. You now get your first view of the rocky pinnacles of Pla de la Casa (1379m), another of the Serrella's main four peaks to the west. Finally, you can see the three fortified crags which protect Guadalest.

Turn right (west) onto a surfaced but narrow road along the side of the reservoir, and in a few minutes your next objective, the remote village of Abdet, comes into view ahead. On the left, above, is the picturesque village of Beniarda (with a municipal swimming pool if you need one, and a good restaurant). As soon as the bridge crossing the Rio Beniarda is reached, you have a very rare treat in this drought-ridden area – the sound of running water!   *13.25km – 4hrs 35mins*

Climbing up to Confrides

Here, crystal water plunges down in a pretty little waterfall to join the stream which tumbles and dances between well-worn boulders all the year round. Follow this road all the way to Abdet, first alongside the stream, then crossing it at a large culvert.   *15.25km – 5hrs 25mins*

There is the last steep pull up to Abdet, where there are three bars and two restaurants. On the way, the main bulk of Serrella's twin summits dominate the view ahead.

All that remains now is to walk along the AV1035 up out of the village to join the main road (C3313) in 1.5km, then turn right (west) towards Confrides. Ignore the access road up into the village, keeping on the main road, as the Fonda, El Pirineo, is at the other end of the village on the right-hand side of the road. There is now a *pension* in the village.   *23.5km – 7hrs*

Fiesta – 24th to 27th August.

Bus Service – Once per day to Alicante.

Ridge Route:
CASTILLO DE SERRELLA
TO RINCON DE OLVIDO

Walking time:	**5hrs 30mins**
Distance:	**16km**
Ascent:	**to castle 498m; to Confrides 980m**
Map:	**Alcoy 821 (29–32)**

This natural and inviting line along the entire Serrella ridge has attracted the attention of mountaineers resting on the Serrella Castle summit of Peña Horadlada for a long time. It was, however, initially considered too rough and indistinct a route to include in the Way, most of which it was hoped would be navigable in restricted visibility.

Things have changed in the last 8 years, as many footpaths became roads and some even surfaced. There is nothing wrong with the standard Way, which gives an excellent valley route with extensive views, but after Serrella Castle the walker has to tread a hard surface for the rest of the day.

This route, by comparison, is over very rough, trackless ground for most of the way (I do not count boar and goat tracks as reliable). Route-finding in clear weather is no trouble, just keep on

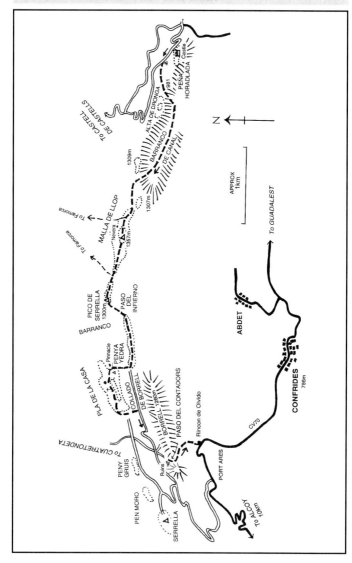

west as high as you can, but in bad visibility navigation will not only be difficult and unrewarding but distinctly dangerous. The ridge route ascends a further 980m (added to the 500m already ascended to the castle) and you will descend a total of nearly 1400m as well. Sufficient to say, for most walkers the effort is well worth the extra effort. This variation is particularly suitable for back-packers, as near Km.25, below the Rincon Olvido Restaurant, a good forestry track leads off directly towards Fuente de Arbols. Those with a support party too will speed down to the comforts of Confrides. Others and purists will have a long 3km rough, downhill walk before dinner (allow an extra hour at least).

From Col de Castillo to Malla De Llop

After your descent from the castle ruins turn left and follow the broad forestry road west, descending at first then climbing to cross a spur, where there is a layby on the left, before the road starts its steady descent towards Castell de Castells.   *2km – 30mins*

Your objective is to enter the Barranco de Canal (the 'glacier'), which we admired from the castle. To do so we head west from a cairn at the back of the layby and head for the crags of Alta de Tronca (881m), then follow the ridge west to gain a small col. The path now splits: the right-hand one continues along the ridge, but the better choice is the one on the left, which follows the easier line down into the dry bed of the Barranco de Canal. Your route is between the majestic crags of the 'glacier', but there is no ice to cool you on this steady grind.

1hr 30mins

On the col you get good views north into the Seta Valley and Famorca. Head west: there are no paths to help you, although the route is obviously well used by animals on your final ascent, towards the trig point, which now comes into view.   *5km – 1hr 50mins*

The Summit of Malla De Llop (1361m)

The views from the summit are most extensive and include most of the peaks in the area; notably Peñon de Ifach is missing. You will also have plenty of time to study the next section of this route, making for the attractive summit of Pla de la Casa to the west. On this section you have the option of ascending to the summit by the scree shoot on the eastern end, or seeking out a track on the south side which joins a foresty road down to Confrides. Looking back over your route you have nice views down the Barranco de Canal towards Serrella Castle. There is also a *nevera* to visit on the north side of the mountain (see Route 19). *2hrs 5mins*

Along the Ridge to Pico De Serrella

Leave the summit and keep to the ridge, moving west with sheer crags below you on the left and more gentle ground to the right, losing height with the summit of Pla de la Casa as your objective. There is no regular path on this section until you reach another craggy summit with a cairn, Pico de Serrella (1300m), where the route down to Famorca descends to the north (Route 19). *8km – 2hrs 35mins*

Descent to Paso Del Infierno

Ahead can be seen a scree shoot descending from the rocky summit of Pla de la Casa, with a prominent pinnacle set in it. This is the route up to the summit as you descend to and reach a broad col, Paso del Infierno, with Barranco del Moro leading down, north to Fachega. Note the small water collecting huts in the barranca.

From the Paso del Infierno a track leads off north, down towards the first water hut and eventually Fachega (2hrs 30mins) (Route 18). You maintain a route on the high ridge until right opposite the pinnacle and the fingerpost in the screes. There is also a cairn.

10km – 3hrs 15mins

First Option: Ascent of Pla De La Casa

Your first objective is to reach the rock pinnacle by way of the screes: not the most pleasant of pastimes. From the pinnacle keep on climbing on very rough ground, but gradually ascend a more stable gully until you stand in the trough below the actual summit.

Above you is the shapely peak with a metal cross on the highest point and below you is the largest, deepest *nevera* that I have found. There is not much room on the summit for large parties, and the cross contains a log book and was installed by Groupo Montanjero de St Joan, Callosa de Seguria.

As if that were not sufficient, the whole level area beneath the summit is covered with large mounds of Hedgehog Broom (Erinacea anthyllis), a mass of blue in the season, but not to be handled.

Now you can add views of the Alcoy mountains to the west.

12km – 4hrs 25mins

Back Down to Collado De Borrell

Walk generally west to south-west along the small plateau to seek out waymarkings which show you the way down south on a rocky path to join a broad forestry road seen below.

Down to Confrides

The forestry road, signposted Cuatretondeta, leads south-west until it reaches the motor road at Puerto Confrides (Ares). There is a variation which you will take, which leads off south towards the ridge of Borrell. When you reach a five-way junction in the road turn left, traversing under the summits of the Serrella until you reach the small cleft in the ridge of Borrell, which is the Paso del Contadores. Negotiate this gap and then descend the south side towards the motor road and the Restaurant del Olvido, which can be seen below. This part of the route is covered also by Route 16. There is no continuous track down steep slopes, but there are a few well-spaced cairns. Move east then south to a large flat area from where a descent track takes you to the road next to the restaurant.

16km – 5hrs 30mins

Second Option:
Avoiding Summit of Pla De La Casa Back to Puerto Ares

From the base of the scree run move south and eventually you will locate a path leading west under the summit of Pla de la Casa.

Summits of Serrella (1359m)

There will surely be some purists with sufficient stamina to ascend to these twin summits by reversing the route shown in Route 16, from the forestry track, which now runs along the rest of the ridge from Peña de Yedra to the summits of Serrella, then rejoining the road at the pass. Add another hour at least.

STAGE 5: CONFRIDES TO
FONT MOLI VIA AITANA

Overall time:	7hrs 30mins
Walking time:	7hrs
Distance:	21km
Ascent:	772m
Maps:	Alcoy 821 (29–32), Villajoyosa 847 (29–33)

This is the last day of the Costa Blanca Mountain Way, and a lovely day it is. Not too demanding, the route passes through beautiful scenery to reach the crowning glory of Alicante province, Aitana (1558m), then provides an amble down to a hostal nestling on the slopes of the mountain which specialises in Valencian cooking.

To Fuente Arbols

Leave the *hostal*, cross the road, and go up the main street of the village, Calle St Antonio, passing the *fuente* on the left, and take the first narrow street on the right, which goes up through the houses to reach a surfaced road. In 5 minutes, fork right, with a mesh fence on the right-hand side, and pass the gate of El Pouet San Ignacio. Ahead you can see Confrides Castle on a jagged spur of Aitana. Over to the left, yesterday's route over the Serrella Pass can be seen. Bear right at a junction and ignore a track to the right, settling down to some well-spaced zig-zags as you start on a western tack to gain height. Behind, the end of the Bernia Ridge has a look of the Matterhorn seen from this angle.

2km – 25mins

Now the antennae on the summit of Aitana are in view ahead. Below, to the right, will appear the road climbing up towards Puerto Confrides and Alcoy. Serrella's two summits appear, with Pla de la Casa behind them. The road contours round a barranca. You pass a small casita, and Monte Cabrer appears in the distant west.

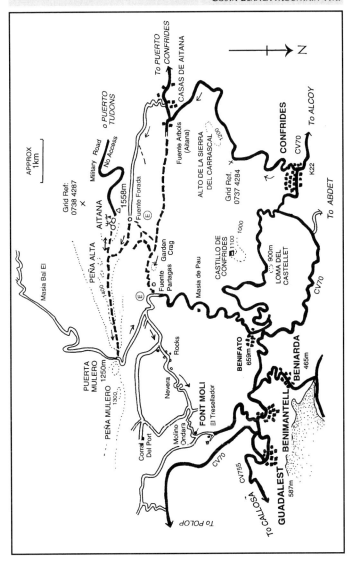

Down below is an old ruined *finca* with an *era*. As you breast a rise, there are more little casitas near Casas de Aitana. Still moving west, you see the western buttress of Aitana and swing left (east) parallel to the ridge. All the summit is now visible, and across the level cultivated area with its casitas can be seen another track climbing towards Aitana. This is the next section of the route.

The road now levels out, and below can be seen the hamlet of Casas de Aitana and the *Fuente* Arbols (*Fuente* Aitana on the map). In 15 minutes, at a large walnut tree, turn right onto a road leading to the *fuente*, with its tables and benches. This is a popular place for Spaniards to hold paella picnics at weekends and fiestas, and for walkers to camp in the summer. The trough of the *fuente* is often full of cans of beer and bottles of wine, keeping cool whilst a barbecue is being prepared on the stone shelves. *6km – 1hr 30mins*

To Fuente Forata

Leave the *fuente*, taking the forestry road which climbs up towards Aitana (south) and zig-zags steeply, gaining height, then turns east below the northern crags. Climb steadily, ignoring two tracks which lead downhill on the left. Note the large split boulder on the right, and the missing section of it below on the left. On this section, you pass four *neveras* (ice-pits), so keep a look out for them.

The road finally makes one or two zig-zags to gain more height, and in half an hour you will be directly under the main masts of the transmitters. You may be tempted to go up directly to the summit, but even if there is a viable route, there is no saying what the effect would be on the military guards as your head appeared at the perimeter fence! *8km – 2hrs 25mins*

Look over your shoulder (north-west) to see Benicadell appear, and ahead, the Bernia Ridge, Montgo, Col de Rates, Segaria and Llorensa are visible on the coast near Moraira.

In 10 minutes, you are directly under the radar domes, and the track drops a little to a flat area with the third *nevera* and the *fuente* with its trough. On this section you get your first view of the *forat* – a hole in the rocks high up ahead of you. *9.5km – 2hrs 40mins*

To Fat Man's Agony

Go up right of the *nevera* on broken ground and scree without a regular path. Head for a cleft crag, which you pass on the right-hand side (east). The fourth *nevera* is below the crag.   *10km – 2hrs 50mins*

The track moves slowly upwards towards another small col, but soon has to cross some scree, and you can now actually touch the crags. Ahead is a jumble of rocks filling a gully. A prominent yew tree will be seen high up and a gap in the rocks to the left of it. This is Fat Man's Agony, and the route. Behind you, high up on the ridge, is a small rock *forat*.

Scramble up the rocks, pass left under the tree, go through the gap, and you have crossed one of the Simas de Partagas. Turn left as you leave the gap, and traverse until you meet a path near some painted rocks – souvenirs of past speleological explorations. Look back into the fissures; they are very impressive. At these painted rocks, turn right (due west) and climb along the edge of the fissures to reach the broad summit of Aitana, the highest point (not quite 1558m, but near enough) accessible to the public in the whole province.   *1km – 3hrs 40mins*

Wonderful Views

From the summit can be seen the second- and third-highest peaks in the province: Puig Campaña (1410m), looking south-east, and Mont Cabrer (1389m) to the north-west. Further access to the west is prohibited, so views in the direction of Alcoy are limited. In all other directions, however, the vistas seem endless. It is not often that you can pick out the square tower of Cocentaina Castle (north-north-west) from walks in this area. Confrides, Serrella and Guadalest castles are also visible to the north-east. The ice-pit, or *nevera*, was a necessity in ancient times for keeping meat fresh. Below, on the northern flanks, see how many of these circular pits you can spot. You will visit one on your descent. You have now successfully completed the Costa Blanca Mountain Way.

Descents

If you have become hooked on Fat Man's Agony, then by all means reverse the ascent route. Campers may wish to return to *Fuente* Partagas for the night. A recommended alternative is to follow the ridge down and over Peña Alta to Paso Mulero.

To Paso Mulero via Peña Alta

Return first to the painted rocks, and follow a reasonable path going up east, keeping to the left of a large fissure.   *11.5km – 3hrs 55mins*

The traverse along the edge of the escarpment east towards the sea provides exceptional views along the ridge to Peña Roc at its end, with Ponoch and Puig Campaña in the distance. Eventually, the coastal mountains of Sierra Helada (near Benidorm) and Peñon d'Ifach and Toix (near Calpe) will come into view. Below you on the north side are glorious views of the Guadalest Valley, and you may be able to pick out your route down to Font Moli. Behind you to the west, you get fine views of the massive fissures and land slips which form Aitana's northern face. To the south there are views of the *barrancas* which lead down to Sella (Stage 6). There is no reliable path over the five buttresses, which have to be traversed to gain the pass. Try to keep as near to the edge of the escarpment as prudence permits, not only to admire the views, but there is usually less vegetation on the bare rocks of the lip. You will soon get tantalising views of the forestry road coming up to the pass from Sella (Stage 6), but the pass itself remains hidden until the very last moment, as you negotiate the last steep slope to the forestry road.   *15km – 5hrs 15mins*

To Fuente Partagas

Turn left and start a long descent west, with Confrides Castle and Partagas ahead of you. You pass under some pinnacles, and when they give way to gentler slopes (in about 15 minutes), look ahead and upwards about 200m from the road to locate a large *nevera*, which is well worth a visit. At the end of this straight section are a number of zig-zags leading to *Fuente* Partagas. At the second one are two small roads leading off to the right. Take the first of these, which heads east parallel to the ridge of Peña Alta.   *16.5km – 5hrs 45mins*

To Font Moli

First avoid a track going right, then avoid two others which go down left (red markers), and you will reach in 20 minutes a small cultivated hollow with a small shelter on your left, and the road drops towards a ruined *finca*.   *17.5km – 6hrs 10mins*

Ahead, behind the ruins, are some crags, and the route descends just to the right of them. Turn left at the old ruined *finca*, and go down to and pass between some picturesque rocky pinnacles. As you emerge from them, note a last *nevera* on the left-hand side, then continue on to reach a concrete road.   *20km – 6hrs 40mins*

Turn left down this road, and in 10 minutes approach the hamlet of Font Moli, with the Font below on the left. Either descend by the small track direct to the Font, or follow the surfaced road down to it.
20.5km – 6hrs 50mins

Now, follow the road, which goes west, passing a large house on the right with a sun-dial on its wall and a small *lavadero* (wash-house) under a tree on the left. In 10 minutes, turn right up the drive to the Pension El Trestellador, where a warm welcome awaits you at the end of a wonderful day on Alicante province's highest mountain.
21km – 7hrs

STAGE 6: FONT MOLI TO SELLA (optional)

Overall time:	**7hrs**
Walking time:	**6hrs 30mins (by direct route)**
Distance:	**20km**
Ascent:	**640m**
Maps:	**Villajoyosa 847 (29–33)**

This section is an optional finish to the Costa Blanca Mountain Way, which allows those with sufficient time and energy to finish the walk further south at Sella, from where there is a bus service to Alicante. For those who do not wish to retrace the route up to Paso Mulero via Partagas, an alternative is provided, which will allow a visit to Peña Mulero.

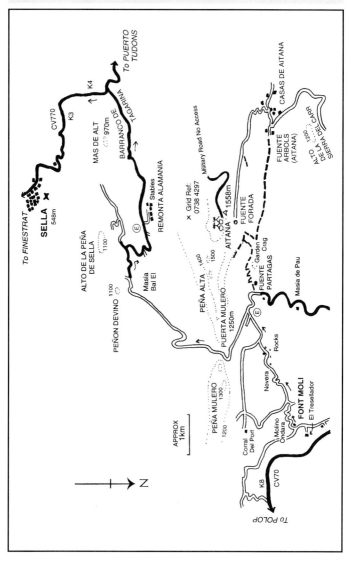

Direct Route to Paso Mulero   *6km – 1hr 30mins*

From the Font Moli to the Nevera

Either climb up a path to the left of the Font or walk round by the road which leads behind the Font, in a generally north-westerly direction, but only for a few minutes. On a concrete section of the road, at a sharp left-hand bend, look for a red arrow on the road surface, indicating the route to the Peña Mulero. Ignore this sign, but look to the right and you will see a good track with a red marker on the wall. The track continues through almond terraces with views of Confrides Castle and Aitana. After a few minutes, note a well-preserved *nevera* (ice-pit) on the right-hand side of the track. Above you and ahead are some very attractive rock pinnacles, and your path winds and climbs through them, eventually reaching the ruins of a large *finca*.   30mins

To the Partagas

Behind the *finca* ruins, there is a good broad track which continues in a generally south-westerly direction towards a small col, from which good views can be had of the summit of Aitana, with its array of aerials and the two radar domes. Below the summit, note the impressive crags of Las Simas de Partagas. Pass a small cultivated hollow with a tiny shelter, and a ruined *finca* comes into view on the skyline on the right. You are now nearing the end of your western 'tack', and on your left can be seen your next section, the road leading east up along the flank of the mountain towards the col (Paso Mulero). In another 15 minutes, join the unsurfaced road coming up from the *Fuente* Partagas and Benifato.   1hr

To the Col

Stop here for a rest and take in the majestic scenery, then settle down to a half-hour steady climb on a well-engineered forestry road up the col between Peña Alta and Peña Mulero. As you gain height, your views are extended as more and more mountains come into sight, including Montgo, near Javea.

After half an hour and one tight hair-pin bend you are on the broad col.   1hr 30mins

(This direct route continues at 'Down into the Barranco de Tagarina', below.)

Alternative Ridge Route to Paso Mulero Via Peña Mulero
6km – 2hrs 30mins

Leave the Font Moli and follow the road which you used to descend on Stage 5 until, on a bend with a concrete surface, the track to the Partagas forks right. You keep straight on upwards. Views are of the Bernia Ridge, and the coastal mountains of Toix and Peñon d'Ifach at Calpe. Peña Mulero, a large buttress, can be seen ahead, and you will reach the ridge to the east of its summit. Ignore a track on the right, and one which leads off north-west to the Partagas. You keep generally to a south-easterly course towards the eastern edge of the ridge, where you can see a narrow path leading across scree towards a rock gateway. This is the route. *40mins*

You are helped on this section by red square markers nailed to the trees, which are boundary markers. At a crossroads, keep to the right and later, when the road forks, also keep to the right. There are views now of Llorensa and Montgo. Eventually leave the track in an almond grove to take to a narrow path which can be seen making for the ridge. In 5 minutes the path crosses scree and emerges onto the ridge by means of a rock gateway (red markers on rock). *1hr*

Views to the south are revealed of the Barranco de Arcos which leads down to Sella, Puig Campaña and El Realet (the beautiful sharp ridge). Turn right (west) to seek out a fairly good path which keeps to the northern edge of the escarpment, where possible, to avoid the vegetation. On this section look to the north just right of Serrella Castle (on its blade of rock) for a view again of Almisira. This is the last view of the mountain which you scaled on the first stage. In 20 minutes, find a depression with a 'pot-hole', a good place to shelter from the wind, and as you gain height you will see Albir Lighthouse at the northern end of Sierra Helada appear to the south-east, and you get your first views of the summit buttress of Peña Mulero. The broad summit is marked by a number of cairns, and you can see, to the south, the city of Alicante with its castle of Santa Barbara, with the mountains of Murcia beyond. To the west are Monte Cabrer and Peña Alta. *2hrs*

Down to Paso Mulero

This is the last summit on the Costa Blanca Mountain Way, and the start of the final descent to Sella. Drop down to the west, without the benefit of a path, to the pass. New mountains appear below, Alta de Sella and Peña Divino, as well as the reservoir of Amadorio near Villajoyosa. *2hrs 30mins*

This route then joins the direct route down into the Barranco De Tagarina.

Down into the Barranco De Tagarina

There is a long walk down to the main road on a good forestry road. As you descend, there is only one possible place to take a wrong turning. In 45 minutes, a road goes off left just after the road gains a surface. Take the right-hand one, and immediately pass a large well-preserved *finca* on the right, with an *era* and its stone still in place. Above are the summit installations of Aitana, as you cross the head of the barranca, and the road improves a little. *4hrs*

In 1km, you pass through a cluster of casitas, and *Remonta* Alemana (German riding stables), and in another hour, reach the main road near Km.5. *5hrs*

If your support party is waiting, you can, I am sure, indulge yourself by accepting a lift after over 100km of walking. Purists, of course, will insist on walking the last 5km down through a gorge to the pretty village of Sella, with its ancient castle, with an *ermita* built into it. Sadly, most of the village houses have become weekend homes for Spaniards and foreigners, but the village bars and restaurants are geared to providing meals and refreshments for holidaymakers from the coast. There are only two buses each day to Villajoyosa (at present 9.30am and 5pm). So, there are no more mountains to climb, only a return to the coast – 'civilisation' – with, I hope, happy memories of a long walk, with all its varied scenery and experiences. There is accommodation in the village at Pension El Mirador. *6 hrs (direct route) 6hrs 30mins*
(alternative route)

SUPPORT PARTY NOTES

For those not undertaking the walk, but who wish to keep in touch with those who are, here are some useful notes about walks, accommodation, and so on.

Stage 1: Villalonga to Val D'Ebo

To Villalonga (Valencia Province)

This large town (pop. 3696) is a good place to stock up with supplies before the walk, and is 12km due south of the larger town and holiday resort of Gandia.

Leave the CN332 about 1km south of Gandia, and take the road on the right signposted to Villalonga (CV685) near the village of Bellrequart, and in 8km enter the town of Villalonga.

Villalonga To Forna   *Walking time 3hrs; driving time 1hr*

Return to the CN332 and turn south-east for Oliva and a turn-off right (south) on to the CV700 to Pego (pop. 9415). In Pego, follow signs CV700 to Cocentaina via Adsubia (pop. 557), 1km west of Adsubia, turn right (north-west) on to the CV717, and in 4km reach Forna. In the village there is a restaurant, the Nautilus.   *Total driving 30km*

Forna To Pla De Almisira   *Walking time 4hrs 30mins*

Return via the CV700 to Pego, and make for the Pla de la Font and the Paseo Cervantes, which is a shady park near the football ground in the south-west of the old town. From here a narrow, undistinguished and unsigned road leads off left, heading for Val d'Alcala, passing the *Ermita* St Joachim, crossing Barranco de la Canal, and winds its tortuous way up to the Pla de Almisira. In 7km, at a col, the service road to the summit transmitters goes off right to the top of the mountain (757m). In an emergency, a car can be driven along the walkers' route until it becomes a footpath. A car can also be driven up to the Castillo de Gallinera from Beniarrama.   *Walking distance 15km*

Pla De Almisira To Val D'Ebo   *Walking time 2hrs 30mins*

Most cars will, in dry conditions, be able to negotiate the walkers' route as only 1.5km of it is unsurfaced.

Retrace your route east for 2km, and at a small casita (waymarking) turn off south on a good broad track for 1.5km until the surfaced section starts, which leads to Val d'Ebo.   *Driving distance 5km*

For those with delicate cars, or in bad conditions, retrace the route to Pego (10km), and leave the town by the CV715 going south until, at

Km.1, you turn right (south-west) on to the CV721, and in 12km reach Val d'Ebo (pop. 368).

There are three bars in the village, and some rudimentary accommodation is available in private houses. Juan Frau at Bar de Plaza is your contact.

Alternative accommodation is in Pego (*hostal*), Vergel (*pensions* – Km.176 on the CN332 is a hostal with 19 rooms), Gandia (many hotels and *pensions*) and Oliva (*pensions* on the CN332).

Stage 2: Val D'Ebo To Fleix   *Walking time 5hrs*

The walking route will take an hour to get to the top of the col (Pla de Molinos) (Km.8), so you may pass your walkers on the route to Fleix. Retrace yesterday's route from Val d'Ebo – east along the CV718, signed Val de Laguart and Fontilles, for 6.8km to Fleix.

Val de Laguart is a collection of four small villages, of which Fleix is the administrative centre. The walkers' route will join the main road just to the west of the village, coming up past the *lavadero* from the depths of the Val de Infierno. The only access point is to follow the walkers' route for 10km as far as the *Fuente* de Juvias on a surfaced road. There is a large hotel at Benimarell (Alhuar), and a *casa rural* (Le Caista) and camping Val Laguar at Campell.

Stage 3: Fleix To Castell de Castells

(1) Fleix To Garga   *Walking time 4hrs*

Follow the CV718 west up the valley (2km) to Benimaurell, skirt the centre on the northern side by following the signs for the Bar Oasis, and keep going upwards (west) on a narrow road. In 2.5km you reach the Col de Garga. The walking route joins the road here near a small casita (waymarkings).   *4.5km*

Access by surfaced road to the quarry is by following the walkers' route from the Church Square at Fleix or from *Fuente* Cambesot at (Km.1) just outside Benimaurell.

(2) Col De Garga To Val De Pop   *Walking time 2hrs*

The walkers' route follows the road down into the valley for 5.5km, where it joins the CV720, Jalon to Castell de Castells road.

(3) Val De Pop To Castell De Castells   *Walking time 5hrs*

Follow the CV720 for 6km, go through the village, and at its western end, where the bridge crosses the river, turn left (south-east) along a narrow road, AV752, for 4km to Corral de Alt to meet the walkers, who will come over the hill to the north, passing an isolated casita. Castell de Castells (pop. 562) has bars, restaurants, a *hostal*, the Hotel Serrella and a motel, the Viel Bigot.

All of this section is on forestry roads, so in good conditions there is access for normal cars. From Innominate Crags, the gradients are steep with loose surface in the Barranco del Molino section.

Stage 4: Castell De Castells To Confrides   *Walking time 8hrs*

Today's route is all on forestry roads, so it may be possible for those with four-wheel drive vehicles to follow the walkers.

Normal Route

(1) Castell De Castells To Beniarda   *Walking time 5hrs 10mins*

Leave Castell de Castells and turn up the minor road from the river bridge, CV752, to climb in 4km to Corral del Somo, and continue east to Tarbena. In a further 7km, turn right on to the CV755 near Km.30, and drive south to Callosa d'Ensarria. In the town centre, turn right with signs Guadalest on the CV755, and turn right (north) down a minor road to the village of Beniarda. You have now to negotiate very narrow streets, passing through the main square, and under the pretty shrine to San Francisco, and in a further kilometre reach the valley bottom, and a bridge over the river. Turn right along a surfaced but narrow road for 3km, and the walkers' route comes down a surfaced road from the north (left), where an inlet of the reservoir indicates a valley, Barranca de Cuevas. Note: This road is subject to devastation every year during the Gota Fria, and landslips bury and carry away part of it. There are bars and a good restaurant in Beniarda. The road up to the Puerta de Castillo is now surfaced.   *45km*

(2) Beniarda To Confrides   *Walking time 2hrs 50mins*

Return to the CV70 and turn right (west) to reach Confrides in 7km. The *hostal* El Pirineo is at the west end of the village, on the right, on the main road. There are numerous restaurants in the village. If preferred, normal cars can follow the walkers' route via Abdet to Confrides which has now been surfaced.

From the south in emergency normal cars can be taken to the pumping station on a narrow surfaced road. Beyond this, gradients are very severe, and the surface often loose and subject to landslip in winter or bad weather.

From the north some normal cars have been seen driving up to the castle, but it is really for four-wheel drive vehicles, although in good conditions a normal car should get you to the forest below the zig-zags.

Accommodation: Fonda El Pirineo, main road, Confrides; Casa Rural Can Pilar, Calle Enmig 1, Confrides.

Stage 5: Confrides To Font Moli   *Walking time 7hrs*

Leave Confrides and go east on the CV70, through Benimantell, and as you leave the village, nearing Km.13, turn right (south) onto a very steep and narrow road signposted Restaurant el Trestellador. In 1km reach the Hostal/Rest El Trestellador, which is marked on the map as Molino de Ondara. Font Moli is the spring nearby, by way of which the walkers will arrive at the end of the day.

Hostal: El Trestellador

IN EMERGENCY

- A normal car can easily reach the *Fuente* Arboles in good conditions and, with care, the *Fuente Forat* by following the walkers' route.

- A normal car can also get to *Fuente* Partagas by leaving the CV70 near Km.31 and turning off south on an unclassified road to Benifato. At the entrance to the village, turn off right (House – La Foya) and follow a narrow country road for 3km to the *fuente*. Four-wheel drive vehicles can easily go further to Puerta Mulero, and so can normal cars in good conditions.

Stage 6: Font Moli To Sella (optional)   *Walking time 5hrs*

Font Moli (Benimaurell)

The walkers' route is on good forestry roads all the way to Sella, so is passable by four-wheel drive vehicles. Be warned of Jeep Safaris which also use this route.

Normal Route

Return to the CV70, and turn west through Confrides, over the Puerta de Confrides (Km.26), and on the descent turn off left (Km.31) near Benasau. Go south over Puerta Tudons and drop down to Sella (pop. 419) on the CV770.   *42km*

IN EMERGENCY

From Km.5 follow the walkers' route for 6km until the surface ends.

Four-wheel drive vehicles can go up to Puerta Mulero.

BACK-PACKERS' VARIATIONS

The camping back-packers, being self-sufficient, and not needing to seek accommodation at the end of the day, have the freedom to really enjoy the route without having to worry about reaching a village for the night. They can also use one or two variations to the route, which are now described.

Stage 3

Can be ended at Corral del Somo, where there is a good well and plenty of scope for a camp-site.

Stage 4

Stage 4(a) can be started from Corral del Somo, joining the normal route at Serrella Castle. If there is no objection to using a road, Stage 4(b) is a direct route with 550m of ascent to *Fuente* Partagas, where there is excellent camping.

Stage 4(a) Corral Del Somo To Serrella Castle
5km – 300m ascent – 2hrs

Red markers show where the track leaves the main road on the south side (CV752, Corral to Tarbena, Km.7.5), 5km from the river bridge at Castell de Castells. Follow a broad track generally south, and in 10 minutes go across a crossroads heading straight for Aixorta and a prominent crag. High above can be seen a forestry road which is your objective. Pass the ruins of an old *finca* with a well on the left, and zig-zag down a little to join a broad forestry road (15 minutes) near a casita on the left. Ignore a road on the right-hand side, and pass another casita on the left before turning off right at another junction. There are good views ahead of the Sierra Ferrer, Passo Tancat and Rates as your road merges with another coming up from the valley. The Bernia Ridge can be seen to the north-west.

Climb gently through pines and bear right at a junction (50mins) to drop slightly, going west to reach *Fuente* Umbria (on the right). Continue towards your first objective, Serrella Castle, which is visible ahead, and join the walkers' route at Puerta de Castillo.

Stage 4(b) Beniarda Bridge To Fuente Partagas
10km – 2hrs 30mins

This is a direct and unremitting climb on a minor road to an excellent camping area. The variation extends this stage by 2km but shortens the ascent of Aitana by over an hour. You pass through the picturesque village of Beniarda, where there are shops and a good restaurant. It is a totally different sort of walk from the normal route, which ascends the valley by easy stages.

Leave the normal route and walk up the narrow surfaced road to the south. It climbs steeply out of the valley, passing a *fuente* on the right and the municipal swimming pool on the left. There are excellent views of the reservoir and Guadalest, and as you pass through an archway look back to see the shrine on San Francisco. Go through the main square with the church and a fountain to an upper square near the school, where there is a bar. Now you must use the road, passing a good restaurant on the right, and in 1km you reach the main CV70 road, on which you turn right. This road can be very busy at times, so make sure you walk on the left, facing the traffic. In 1km pass another good restaurant on the left, and just round the bend go off left (south) to climb to the village of Benifato. You are now on a country road again, free of traffic. As you are about to enter the village, turn off right at a house (La Foya) onto an access road which twists and turns for 3km to reach the *Fuente* Partagas, where you can camp for the night under the protection of the crags. The views over the Guadalest Valley and the day's route over Serrella are outstanding. The road continues upwards to Puerta Mulero, and after 15 minutes there is a deep ice-pit on the south side, about 100m from the road.

Towards the Partagas Rocks

Behind the *Fuente* Partagas can be seen the solid wall of double cliffs which are the Partagas, and it is necessary to first outflank them by turning them on their eastern end. To do this, strike up west-south-west keeping a prominent crag (Garden Crag) on your right, towards a small col, then seek out an indistinct path with zig-zags upwards in the same direction, until the masts on the summit of Aitana are visible. Look back now, and see that the impressive Garden Crag is, in fact, cultivated nearly to the summit, and you have glorious views of the coast, Peñon d'Ifach, the Bernia and Mala del Llop, with Confrides Castle just below the ridge. Carry on heading for the summit masts for a while, passing a *deposito* and a spring, until you reach a large flat area, which gives onto a broad shelf running almost parallel with the main ridge. You can now see all the summit installations.

To Fat Man's Agony

Change direction to south-east to follow below the Partagas cliffs away from the summit. You have outflanked the lower cliffs, and have to cross another band to join the main ridge of Aitana itself. Rejoin the walkers' route to Fat Man's Agony.

Stage 5

From *Fuente* Partagas there is a good route up to Fat Man's Agony, where the normal route is joined.

Appendixes

Appendix 1

Costa Blanca Mountain Walkers

'An informal group of those happy people who enjoy taking strenuous exercise in the magnificent Sierras of the Levant, formed to provide companionship on the mountains, sharing enjoyment and knowledge of the high places of the Costa Blanca.'

What was true in May 1987, when the group was formed on the summit of the Peñon d'Ifach, is still true today. We have always resisted the temptation to form a 'club', and remain still extremely informal. There is no membership, therefore no membership fee. The modest expenses of organising the group are provided for by members donating 200 pesetas (twice per year), for which they receive a full programme of walks and a comprehensive newsletter, which keeps them in touch with group activities. All other publications, badges, etc., are the responsibility of individual members who voluntarily accept this work, subject only to two criteria: (a) that the items be supplied at cost to members, and (b) that no charge falls on the group.

The group comprises about 50 regular residents of the Costa Blanca, supplemented by an increasing number of 'Winterers' and, of course, holiday-makers.

Every season, from the beginning of October to the end of May, the 20 Leaders of the Group (Cuerpo del Guias) take over 2000 walkers into the mountains and, what is more important, bring them back again, tired but elated. We basically still remain an English-speaking group but, at the last count, 21 nationalities were identified. In 1993, we welcomed our first Spanish leader, with the distinguished name of Cristobal Colon (Christopher Columbus).

We maintain friendly relations with all other walking groups on the Costa Blanca, especially the Spanish Mountaineering Clubs at Alcoy, Altea and Calpe.

In 1992, the group celebrated its fifth anniversary in grand style, again on the summit of the Peñon d'Ifach. Founder members were invested with special souvenir medals, and the chairman was pleased to present certificates to those who had completed the Costa Blanca Mountain Way. This 100–150km long-distance walk, right across our walking area, Las Marinas, was instituted especially to celebrate our fifth anniversary.

In our fifth anniversary year, we were flattered and gratified to find that *Lookout Magazine* (the premier English-language magazine in Spain) had chosen our Group out of 80 others to feature on the cover and in the main article as 'an example of a new type of Club and a new type of resident, a Group of active people who desire to know Spain better'.

Walking is probably the most popular recreation on the Costa Blanca, and mountain walking is the quintessence of this pastime. Although we are the oldest-established walking group in this area, there are now many more informal groups, some founded by our own members who were dissatisfied with only one walk in the mountains per week. *Costa Blanca News* (Friday) and the *Weekly Post* (Sunday) are published weekly, and *The Entertainer* (Fridays) is available free at supermarkets and some newsagents. All these publications give details of walks by Costa Blanca Mountain Walkers and other walking groups.

The walking season starts at the end of September, and usually over 50 walks are provided before the season ends, with our AGM on the last Wednesday in May. During the summer months, leaders meet once each month for lunch, sometimes including a short stroll, and those members who are still in Spain are more than welcome to join them.

Anyone who completes the first five sections of the Costa Blanca Way is entitled to become a *compañero*. Certificates are available if details and an s.a.e of 24x20cm are sent to the registrar c/o Cicerone Press.

Appendix 2

USEFUL READING

Recommended Guidebooks In English

Michelin Guide to Spain
Berlitz Guide to the Costa Blanca
Guide to Costa Blanca (Alicante Tourist Board)
Alicante & Costa Blanca Guide (ANAY Touring Publications)

Recommended Rock Climbing Guides

Rock Climbing Guide to the Peñon d'Ifach by Juan Antonio Andres Martinez (published by the author in Spanish, English, French and German): illustrated in colour, but no written descriptions of the routes.

Costa Blanca Climbs by Chris Craggs (Cicerone Press): excellent guidebook in the traditional English style and gradings.

Topo guides to one of the most popular rock climbing locations in the area, Sella, can be purchased at the bar in the village square, or up the valley at a climbers' refuge below the crags. See also www.geocities.com/costablancaclimbing

Geology

The Geological Field Guide to the Costa Blanca by C.B. Moseley (Geologists' Association)

Ornithology

Country Life Guide to the Birds of Britain and Europe by Bertel Bruun (Country Life)

Botany

Flowers of South-West Europe by Oleg Polunin and B.G. Smythes (Oxford)

Flowers of the Mediterranean by Oleg Polunin and Anthony Huxley (Chatto and Windus)

Wild flowers of Spain (3 booklets) by Clive Innes (Cockatrice)

Wild flowers of Southern Spain by Betty Molesworth Allen (Mirador Books, Malaga, 1993): covers Andalucia but applicable to Costa Blanca area.

Wildlife

Wildlife in Spain by John Measures (Crowood Press)

General Reading

Iberia by James Michener (Fawcett)

Spain by Jan Morris (Penguin)

As I walked out one Midsummer Morning by Laurie Lee (Penguin)

The Spaniards by John Hooper (Penguin)

The Spaniard and the Seven Deadly Sins by Fernando Diaz Plaja (Pan)

Culture Shock Spain by Marie L. Grafe (Kupera)

Spain by Dominique Aubler and Manuel Tunon de la Lara (Vista Books Longmans)

Marching Spain by V.S. Prichett (Hogarth Press)

The Face of Spain by Gerald Brenan (Penguin)

Lookout Magazine: publishes handy books on many topics relating to living in Spain, from cooking to the law, but most of the guidebooks relate to Andalucia.

The Story of Spain by Mark Williams: covers the whole country.

Appendix 3

GLOSSARY

The Mapas Militar normally use Castellano as their language, except for some place names which are in the Valenciano language. In recent editions of the maps, however, there is an increasing tendency to replace Castellano with Valenciano, no doubt in sympathy with the revival of this ancient language. This short glossary includes those terms which occur most often on maps and in guides.

CASTELLANO	VALENCIANO	ENGLISH
Alto/Collado	Alt	High Place
Arroyo	Rierra	Stream
Bancal	Bancal	Terrace
Barranco	Canal	Gully or ravine
Camino	Cami	Road
Casa	Casa	House
Casa de la Branza	-	Farmhouse
Casa de Molino	Moli	Mill
Cascada	Cascada	Waterfall
Castillo	Castell	Castle
Cauce Seco	Caixer Sec	Dry river bed
Cima/Cumbre	Cim	Summit
Colina	Tossal	Hill
Collado	Col	Col
Cordillera/Sierra/ Cadena	Serra	Mountain range
Corral	Corral	Cattle pen/small farm or hamlet

Embalse	Embassament	Reservoir
Finca	Finca	Country house/ Farm
Fuente	Font	Fountain or spring
Hoyo	Forat	Hole
Lago	Llac	Lake
Lomo	Llom	Shoulder
Montana	Muntanya	Mountain
Nevera	Nevera	Ice-pit
Paso/Puerta	Pass/Port	Pass
Penn/Peñon	Penja/Penyal	Cliff, crag, or mass of rock
Pennaco	Penyal	Crag
Pozo	Pou	Well
Presa	Presa	Dam
Punta/Pico	Punta/Punuxa/Pic	Peak
Rio	Riu	River
Ruinas	Ruinas	Ruins
Senda	Sender	Footpath
Simas	Avenc	Pot-holes & fissures
Valle	Val	Valley

Appendix 4

THE COUNTRYSIDE

One of the main differences between the countryside and that of Britain is the almost total absence of manor houses and stately homes, set in parkland. Throughout its history, Valencia has never been a particularly wealthy province, and the Senorios (feudal landlords, tenants of the king), were usually absentees, preferring to live in their palacios in the cities. There were, however, one or two exceptions: at Alcalali, Penaguilla, Calpe, for example, the remains of fortified palacios can still be seen. Most mountain villages seem to have been left to themselves to scratch a meagre living from a poor soil and a harsh climate. It is remarkable how little the life of the campesino has changed whilst his children go on to become computer analysts, bankers, and public relations advisers, leaving most villages solely occupied by the very young and the very old.

You will find that, many of the villages have strange sounding names, a reminder of the long centuries of Moorish occupation.

Fuentes (Springs)

In ancient times, a good and reliable water supply was essential for survival in this arid region, and the site of a farm or a village depended on the springs issuing from subterranean reservoirs. These village *fuentes* were well maintained, and usually included a lavadero (wash-house) for the housewives. Surprisingly, many are still in use, and not only by the older ladies. Nearby can sometimes be found the remains of old watermills, especially where a reliable flow of water existed (Bolulla). At Font Moli, above the village of Benimantell, however, the *fuente* feeds a reservoir which once provided a head of water for the mill. Today, many villages have refurbished their *fuentes*, embellishing them with ceramics, and providing shade trees, barbecues and picnic sites, much loved by the Spaniards at weekends and fiestas for holding paella parties. Don't be surprised if you find people filling the boots of their cars with plastic bottles of the spring water. Spaniards and others seem to have a distinct distrust of the public water supply, despite the fact that most coastal resorts have a reliable supply of excellent water.

Irrigation

The regulation and allocation of water to those landowners whose deeds give them the right to irrigation is vested in a committee of landowners in each village. Each farmer is annually allocated a time when he may open the sluice gates, and allow the precious water to flow on to his land. This, if he is unlucky, could be in the middle of the night, nevertheless, at the exact time when his allotted period expires, you may rest assured that his neighbour will be waiting to ensure that the sluice gates are closed, ready for him to get his share of the water. Serious disputes concerning water rights are settled by an ancient court, which sits on the steps of the cathedral in Valencia.

When the A150 between Altea la Vieja and Callosa d'Ensarria was widened, it was necessary to reconstruct the water conduits alongside it, and this is a good place for those who wish to study these irrigation systems, which nourish the extensive crops of nispero and citrus fruits. The Moors seem to be credited with the introduction of irrigation during their occupation of the area.

The Huerta

This means, literally, irrigated land, used for vegetables. *Huerto* means an orchard of citrus fruit, and, where the land levels out on the coastal plain, vast areas of rich soil have been irrigated all along the coast of Valencia, diverting the water of the rivers by means of pumps and irrigation channels since Moorish times. The huerta inland from Denia is particularly interesting. Rising from the vast sea of orange and lemon trees the tall chimneys of the old steam pumping stations can still be seen. Further north, near Sagra, can be found an old Moorish water mill, still in reasonable condition.

Fincas and *Casitas*

The ruins of these farms and cottages are to be found high in the mountains, and show how hard these farmers had to work to wrest a living from this harsh land. You will hardly find any dressed wood, except perhaps, the door. All beams and lintels are rough-hewn. Windows are usually small and unglazed, and generally only on the north side. Roofs were lined with bamboo from the river, and then tiled. The space was then filled with almond shells to provide insulation; sometimes the traditional Valencian arches between the beams are plastered. Not far from the back door you will find the housewife's beehive-shaped oven, which was heated with brushwood until a sufficient temperature had been reached then sealed with a stone. The nearby well, with its lavadero, and troughs for the animals, completed the facilities available.

Not all these remote *finca*s were occupied the whole year. Some, like the old village under the crags of Bolulla Castle, were used as shelters when the herdsmen and shepherds took their animals to summer pasture. Others were used by the family when it was necessary to work on the land. Today, with the advantage of motor transport, the land is cultivated on a daily basis, with the farmer living in his village house.

Riu-Raus

This is a distinctive type of architecture, to be found only where the Muscatel grape is cultivated for the manufacture of raisins. They are long, arched porches along the wall of a single-storey building, and are so attractive that they have been incorporated in many modern villas. Their purpose, however, is strictly practical, in that the long loggia provides shelter from the weather for the trays of ripening raisins.

Village Bars

Sadly I have recently noticed a change in attitude amongst a small minority of bar owners, no doubt inspired by tales of a quick fortune to be made by adopting the inflated prices of the coast. They seem to treat all foreigners as eccentric millionaires, who do not know the value of Spanish money, and don't care if they don't get any change. It is not my intention to suggest that you spoil your holiday by haggling over every drink, but it might be prudent to learn a few Spanish phrases to use in the situations outlined above, such as:

Cuanto es?	How much is it?
Es muy caro	It's very expensive
A donde es mi cambio?	Where is my change?
Madre mia, caramba	My goodness, tut-tut, general displeasure

| Yo no estoy contento | I am not happy (shrug shoulders, beat forehead, stamp feet) |
| Vamonos | We are leaving |

Village Houses

As might be expected, these are a little grander, with tiled balconies and rejas (grilles) over the windows, a left-over from the Moorish preoccupation with protecting the female members of the family. Note the large double doors, which allowed horses, mules and carts, to be taken through the house to the courtyard at the rear. Even today, in the villages and larger towns, you can still see the ruts in some of the doorsteps, worn by the cartwheels, and the small stone pillars placed on each side of the door arch, to protect the masonry from damage from the cartwheels. The stone used in town and village houses is a coloured limestone called 'tosca', and very attractive it is, when carved to form arches and doorways.

Churches

Mountain villages are usually poor, without benefactors, and on the surface, the outside of the churches sometimes seem sadly neglected. There are, however, exceptions, and the beautiful domed church of Jalon has a Grandee of Spain for its benefactress, who, amongst her other titles, is Baroness of Jalon and Lliber. The insides of churches are usually particularly beautiful, but you will, except on Sundays and fiestas, have to seek out the guardian to obtain the key. They are all kept locked, due, no doubt, to the Spanish propensity for burning down churches in time of revolt. The tower of the church at Murla was built on the base of the old Moorish castle. It fell down during a recent storm, killing two elderly ladies.

In addition to the village church, there is usually a sanctuario, or a hermita, dramatically situated on the mountainside above the village.

Spanish village cemeteries are easily identified by an avenue of the tall Mediterranean cypress trees, and normally include a calvary (Stations of the Cross). Some are beautifully decorated with ceramics. The cemeteries are interesting places to study the history of the village, especially the names of the main families. It is traditional to place the dead in brick cubicles built into walls around the cemetery, rather than bury them in the earth. Only the very important families have vaults.

Crops

On the dry land, olives, vines, carobs and almonds prosper, often with a spring catch crop of vegetables sown between the lines of trees. The olives, almonds and carobs are harvested, as they were centuries ago, by spreading a net on the ground, and knocking the fruit down with a long bamboo pole. Green olives are picked first, then cured, a long and tedious process. Most of the olives sold in the shops are the produce of Andalucia, but in mountain restaurants, you will probably be served with a local product.

Ripe purple olives are crushed in an almazara (olive press). The oil extracted is usually for home consumption, or sold in village shops.

Almonds, for which the Jalon Valley is rightly famous, are grown in a great number of varieties. The blossom ranges in colour from white to deep purple, and this indicates whether the almond is sweet or bitter, and used either for eating, making turron (nougat), or for extracting oil. There are a number of cooperatives where the farmers can take their crops, and there are crushing plants in Altea, Fleix and Tormos, identified by the great mounds of almond shells in the factory yard. In remote villages, the mobile shelling machine is set up in the village square. You cannot miss it, the noise is ear-shattering.

The carob (locust bean) makes good animal fodder, and is useful for making chocolate substitute. Wherever the Muscatel grape is grown, eg., Calpe, Teulada and the Jalon Valley, some of the crop was made into raisins, by scalding with caustic soda, and leaving in the sun on wicker mats to dry. This practice is now only carried on in a few villages, eg., Lliber. The production of raisins gave rise to the distinctive architecture of Riu-Raus (see *Fincas* and *Casitas*).

Nature's Bounty

Mountain villagers have always been adept at living off the land. After rainfall, you may see groups of women and children foraging in the ditches by the roadside, seeking wild asparagus and snails. On the high mountains, the men will probably be collecting mushrooms, especially the large brown ones, a much sought-after delicacy.

Livestock

The further inland you go from the coast, the more chance there is that you will see long-legged mules, donkeys, and the lovely miniature shire horses, used by the farmers in cultivating their land. Although most farmers have turned to tractors, the mule and donkey have a distinct advantage when it comes to cultivating narrow terraces, or using the Mozarabic trails.

Cattle, including bulls, are often grazed in some valley bottoms, where there is a reliable water supply, eg., Maserof, Almadich and the Val de Infierno near Isbert's dam. Thankfully, they are always supervised by the vaquero (herdsman).

The mixed flocks of sheep and goats can still be seen grazing under the care of the pastor (shepherd), and his motley collection of dogs, whose purpose is to protect the flock against wolves! The shepherd guides his flock by throwing stones and shouting, but the lead ewe seems to decide where the flock will go, whilst the dogs mill about showing off. The flocks are corralled at night.

Other livestock, pigs, chicken, ducks, rabbits etc. are, it seems, raised in secret by the little old ladies you see returning home with baskets of grass and herbs.

Appendix 5

FIESTAS

Be prepared to find the village shop and even the bakery closed on fiesta days. The more local the fiesta, the less likely you are to find supplies, although the village bar will remain open as usual. The Patronal Festival is the most important. Village fiestas are modest, intimate affairs, unlike the more affluent towns where impressive processions, concerts, bull-running and extensive sports pro-grammes are the norm. Valencia was the last province to be reconquered by the Christian kings, so the fiestas of Moors and Christians are impressive sights. One of the most famous is in Alcoy, an industrial town some 40km inland, where in 1276 St George is alleged to have appeared to inspire the Christian troops, who then overcame the beseiging Moors led by Al Azraq. Since then they have celebrated their victory over the Moors. The museum has costumes and photographs dating from the 19th century. In recent times, the developing coastal resorts have followed this example, and there are spectacular celebrations in Villajoyosa, Benidorm, Altea, Callosa Ensarria, Calpe, Javea, Denia and Pego.

Volta En Carro

In Las Marinas in July each year, there is an unusual expedition through the mountains of old 'covered wagons' pulled by teams of mules or horses. Their owners are farmers or businessmen determined to keep up the old traditions, and each night they camp and accept the hospitality of a mountain village for a paella and a fiesta.

Tira Y Arrastre

This is a most unusual sport, a trial of strength, practised by Valencians. Each team of horses and men together pull a weighted cart along the shingle bed of a river in competition with each other. It is reported that it is only the men who need reviving after their exertions; apparently the horses take it in their stride!

El Bous

Bull-running is now not confined to Pamplona, but has been adopted as part of most fiestas. It seems, on the face of it, a harmless sport and an opportunity for the young to show their mettle. Whilst accepting that the Spaniards are not as sensitive as others about animals, this activity often gets out of hand with young people, sometimes the worse for drink, goading the frightened animals with sharp instruments, letting off fireworks and throwing bottles and cans at them. The Civil Governor has regularly threatened local mayors that if his local inspectors (retired matadors!) report any cruelty, he will ban the event in future (but he never does).

Bous a Carre

A street is closed off, stands erected for spectators, and boards behind which a hard-pressed 'torero' can hide.

Bous a Mar

The same, except that the event is held on the harbour wall, and refuge taken in the sea.

Bous Embolat

This is often the end of the event, with all lights being extinguished, and the poor animal, with flaming torches fixed to its horns, chased down the street.

Hogueras and Fallas

In Valencia, since the middle ages, carpenters have celebrated the day of St Joseph (19th March), their patron, by spring cleaning their workshops, and burning all the old wood and shavings, including the rough racks on which they hung their outdoor clothes. In later years crude effigies of local personalities were added, and today it has developed into a major art form. A huge industry exists in Valencia to produce giant displays of papier maché sculptures on wooden frames, often with a humorous or political message, as local personalities are mercilessly caricatured. All year round the Filas (clubs) of the various districts of the city work to raise funds so that they can commission the many artisans who will make the giant tableaux. With great festivity, a display of fireworks, and the many bands competing with each other, the whole lot goes up in flames at midnight, as the poor fireman try to prevent the nearby buildings from catching fire. Only one Falla, the one judged to be the best, is saved for display in the museum.

In Alicante, they celebrate the day of their patron St Juan (June) in a similar manner but the displays are called Hogueras, and many of the resorts along the Costa have added the Fallas to their lists of fiestas.

La Pilota Valenciana

This is a Valencian version of the Basque game of handball, but not using a basket, strapped to the hand to give velocity to the ball. There are two versions, Raspat, where the ball is skimmed over the surface of a street, and Llarges, where it is bounded off a high wall. The game is still played in Calle Garcia Ortiz at Calpe every Sunday afternoon, but even small mountain villages have their purpose-built court, recognised by its high, green painted walls set at 90 degrees.

Tourist offices will supply full details of local fiestas, and publish a monthly leaflet for the whole of the province. Details of all local events appear in the three English-language newspapers.

Religious Fiestas

Spaniards observe many more religious holidays than we do in the UK. In addition to the Patronal fiestas of villages and towns the main ones are:

6th January	Epiphany. Known as the Three Kings, when children receive their presents. Normally lasts for a whole week.
March	San Jose, patron saint of carpenters. Burning of Fallas in Valencia. Wooden and papier maché effigies burned are sometimes 15m high.
March/April	Semana Santa (Holy week). Very important in Spain.
May	Ascension, Pentecost and Corpus Christi.
June	St Juan – burning of Fallas – Alicante and Costa.
25th July	Santiago.
August	Assumption of the Virgin Mary.
November	All Saints.
8th December	Immaculate Conception.

25th December   Christmas Day (one day only).

In addition, the following secular fiestas are held:

1st January   New Year's Day. Traditional to eat one grape for each
                   chime as midnight sounds.

1st May   Labour Day.

9th October   Valencian Day.

12th October   Columbus Day (Dia de la Hispanidad).

6th December   Spanish Constitutional Day.

Appendix 6

RELICS OF THE PAST

Castles

Valencia is rich in castles, and there are many ruins in the mountains, not all of them marked on maps. 'Castle' is rather a grand name, as some of them were only fortified lookouts. All date from the Moorish occupation and Reconquest in the 13th century, and whilst some of them are in reasonable repair (ie. Forna), others are just a few dressed stones or a single wall. Serrella has a cistern which still holds water, and in which mountain toads breed each year.

Eras

Where there is an extensive farmhouse, you will always find a well, an oven, and an *era*. This last is a flat surface for threshing and crushing cereals, by means of a metre-long tapered stone with a metal rod running through it. The stone was pulled over the grain by man or mule. When I first started walking in the area, most *eras* had at least one stone, left after the last harvest some hundred years ago. Sadly, most of them have now been taken away as souvenirs.

There is a gigantic *era* stone at the entrance to the village of Guadalest, and the Ponsoda restaurant on the road from Benimantell to Polop has lined the edge of the car park with them. At the Jami restaurant in Confrides, there is another good specimen, and you will park on what was once the *era* of an old *finca* (now the restaurant).

Almazeras

These are the old presses, normally used for crushing olives, but occasionally used for grapes. One or sometimes two conical stones ran in a circular stone trough, and were powered by mule or donkey. The stones were supported by a metal frame and cogwheel, and a good example can be seen at Km 169.7 next to the old venta (inn) on the CN332 at Calpe. The old inn is now a disco. There was another one in working order in the Val de Gallinera, in the remote village of Lombay, but this year, the roof fell in and buried it. The stones, along with millstones and old wine presses, are much sought after to decorate *fuentebancales* and glorietas in the villages, eg. Lorcha and Cuatretondeta.

Mozarabic Trails

'Mozarabic' is a term reserved for those Christians who accepted Moorish rule, and were allowed to follow their religion. Moors who, after the reconquest, were baptised were known as Mudejars.

The Spaniards use the term 'Mozarabic' to describe the narrow stepped trails which cross our mountains, zig-zagging down into the depths of the deepest ravines, and up the other side. They are truly marvels of engineering, with revetments used to support the trail in desperate places. Surprisingly, many of them have withstood the ravages of time, nature, and lack of maintenance. They are best seen in the Val de Laguart, where the Camino de Juvias first descends the sheer sides of the Barranco del Infierno, and then climbs out of the valley on the other side, towards the Val d'Ebo.

Neveras

These are deep cylindrical ice-pits, usually constructed on the northern slopes of the high mountains, for the purpose of making ice from snow. They are normally about 15m deep, and 10m in diameter. The larger ones had supporting stone beams, and a wooden roof which was tiled. Smaller ones were corbelled, built up in steps from bricks and stones, to make a dome. They were mainly used during the 17th and 18th centuries, and fell into decay with the introduction of refrigeration by electricity.

In winter, the pits were filled with snow, sometimes in sacks, and sometimes layered in straw. During the summer men with mules spent the night at the *nevera* cutting the ice into blocks, insulating it with straw, and transporting it by mule down the hazardous trails to the villages before the sun rose. Whether it is true or not I do not know, but an old villager in Fachega told me that his father remembered seeing the fires lit by the ice-cutters on the mountain Pla de la Casa, and could describe to me the route taken back to the village down the Barranco del Moro.

There is an excellent example of an arched *nevera* above Agres on the Moro del Contador, near the *Refugio* Santiago Reig del Mural, on the way to climb Monte Cabrer. Next to the *Refugio* is a small corbelled *nevera*, with the roof intact. There are also good examples on the Peña Mulero route and the biggest, deepest and highest is a few metres below the summit of Pla de la Casa.

Salinas (salt pans)

The only place in the area where salt was produced by evaporation are the salinas on the isthmus, under the Peñon d'Ifach at Calpe. Salt was last produced here in 1988, by pumping sea water from a point near the Queen's Baths (Roman remains) on the Arenal beach. The area of the salinas has now turned into a freshwater lake, and attracts a great many water birds, including the colourful flamingos from the Camargue in France, who winter here. One day, it is hoped that plans to turn the area into a Natural Park may soon materialise. Salt is still produced commercially further south in Torrevieja and Santa Pola.

Mountain Crosses

On a prominent crag above many mountain villages can be found a stone or metal cross, which protects the village, from Moors, lightning and tempests. In 1952, the cross on top of Perereta (826m) above the tiny village of Benimaurell, was restored by the young men of the village, no doubt at the instigation of the old people, who felt they still needed the protection of the old cross, which had disintegrated.

Windmills

Water mills, mentioned in the section 'Springs', needed to be near a reliable source of water. Windmills, which were more numerous, needed the best possible position to tap their power source, the wind. You will find them on any piece of high ground near a village, on the coast (Calpe) and even the top of cliffs (Javea). They are gregarious, like the company of other mills, and on Cabo St Antonio, near Javea, there are over ten of them on the cliff edge. They were used to grind wheat and indicate the amount of cereals which were grown on the narrow terraces in ancient times. Many of the mills, date from pre-Moorish times but today only the ruined towers remain, unused for over 100 years. When in use the mill had a conical cap, which could be rotated to catch the wind, and which accommodated the sails which were sometimes of wood, but more often of canvas. Wooden shafts and gears drove the large grinding stones on the ground floor. Some mills were also used as early lookout towers.

Watch Towers

These round lookouts were built in the 16th century on the coast to provide an early warning of raids by pirates. Piracy had always been rife in this part of the Mediterranean, even in the 14th century. Raids by ships from Africa and even from the one remaining Moorish kingdom, Granada, were quite common. After the final expulsion of the Moors in 1609, the raids became more frequent and the authorities had to take steps to combat them by building the towers and by providing a fleet of defensive ships. The costal towns were, of course, the most vulnerable to attack. In 1636, the pirates, after pillaging the village of Calpe, took nearly all the population back to Algiers as slaves. They were released many years later, when a ransom had been paid. We even know the names of some of these desperados: Dragut, Barberroja (red beard) and Picelilli Pacha. Moraira has restored its tower on the beach, and one of the many windmills on Cabo St Antonio near Javea, was also used as a lookout.

LISTING OF CICERONE GUIDES (International)

Cicerone's mission is to inform and inspire by providing the best guides to exploring the world

Since its foundation over 30 years ago, Cicerone has specialised in publishing guidebooks and has built a reputation for quality and reliability. It now publishes nearly 300 guides to the major destinations for outdoor enthusiasts, including Europe, UK and the rest of the world.

Written by leading and committed specialists, Cicerone guides are recognised as the most authoritative. They are full of information, maps and illustrations so that the user can plan and complete a successful and safe trip or expedition – be it a long face climb, a walk over Lakeland fells, an alpine traverse, a Himalayan trek or a ramble in the countryside.

With a thorough introduction to assist planning, clear diagrams, maps and colour photographs to illustrate the terrain and route, and accurate and detailed text, Cicerone guides are designed for ease of use and access to the information.

If the facts on the ground change, or there is any aspect of a guide that you think we can improve, we are always delighted to hear from you.

Cicerone Press, 2 Police Square, Milnthorpe, Cumbria LA7 7PY

Tel 01539 562 069   Fax 01539 563 417
email info@cicerone.co.uk   web: www.cicerone.co.uk